TOTALLY
SAVED

TOTALLY SAVED

*Understanding, Experiencing and
Enjoying the Greatness of Your Salvation*

Tony Evans

MOODY PRESS

CHICAGO

ISBN: 0-8024-6819-5

3 5 7 9 10 8 6 4 2
Printed in the United States of America

*This book is gratefully dedicated to
Professor Zane Hodges,
who has greatly influenced me
as a mentor, teacher, and friend*

CONTENTS

WITH
GRATITUDE

I want to say a word of thanks to my friend and editor, Philip Rawley, for his excellent help in the preparation of this manuscript; and to Greg Thornton, Cheryl Dunlop, and the rest of the team at Moody Press for their encouragement and quality work on this project.

INTRODUCTION

The humorous story is told of a baseball manager who decided to play a rookie in right field one day. The regular right fielder wasn't happy about it and loudly made it known from the bench that it was a mistake to play the kid.

Well, as it turned out the rookie was so nervous that he messed up big-time. He made a couple of errors and misjudged several other fly balls that could have been called errors. And each time he messed up, the veteran complained loudly on the bench.

Finally, late in the game the manager replaced the rookie with the veteran, mostly to shut the veteran up. Sure enough, he muffed the first ball hit to him for an error. As he came off the field at the end of the inning, everyone on the bench got very quiet to hear what he would say.

The manager was waiting for the veteran too, but before the manager could say anything the man slammed his glove down in disgust and said, "Skip, that kid has right field so messed up nobody can play it!"

That's the way many Christians feel about the teachings surrounding the great doctrine of salvation in Jesus Christ. They feel as if church "professionals" have so mixed up and complicated the issues that no one can get them straight anymore. Too many pastors, teachers, and theologians have added to the problem by failing to communicate the wonder of the unspeakable gift of salvation in Christ in language the everyday person can relate to. As a result, this truth is far too misunderstood, underappreciated, and even abused.

That's unfortunate, because there are few teachings in the Bible more glorious than the truth that God has delivered us from His wrath and given us the guarantee of heaven in the salvation He has provided through the death and resurrection of Jesus Christ. I have written *Totally Saved* in an attempt to explain the doctrine of salvation in words that I hope my readers can readily grasp and apply, while not losing any of the strength and depth that is a part of this great biblical teaching.

I have also sought to address some of the more controversial issues such as election, eternal security, grace, discipleship, assurance, and many other subjects related to our great salvation. It is my prayer that this inexhaustible subject is addressed in such a way that you will not only understand it better, but most importantly love, appreciate, and worship our God more, since He has provided us this awesome privilege of being called His children.

I also pray that by the time you have completed this book, you will either make sure about your relationship with Christ, or experience a fresh awakening to the exciting truth that you are totally saved.

OUR
GREAT
SALVATION

①
SIN: THE NEED FOR SALVATION

It's safe to say that some words don't mean what they used to mean.

Modern technology is responsible for a lot of these changes in meaning. For instance, if you stop a person on the street and ask what *windows* are, the chances are good that the answer will relate to a computer program instead of clear panes of glass that people look through.

The word *help* is another example. It used to mean a cry of desperation by someone in trouble. But today it's just an option on a computer's toolbar (although for some computer users, clicking on the help icon still represents a cry of desperation by someone in trouble!).

Here's one more example: the words *save* or *saved*. To a twenty-first century mind, "save" is a command whereby the data in a computer file is preserved, and "saved" describes the condition of the file after this command is performed. The world may consider the spiritual meaning of the word *saved* to be a relic from a previous generation, but it's a good biblical word that we ought not abandon.

The Philippian jailer who fell down before the apostle Paul and cried, "What must I do to be saved?" (Acts 16:30) knew that something was radically wrong and that he needed a radical solution. When the Bible says that people need to be saved, it communicates the message that they are lost. Jesus Himself said He came "to seek and to save that which was lost" (Luke 19:10).

It is vital that people understand that they are eternally lost without Jesus Christ and they desperately need to be saved. In fact, the basic thesis of this book is that we need to be totally saved because we are totally lost and without hope for eternity apart from Christ.

The biblical teaching of salvation not only makes many people in the world uncomfortable, but it has also made some liberal theologians and church people feel embarrassed. Over the years, liberal teachers have tried to move away from the idea of "being saved" because they think it smacks too much of the backwoods, sawdust-trail evangelism of an earlier era. These folk want us to talk nice to people about joining the church or discovering the god within them, and not get them all upset talking about their lost condition.

But let me tell you something: Lost people had better be walking on *something*, whether it's sawdust or plush carpet, to get to Jesus, because the Bible says, "There is salvation in no one else" (Acts 4:12)! After pointing out that God held the people of Israel responsible to obey the Mosaic Law, the writer of Hebrews asked this important question about our greater responsibility to turn to Christ: "How will we escape if we neglect so great a salvation?" (2:3).

This salvation we have is a great salvation. It's beyond human description, and yet God has given us the means to describe and understand it to the degree that we're able. So in this first section of the book, I want to consider our great salvation as we study great concepts such as justification, propitiation, redemption, reconciliation, forgiveness, and other biblical terms that are replete with depth and meaning and significance.

We'll explore each of these truths in turn as we consider what it means to be totally saved. But first I want to talk about the reality of sin and our need for salvation. This is one place where the Bible's teaching and the world's view part company, because the prevailing view today is that sin isn't all that bad.

THE CONCEPT OF SIN

One observer said that contemporary America has "defined deviancy downward." Our culture has made sin seem so acceptable that things that used to be considered deviant are now considered almost normal.

But make no mistake. God has not defined sin downward. His concept of sin is the same today as it was in eternity past when Lucifer and one-third of the angels rebelled against Him. Sin is anything that fails to conform to the holy and perfect character of God.

Failing to Measure Up

God said to Moses, "You shall be holy, for I the Lord your God am holy" (Leviticus 19:2). Sin becomes sin when it is measured against the standard of God. When the prophet Habakkuk encountered God, he said, "My inward parts trembled, at the sound [of God] my lips quivered. Decay enters my bones, and in my place I tremble" (3:16). Isaiah had a similar experience in God's holy presence. The prophet saw the Lord in His holy temple and cried out, "Woe is me" (Isaiah 6:5).

One reason we don't have a high view of sin today is that we have a low view of God. We haven't visited Him lately in His holy temple, because when we are in His presence we don't feel so good about ourselves anymore. We've become too comfortable living in an age that devalues God's standard and makes acceptable that which He hates.

David understood the seriousness of sin in relation to God's holiness. Following his sin with Bathsheba and the arranged murder of

Uriah, David confessed to God, "Against You, You only, I have sinned and done what is evil in Your sight" (Psalm 51:4). David knew that sin is first and foremost an offense against a holy God.

The apostle John wrote, "God is Light, and in Him there is no darkness at all" (1 John 1:5). He is absolute perfection in every detail. Some theologians consider the holiness of God to be His controlling attribute. That is, all the other divine attributes are referenced from God's holiness. He is totally set apart from sin.

In the same epistle, John gave a more formal definition of sin. "Everyone who practices sin also practices lawlessness; and sin is lawlessness. You know that He appeared in order to take away sins; and in Him there is no sin" (1 John 3:4–5). These verses not only characterize sin as rebellion against God by the breaking of His law. They also teach that sin is anything in creation that is contrary to the nature of the Creator.

Sin makes us self-centered and self-dependent instead of God-centered and God-dependent. You know you're getting deeper into sin the deeper you get into independence—the idea that you can run your own life and don't need God. The less you need God, the more sinful you have become, because you are trying to function independently of the Creator.

Therefore, we can say that sin is the failure to reflect God's holy character and obey His righteous laws. "All have sinned and fall short of the glory of God" (Romans 3:23). We may come off looking pretty good when we compare ourselves to other people. But when God is the standard, we all come so far short of measuring up that it's a waste of time to compare ourselves to each other.

Like most big cities, Dallas has some tall buildings. We could compare one building to another and say, for instance, that building A is thirty stories taller than building B. That's a big difference from our perspective. But if we're talking about the distance from these two buildings to the moon, our comparison means nothing because the moon is so far away that a few hundred feet of difference means nothing.

That's the problem with using the wrong standard of measurement. You may be a nicer person than your neighbor, but when God is the standard, we all come up short. All of us have sinned, whereas in God there is no sin at all.

The Deep Roots of Sin

Where does sin finds its roots? This question takes us all the way back to some point in eternity past, before the creation of the world, when the angel Lucifer decided he was tired of being less than God. This beautiful being, the highest-ranking of all God's angels, led one-third of the angelic host in a rebellion designed to topple God from His throne.

Lucifer's rebellion is described in Ezekiel 28:11–19 and Isaiah 14:12–14. We learn that God created him with stunning beauty and that his heart welled up with pride. Lucifer decided to assert his independence by making his famous "I will" statements in Isaiah 14. Lucifer tried to impose his will in opposition to God, but he was defeated and judged and became Satan, the deceiver and "the accuser of [the] brethren" (Revelation 12:9–10).

Satan's rebellion shows that the root of sin is pride, the creature thinking more highly of himself than he ought to think (see Romans 12:3). Sin began in heaven, and it began with pride. Satan allowed pride to grow in his heart and he tried to make himself equal with God because he forgot that he was a creature, not the Creator. Satan was totally dependent on God for his existence, just as we are.

Pride is such a pervasive thing that it's good for us to remind ourselves regularly who is in charge here. If the Creator ever decided to withhold oxygen, water, or food, you and I wouldn't even be here, let alone start acting like we're the Creator. Everything we enjoy comes from something that God made.

Only pride could make any creature claim equality with God, as Satan did. Paul warned of this when he cautioned Timothy not to appoint a new believer to leadership in the church, "so that he will not become conceited and fall into the condemnation incurred by the devil" (1 Timothy 3:6).

The Bible says that Satan was beautiful and had great musical ability as he led the angels in worshiping God. Satan was called "the anointed cherub" (Ezekiel 28:14). But he forgot who he was, and the root of sin sprang up in his heart.

Satan's pride and desire for independence from God spread to others in the angelic world, and then to the human race when the serpent came to Eve in Eden. Here again, sin's root can be traced to pride and a desire for independence from God.

God had commanded Adam and Eve not to eat of the tree of the knowledge of good and evil, because "in the day that you eat from it you will surely die" (Genesis 2:17).

The question that everybody asks is why God put the forbidden tree in the garden in the first place. The presence of this tree was a test of Adam's and Eve's obedience, and a reminder of the Creator/creature distinction we have been talking about. That is, the forbidden tree reminded our first parents that they could not do whatever they wanted to do whenever they wanted to do it, because they were limited, created beings who owed obedience and loyalty to their Creator. The tree reminded Adam and Eve of their "creatureliness" in contrast to God.

People focus on the one prohibition that God established in Eden, but that still left every other tree in the garden for Adam and Eve to enjoy. There may have been one hundred or one thousand trees in the garden, but whatever the number Adam and Eve still had the run of the place.

But when Satan approached Eve in the form of the serpent, he focused on the one prohibition God had made to teach Adam and Eve that they were not their own gods. Satan had tried to make himself equal with God and had failed, so he used the same tactic on Eve because he knew how seductive the temptation is to imagine that we can be like God, having His knowledge and power.

The serpent was too "crafty" (Genesis 3:1) to call God an outright liar. He questioned God's goodness in putting this tree off-limits for Adam and Eve (v. 5), suggesting that God was being selfish in keeping His deity to Himself. The serpent also promised Eve the opposite of death, the judgment God had decreed for disobedience. Eve was promised godlike status that would erase the Creator/creature distinction. Satan was saying to Eve, "There's no reason that God has to be up high while you're down low. You can erase that line by eating this fruit."

According to Genesis 3:6, Eve bought the lie and sinned. Not wanting to go down alone, she got Adam to sin with her. Adam allowed Eve to be god in his life at that moment, and it cost dearly. Anytime we let another human being become more important to us than God, that's sin.

Sin on Mankind's Charge Account

Now when Adam ate of the forbidden fruit and sinned against God, something very important happened. His sin was imputed, or charged, to the whole human race. Paul wrote, "Through one man sin entered into the world, and death through sin, and so death spread to all men, because all sinned" (Romans 5:12). This is the doctrine known as imputation, which simply means to post a charge against someone's account.

All of us understand how a charge account works. You accumulate a debt on your account, which must be paid off in full in order to clear your account. That's the basic idea here. When Adam sinned, God posted a debt of sin to the account of every person who would ever be born.

The reason is that Adam was acting as the covenantal representative of the human race. Adam was given a position of headship by God, so his sin affected all who would come after him. That's why Paul said sin passed to every person through Adam, the "one man" the apostle was talking about.

The usual reaction to the teaching of Adam's representative status is that it's not fair for one person's sin to corrupt the race. After all, you and I didn't ask Adam to represent us. We're in this mess because of what he did. Most people want to be their own representatives because they figure they can do a better job than Adam did.

Let me make several observations here. First, God has the pre-rogative to establish the conditions under which His creatures will function. He's God, and we're not. Besides, Adam was a lot better representative than you and I would be. Why? Because Adam was created perfectly in a perfect environment. If he fell into sin in that setting, how long do you think we would last? Satan wouldn't have needed a serpent to seduce us. Don't ever think you'd be better off if you could have been your own representative.

Here's something else to think about: The principle of repre-sentation is a well-established part of human life. We call our elected officials our representatives, and when they make decisions for us we have to live with the consequences. If the Congress declares war, for example, all Americans are affected. We can't say, "Don't bring me into this. I didn't make that decision." If the president decides to go after a group of terrorists, all Americans become poten-tial targets for retaliation. We're affected because the president made his decision as the duly elected representative head of our nation.

Even the world of team sports operates by the principle of rep-resentation. When a football player jumps offside, the entire team is penalized. You don't see the other players refusing to move back because they weren't the one who committed the penalty. The team is a unit.

Adam sinned as the head of the human race, so his sin was imputed or charged to mankind's account. When this happened, Adam and Eve's sin was inherited by their offspring. We inherited a sin nature from our first parents, and that nature is passed on to every generation. We call this original sin, the nature that was trans-ferred from Adam to every human being. David said in Psalm 51:5, "In sin my mother conceived me." Adam and Eve passed on their spiritual genes to their children.

You look the way you do because you are a combination of the DNA you inherited from your father and mother. Every physical fea-ture you have was passed on to you by your parents.

But your mom and dad passed something else on to you that they inherited from their parents, a spiritual gene called the sin nature. That is, they passed on to you a capacity and a bent to rebel against God. The only thing you lacked at birth was enough knowledge and time to work this sin thing out. But the nature was there. Sin is imputed or charged to the human race and is inherited through conception.

THE CORRUPTION OF SIN

This inherited sin nature we possess brings us to another theological term that's important to understand. It's called depravity, which means that every facet of human nature has been polluted, defiled, and contaminated by sin. We are talking about inborn corruption.

Sin's Corruption Is Complete

Jeremiah 17:9 says of human nature, "The heart [the seat of our being] is more deceitful than all else and is desperately sick; who can understand it?" Jeremiah was referring to this capacity all of us have to function in rebellion against God.

Paul said of himself, "I know that nothing good dwells in me, that is, in my flesh" (Romans 7:18).

And Paul was not alone, because in Ephesians 2:1 he said, "You were dead in your trespasses and sins." The Bible declares that we are spiritually contaminated and are "by nature children of wrath" (v. 3). By nature we are destined to incur God's wrath because depravity also means that there is nothing within us to commend us to God or cause Him to accept us.

We never have to teach our children how to sin. No child ever needed a class on how to be selfish or disobedient. No, we have to teach children how to love, to share, to be kind to one another, to stop fighting. The bad stuff is automatic. The capacity for sin is present when a child is developing in the womb. As I said before, all that's lacking is information and opportunity for sin to express itself.

My family went back to my boyhood home in Baltimore on vacation a couple of years ago. My aunt and uncle came over one night, and we were all sitting around eating crabs.

I don't even know how we got on the subject, but the discussion turned to what a bad child I was. I know, you have a hard time believing that. So do I. But someone recalled a time when I was three or four years old and was sent upstairs to get a clock and bring it downstairs. I was told not to throw it, because apparently I had a propensity to throw things. Whoever was telling the story said that when I got the clock and came to the head of the stairs, I threw it down the steps anyway because there was no one there to take it.

My uncle also told me that I used to hit people and then run. He said I came up to him one time and said, "Uncle Smitty, can I have a quarter?" He reached in his pocket and gave me a quarter, and bam! I hit him and ran. My father never gave me a course on clock-throwing or hitting people. It was inbred.

This is what the Bible calls our depravity or total corruption by sin. People object to this teaching because they think it lumps them in with the Hitlers and the Stalins of this world. Depravity does not mean we are as bad as we could be. But it does mean that we have the potential within us to do anything when it comes to sin.

People console themselves about human nature by saying things like, "Well, Hitler was an animal." No, he was a human being who gave full expression to his depraved nature.

How many times have you told yourself you would never do something, but then you wound up doing that very thing? We all do things like this, and then we say, "I can't believe I did that. That just isn't me." Oh, yes it is. Let's not kid ourselves. Under the right conditions, we are capable of committing murder or any other terrible thing anyone else might do. Why? Because we all have the same corrupt human nature we inherited from Adam. It just doesn't express itself the same way in everyone.

My granddaughter once got some flowers for her mother and put them in a vase. It was a nice gesture to give her mom these lovely flowers. But a day and a half later, those flowers were drooping and the petals were about to fall off. The reason is they were dead—and they died the moment they were picked and disconnected from their life source. The proof that those flowers were already dead is that they drooped over and wilted. Putting them in a vase with water only postponed the full expression of their death.

So ladies, don't get too excited when a man brings you roses, because he's bringing you death. They may be red death, pink death, or white death, but they're nothing but death. As pretty as those roses look, give them time and they will demonstrate that what you have sitting in your den or on your dining room table is death.

God told Adam and Eve that on the day they ate from the tree He commanded them not to eat from, they would die (Genesis 2:17). They died spiritually that same day, and eventually they died physically. In our sinful condition, the human race has been cut off from its life source and is dead. And the proof that we are dead spiritually is the fact that we will die physically someday.

The Bible says that all of us will die "in Adam" (1 Corinthians 15:22), just as Adam himself died. To put it another way, your birth certificate is also your death certificate. "The wages of sin is death" (Romans 6:23).

Sin's Corruption Is Obvious

Sin expresses itself in both personal and corporate ways. We've just talked about the personal expression of sin, which we are all guilty of because of our inherited sin nature and our disposition to sin. We sin because we are sinners, so we can't point the finger at Adam and tell ourselves that if only he hadn't sinned, we'd be all right.

Sin can also be collective, as when an entire nation or group of people systematically participates in and supports evil. Slavery is an example of collective sin. We see in the Bible that God judged whole groups of people for the sins they practiced. That doesn't necessarily mean that every person in that group was guilty of the particular sin, but that the group was so characterized by and corrupted by the sin that the people came under judgment collectively. Sin is also collective in the sense that the entire creation has been affected by sin.

THE CONSEQUENCES OF SIN

The Bible is very clear about the consequences of sin. "The wages of sin is death" (Romans 6:23). Death in the Bible never means the cessation of our existence. Death means separation, and the Bible talks about three kinds of death, all of which have come about as a consequence of sin.

The Death That Results from Sin

One type of death is spiritual death, which we read about in Ephesians 2. Spiritual death is separation from the life of God. The first thing Adam and Eve did after they sinned was to hide from God because their fellowship with Him was severed (see Genesis 3:8–10). All of us are born spiritually dead.

The second manifestation of death, the one we're most familiar with, is physical death or the separation of the soul and spirit from the body. The proof that we are all sinners is the fact that we all die.

There's a third kind of death in Scripture, which is eternal death or separation from God for eternity in the place of punishment and suffering called hell. Spiritual death can be reversed by salvation, and physical death will be reversed by resurrection. But there is no reversal of eternal death. The horror of eternal death is total separation from God.

In hell, there is no presence of God in the sense that there is no righteous provision of His goodness. God is everywhere, including hell, because He is all-present. But in hell there is no experience of God's goodness. There is nothing to balance or temper the presence of pure evil. Hell is the worst form of bondage because people are locked in their sin forever.

Some people live in neighborhoods that are controlled by evil. They live behind locked doors and bars on their windows. The children can't go outside and play; they're trapped inside. These neighborhoods are miserable places to live because of the atmosphere that dominates them. That's a good picture of hell, being locked away in total evil and the total absence of God's goodness.

Sin's Devastation on the Creation

I also want to mention another consequence of sin, which is its impact on the whole of creation. Paul taught in Romans 8 that "the creation itself also will be set free from its slavery to corruption" when Jesus comes to complete our redemption (v. 21).

All of creation, what we call nature, was affected by sin. The reason we have all the disturbances and destructiveness of nature is that sin has spoiled God's creation. God's grace keeps sin from having total domination in nature, but even the natural world "groans" (Romans 8:22) under the weight of sin.

There is a direct relationship between man and nature. When God created Adam, He put him in the Garden of Eden "to cultivate it and keep it" (Genesis 2:15). When Adam sinned, God cursed the ground as one of the consequences (3:17–18). Suddenly, nothing grew right anymore. Thorns and thistles appeared. Sin spoiled every part of God's good creation.

stop.

THE CURE FOR SIN

Sin is a dread disease from which all of creation is crying out for a cure. Now a terrible disease without a cure is bad news, but the news concerning a cure for sin is good. God has a remedy for this scourge, which is found in the atonement of Jesus Christ.

Atonement for Sin Is Necessary

When a disease is ravaging your body, you don't want your doctor to skip over it and send you away, knowing that the illness will ultimately kill you. Disease demands a cure because it's not going to go away by itself. And a truly competent and caring physician will insist that you undergo the cure, no matter what it demands, because of the awful consequences of not dealing with the problem.

It was necessary that sin be atoned for, because God is too holy and just to ignore sin, and too loving to let us plunge headlong into judgment and hell. And as we'll see, Christ is the only One who could pay the terrible price that sin demanded. In other words, just saying "I'm sorry" doesn't atone for sin. Sin must be addressed in a way that is acceptable to the one who has been offended.

If I borrow your car and run it up over the curb, bending the rim and smashing the car into a pole, you're not likely to be completely satisfied if I just hand you the keys and say, "I'm deeply sorry I wrecked your car."

You might say, "Tony, I'm glad you're sorry, and I forgive you. Now let's talk about your insurance coverage, because being sorry won't fix my car. Someone will have to pay for the repairs, and I believe that person is you." You would rightly expect me to atone, or pay, for the damage I caused.

Atonement is paying what must be paid to settle the claim, because damage has been done. Sin is an attack on the character of God and, therefore, it must be atoned for by a payment that is acceptable to Him. The only payment that God ever accepted for sin is death (see Romans 6:23). God told Adam concerning the fruit of the forbidden tree, "In the day that you eat from it you will surely die" (Genesis 2:17). The Bible says, "The Lord will by no means leave the guilty unpunished" (Nahum 1:3).

God Permitted a Substitute to Die

Sin's death penalty would be very bad news for us, except for one exciting truth. Although God didn't lessen the penalty for sin, He did allow a substitute to bear the penalty for guilty sinners. A substitute, of course, is someone who goes out in the place of another person. In sports, a substitute player has to take the place of and fulfill the responsibilities of the player he replaces.

The principle of substitution also goes back to the beginning. After Adam and Eve sinned, God responded by slaying an animal to clothe them. Adam and Eve had their own substitute in mind, but it was a fig leaf substitute, which was completely unacceptable to God. The only sacrifice that He accepts, and that will properly atone for sin, is the shedding of blood.

God's economy has always operated this way. According to Leviticus 17:11, "The life of the flesh is in the blood, and I have given it to you on the altar to make atonement for your souls; for it is the blood by reason of the life that makes atonement."

Blood is the only means of atonement that satisfies God's righteous retribution against sin. Before Christ came, God accepted the blood of sacrificial animals as a substitute for man's blood, and no sinner dared to approach God and seek forgiveness without an acceptable substitute. That's why the writer of Hebrews said, "Without shedding of blood there is no forgiveness" (9:22).

Jesus Is Our Substitute

When Jesus came, the sacrificial system came to an end as He became the final sacrifice for sin. We know that sin must be paid for, and that the penalty is death. We deserved to die on the cross, but Jesus Christ took our place by becoming our Substitute and bearing the penalty for the guilt we had incurred.

This is why we refer to the atonement of Christ as substitutionary. Jesus didn't die just to leave us a good example, or show us how to bear up under suffering. Our guilt was transferred to Him, and therefore He took the death stroke that should have fallen on us for all eternity. That's a great salvation!

I will never forget an incident that happened when I was a student at Dallas Theological Seminary. Two of my classmates were robbed, and the police caught the robbers. They were tried and sentenced to a year and a half in jail.

When the sentence was pronounced, one of my classmates who was a robbery victim stood up in court and said to the judge, "Your

Honor, I would like to take the penalty for the gentlemen who robbed me."

The judge was startled. "Why in the world do you want to do something like that?"

My friend replied, "Because I want to demonstrate to these men what God did for me when Jesus Christ took my penalty on the cross." This student was offering himself as an atonement to satisfy the demands of justice against the guilty parties. This wasn't allowed, but my friend was legally qualified to make the offer because he had no crime of his own to pay for.

This is something you need to know about Jesus Christ. To serve as our Substitute, He had to be free of the guilt of sin Himself. You and I can't depend on another sinner to help us out, because everyone else has the same problem we have. Only the sinless Son of God could stand up in God's court and say, "Your Honor, I would like to take the penalty for these guilty ones."

In the Old Testament, the lambs and other animals that were brought for sacrifice had to be without any spot or blemish. This was a picture of Jesus Christ, the sinless Lamb of God who would be the perfect atoning sacrifice for sin.

Let me tell you something else about your Substitute. He had to be a Man, one of us who wore the same flesh that we wear. Hebrews 10:4 says, "It is impossible for the blood of bulls and goats to take away sins." Animals were only a temporary solution to the problem of sin's guilt.

❷
JUSTIFICATION: THE VERDICT OF SALVATION

More than eighty years ago, a group of major league baseball players left a courtroom in Chicago with smiles on their faces and congratulations all around.

The eight men were members of the Chicago White Sox, and they had just been acquitted of conspiring with gamblers to throw the 1919 World Series to the Cincinnati Reds in what came to be known as the "Black Sox" scandal. Chicago had lost the series although heavily favored, and rumors had swirled around the players for months. The players initially admitted the plot, but some of the evidence against them mysteriously disappeared and they were found not guilty. They completed the 1920 season and looked forward to carrying on with their careers.

But there was another judge these players still had to deal with. Kenesaw Mountain Landis, a former federal judge, had been appointed by the major league team owners to clean up baseball and restore its reputation. Judge Landis issued his verdict: Regardless of their acquittal, the eight players would be banned from baseball for life because of their admitted involvement in the scheme. The men fought the commissioner's decision, but it held up. None of them ever played major league baseball again.

This famous story from American sports history helps to illustrate the human race's predicament before God as sinners. People may be able to tamper with or destroy the evidence of sin, and they may "beat the rap" in terms of human judgment even though they know they're guilty. But there is another court and another Judge we must deal with, and He is not impressed by our standards. Sin must never be measured by our viewpoint, but by the standard of absolute perfection resident in a holy God.

Since God's verdict is the only one that matters, we need to answer the question of how guilty sinners can be made right before a perfectly holy and perfectly just God. Job asked, "How can a man be in the right before God?" (Job 9:2). The psalmist phrased the question this way: "If You, Lord, should mark iniquities, O Lord, who could stand?" (Psalm 130:3).

Have you ever been around people who want everything just right all the time? I'm married to a person like that. Clothes have to be hung up at all times. Any dishes in the sink have to be washed, dried, and put away. Beds always have to be made, because you never know who might drop by.

Some of us have trouble living up to a standard like that. Now if we have a hard time meeting the standards of imperfect, sinful people, imagine what we are dealing with when we're talking about God and His perfect standard. He wants all things right all of the time; in fact, He demands it. When a God like this holds us to His measuring stick and marks every failure, there isn't a person on earth who can stand before Him. So we're back to the issue of how unholy people can be made right before a holy God. We don't have to worry about falling short of our spouse's glory or the neighbor's glory. Our problem is that we have fallen short of God's glory (see Romans 3:23), and He must address sin.

There are three ways God could deal with sin. He could simply issue a verdict condemning all sinners and be done with it, leaving us hopeless. Or, He could compromise His righteousness, lower the standard, and take us just as we are. God could say, "Let bygones be bygones," and skip over our sin—but then He would not be righteous and just. However, God took a third option, providing the means to forgive sinners and declare them righteous in His sight.

THE CONCEPT OF JUSTIFICATION

The biblical term for this glorious verdict is *justification*. I say "verdict" because the Greek word translated "justify" means to announce a favorable verdict, or to declare righteous. It is a legal term taken from the courtroom. A basic definition of *justification* is "a judicial act by which God declares righteous those who believe in Jesus Christ." The Bible is clear that justification comes from God alone, for "God is the one who justifies" (Romans 8:33).

Measured Against the Law

The book of Romans is a good place to start, because Paul had a lot to say there about the doctrine of justification. We saw that in Romans 5 the apostle contrasted the disobedience of Adam in the Garden and its effects with the obedience of Christ on the cross and its effects. In verse 18 we read, "So then as through one transgression there resulted condemnation to all men, even so through one act of righteousness there resulted justification of life to all men."

The opposite of justification is condemnation. Through Adam all people were condemned, but through Jesus Christ the righteous demands of God were met so that sinners can be justified before a holy God. Because Christ's sacrifice dealt with sin, God is now free to reverse His verdict of condemnation toward any sinner who puts his or her faith in Christ for salvation.

As I said earlier, justification as it is used in the Bible is a judicial term, which sets it in the context of law. When you enter a courtroom, you are there to be measured against the law. It's the same in God's courtroom. Paul wrote:

> Now we know that whatever the Law says, it speaks to those who are under the Law, so that every mouth may be closed and all the world may become accountable to God; because by the works of the Law no flesh will be justified in His sight; for through the Law comes the knowledge of sin. But now apart from the Law the righteousness of God has been manifested, being witnessed by the Law and the Prophets, even the righteousness of God through faith in Jesus Christ for all those who believe; for there is no distinction; for all have sinned and fall short of the glory of God. (Romans 3:19–23)

Many people may not be aware of it, but all mankind has already been tried in the tribunal of heaven before God the righteous Judge, and found guilty of sin. We stand before God as guilty sinners, and our guilt is obvious because we have broken God's Law. There is no argument, defense, or debate. Our mouths are closed. The sentence is pronounced. "The wages of sin is death" (Romans 6:23).

A New Plan Introduced in Court

This is serious because the Bible means eternal death, separation from God forever in hell, when it speaks of death as the penalty for sin. But God's court is unlike any human court, because God did what no human judge can do. He conceived the plan of salvation whereby we not only do not have to pay the penalty for our sins, but we are justified—given a declaration of righteousness that means God sees us the same way He sees His sinless Son. When we trust Christ, we move from being totally condemned to totally saved!

No human judge can do this, because once a person is found guilty of a crime, the judge cannot ignore that verdict. A person may later be released if new evidence comes to light, but someone convicted of breaking the law must pay the penalty. The person may be paroled, but that doesn't erase the conviction or remove the guilt of the crime. My point is that human judges cannot simply take matters into their own hands and release the guilty from their guilt.

But God introduced a glorious plan called justification into His court. Therefore, sinners who accept Christ's payment for their sin can walk out forgiven, with their sin debt paid and the righteousness of Christ Himself credited to their account.

THE GIFT OF JUSTIFICATION

Perhaps you have noticed in this discussion that nothing has been said about our doing anything whatsoever to deserve the glorious reality of justification. That's because we didn't earn it. The earlier quotation from Romans 3 ended at verse 23 with the statement of our shortcoming before God. Romans 3:23 is one of the most famous and most quoted verses in the New Testament, but thank the Lord it is not the end of the story. We hardly ever hear Romans 3:24 quoted, but it is necessary because it continues the thought of verse 23.

Candidates for God's Grace

According to verse 24, the same people who fall short of God's glory are candidates to be "justified as a gift by His grace through the redemption which is in Christ Jesus." Paul then went on to say that Jesus made "propitiation" for our sins through His blood (v. 25). We are saving the concepts of redemption and propitiation for later chapters, because they are equally glorious facets of our great salvation.

So justification is a gift of God's grace. That's the only way it could happen, because we had nothing to offer God to make us acceptable to Him. The means by which God's declaration of righteousness is applied to us involves a biblical truth we introduced in the first chapter: imputation, or crediting something to someone's account.

Perfect Righteousness in Our Account

You'll recall that in the Bible, imputation has both a negative and a positive meaning. We read in Romans 5 that Adam's sin brought death to all mankind because God charged the sin of Adam to every person's spiritual account (see Romans 5:12–14). But when Jesus died on the cross to satisfy God's righteous demands, He provided a means whereby those who receive His forgiveness could have His perfect righteousness credited to their accounts.

Now you may want to take a minute or two to sit back and think about that. You can be tried for a crime in court and be found not guilty, but that's as far as the verdict can go. The court is not saying you are perfectly righteous, or that you may not be guilty of other offenses. A "not guilty" verdict only deals with the particular charge under consideration.

But when you are justified by God, it means far more than not guilty. An incredible transfer takes place, described this way by Paul: "He [God] made Him [Jesus Christ] who knew no sin to be sin on our behalf, so that we might become the righteousness of God in Him" (2 Corinthians 5:21). God imputed or charged our sin to Christ's account, even though He didn't deserve it. He paid the terrible debt for that sin, and God credited the righteousness of Christ to our account, which was formerly full of sin we couldn't do anything about. And God did it all as a gift because He loved us and wasn't willing to let us perish.

Some people may think this transaction is not necessary because they are counting on the self-righteousness they have been depositing in their spiritual accounts. These are the people who believe they are accumulating enough goodness to pass God's bar of judgment and make it into heaven. They've been going to church, perhaps, or doing good deeds here and there and not committing any really gross sins, so they look at their account and figure they've got enough in there to be OK.

But none of those things in and of themselves count for anything before God. We don't know our true spiritual condition until God audits our account and says, "There is none righteous, not even one" (Romans 3:10). Until God imputes or credits the perfect righteousness of Christ to our lives, we are utterly bankrupt spiritually.

College students probably understand the blessing of imputation better than anyone, especially when they're broke. When our son Anthony Jr. was in college, he called one night. It didn't take him long to get to the point. He needed seventy dollars for something, so he asked us to do an imputation, although he didn't use that word. The idea was for Lois or me to go to the bank and transfer the seventy dollars from our account to Anthony's. We had the money and he didn't, so he was totally dependent on us for the transaction.

The illustration isn't perfect, because in order to credit the seventy dollars to my son's account, I had to diminish my bank account. Jesus Christ is not diminished one iota when He gives us His righteousness, because He is God. But the point is that Anthony had no way of getting what he needed, so he had to look to me for his provision. As long as he was feeling self-sufficient, he didn't see the need to seek my help. It was only when he realized his need that he picked up the phone.

From Slavery to Freedom

There's a wonderful biblical example of imputation in the little book of Philemon. It's about a slave named Onesimus, who stole from his master, Philemon, and ran away, then encountered Paul and got saved. Paul was sending Onesimus back to Philemon, urging Philemon to receive Onesimus back not as a runaway slave to be punished, but as a brother in Christ. Paul even asked Philemon to treat Onesimus as he would treat Paul himself.

To add more weight to his appeal, Paul made this generous offer to Philemon: "But if [Onesimus] has wronged you in any way or owes you anything, charge that to my account; I, Paul, am writing this with my own hand, I will repay it" (Philemon 18–19). That's a description of the biblical doctrine of imputation.

Meeting God's Demand for Perfection

There came a day when I realized that God demanded perfection if I was going to stand before Him. I looked into my spiritual account and saw that I didn't have what God demanded. So I went to God and said, "I'm broke, and I need You to do a transfer. I need the righteousness of Your Son credited to my account, and I trust Him completely for my salvation."

Once you belong to Christ, God now looks into your account and sees that you have what He demands because Christ has already satisfied God's penalty for sin. This is how God can declare sinners like us righteous without compromising His perfect character or lowering His divine standards. Our sin debt wasn't just ignored or brushed aside. Jesus paid it all as God's gift to us.

It gets even better, because the Bible teaches that when we were saved we were placed into Jesus Christ. Paul called it being "clothed . . . with Christ" (Galatians 3:27) and "hidden with Christ" (Colossians 3:3). This means that when God looks at us He sees not merely justified sinners, but His own dear Son. Those who belong to Christ now stand in the same relationship to God as Jesus Himself.

Nobody else has ever done anything like that for you. Someone may have put some money in your account at some point, but nobody else has ever put perfect righteousness into your account. Paul put the capstone on the awesome goodness of God in salvation when he declared, "Thanks be to God for His indescribable gift!" (2 Corinthians 9:15).

Held Firmly by Christ

I like the story of the three men who decided to go mountain climbing and hired two guides to lead them. It so happened that both guides were named Adam. The first Adam took the lead, and the last Adam was behind the three climbers, with all five people connected by ropes.

As they were trying to climb up the precipice, the first Adam slipped, lost his footing, and slipped down the mountain. As he fell, he pulled the three mountain climbers down with him. But when he saw the others falling, the last Adam dug into the mountain and braced himself. He held on to the rope and kept the others from falling, but as he held against the tremendous weight pulling against him, the rope cut into his hands and the blood began to flow. But finally, the first Adam and the climbers were able to climb back up the rope to safety because the last Adam dug in and held on.

That's a picture of our need and Christ's sacrifice. When the first Adam slipped by eating the forbidden fruit in the garden, we all slipped with him and were hanging over the precipice of hell. But on Calvary Jesus held on, refusing to fall to the temptation of Satan. He refused to come down from the cross, and blood ran from His hands as He held on and provided us with a way back up from the precipice of sin. Anyone who is lifted up by the last Adam can scale the mountain and reach the heights of glory in heaven. That's because "the last Adam became a life-giving spirit" (1 Corinthians 15:45).

THE DEMONSTRATION OF JUSTIFICATION

Justification is a spiritual transformation that takes place in our hearts when we come to Christ for salvation. But that doesn't mean our salvation is strictly a private deal between us and God. Being declared righteous in the sight of God should produce changes in our attitudes and behavior that are visible in the sight of others.

That's what I mean by saying that our justification should be demonstrated. Christians ought to act differently than those who don't know Christ. That's the point the apostle James was making when he wrote, "What use is it, my brethren, if someone says he has faith but he has no works? Can that faith save him?" (James 2:14).

A Faith That Works

This verse introduces a passage (James 2:14–26) that generated a lot of controversy in church history because James seems to be contradicting the biblical teaching of salvation by faith alone (see Romans 4:1–8; Ephesians 2:8–9). But James is *complementing,* not contradicting, the truth that we are justified in God's sight through faith alone. James is giving us the human perspective of a divine transaction.

This difference in perspective is the key to understanding James 2. His illustration of a brother or sister in need who is turned away without receiving what he or she needs (vv. 15–17) shows that James was writing about justification not in terms of our standing before God, but in terms of our standing before other people, particularly fellow Christians. James was simply saying that justification should make a difference in the way we live.

What really stirred up the controversy is James's use of Abraham to illustrate his point. "Was not Abraham our father justified by works when he offered up Isaac his son on the altar?" (James 2:21). Paul said in Romans 4:2, "For if Abraham was justified by works, he has something to boast about, but not before God."

Once again, the key to understanding these two passages is the writer's perspective. Note that Paul's concern was being justified "before God." The only way to be right before God is by faith—and James wasn't denying that. He acknowledged that Abraham had faith (James 2:22), but he was saying that the only way the rest of us knew Abraham had faith was when he put his faith into action and offered Isaac in obedience to God. James said Abraham's act of faith brought to fulfillment the Scripture that said, "Abraham believed God, and it was reckoned to him as righteousness" (quoted in James 2:23).

This was written of Abraham in Genesis 15:6, years before his offering of Isaac in Genesis 22. Abraham was justified before God in Genesis 15 based solely on his faith, but he declared his justification to the world years later when he put Isaac on that altar and raised the knife because God told him to. Paul's focus in Romans 4 was on what God did for Abraham in justifying him. James was interested in what Abraham did to demonstrate that he was a justified man.

Saints Who Look Like Saints

Paul was talking about how sinners become saints. James was talking about how saints can look like saints before others.

We can tell people that we are saved, but they can't see what happened in our hearts between God and us. They can only see what we do. A faith that stays private and never reaches our mouths and hands and feet isn't worth much if we're sending our destitute brothers and sisters away with nothing but a blessing when they're hungry and cold. There is definitely a sense in which our good works help to perfect our salvation.

James also said that because Abraham put his faith into action, "He was called the friend of God" (James 2:23). Now this is interesting because it wasn't only God who called Abraham His friend. Other people called Abraham God's friend (see 2 Chronicles 20:7 for an example) because his faith was made visible. An invisible faith is a useless faith, just as a car without gas is a useless vehicle. It's there, but it's of no benefit to anyone.

People argue about the theology of James 2, but our real problem in the church is that we have a lot of people who've been justified by faith but haven't been justified by works. Their faith is hidden. No one knows about it because no one can see that visible validation of the justification they proclaim. So it's possible for us to be saved but not *look like* we're saved because there are no visible good works in our lives. And Paul said that those who are saved by faith alone become God's workmanship, "created in Christ Jesus for good works" (Ephesians 2:10).

Now of course, it's possible for a person to act and look like a Christian and yet not be saved at all, just as it's possible to teach a chimpanzee to mimic human behavior. Chimps can perform all kinds of humanlike behaviors, but it's only an act because they lack the life principle of humanity within. So it is with non-Christians who do not have the life of Christ within, but still look and act like Christians. They do not have the life principle in them. They have not been justified by faith, so their works have no meaning to God because they are not in a right relationship before Him. Therefore, let's be clear that justification by works is real only when it flows out of a life that has been justified before God by faith. It's not a matter of having one without the other. These two aspects of justification are not something we have to choose between.

Making It Real in Today's World

Justification by works is important first of all because God has called us and commanded us to live a life of service to others. Let me give you another reason that it's important for us to validate our faith before others. This has to do with the culture in which we live.

Our day is being called a post-Christian era, and that's true in the sense that Christian values are no longer normative in the wider culture. In our parents' day, even unbelievers generally acknowledged and accepted Christian values as the way a society ought to operate.

But those days are long gone. The Bible is not respected anymore as the Word of God. Pastors and Christian leaders aren't considered worthy of respect by the culture at large. It's no longer honorable, or even OK, to be a Christian in the world's eyes. In a cultural climate like this that distorts real Christianity, confuses the issue of salvation, and teaches people to devalue Christians, it's more important than ever that people see genuine faith at work.

So when people see you being faithful to your wedding vows when no one else is being faithful and they ask you why, you have the opportunity to tell them what motivates you. When your faith leads you to live a life of self-sacrifice when everyone else is into self-aggrandizement, your life becomes a visible demonstration of the difference Christ can make.

THE BENEFITS OF JUSTIFICATION

Now if justification produces a radical change within us and leads to what should be a radical change in our behavior, there ought to be some benefits of this that we can enjoy. And there are. I want to end this chapter by considering just a few of the primary benefits of justification. What can we expect to receive from God when we are brought into a right standing before Him?

Incredible Peace

Everybody wants peace at some level, but peace only comes as the result of a process. "Therefore, having been justified by faith, we have peace with God through our Lord Jesus Christ" (Romans 5:1). This is the peace that comes at the cessation of hostilities. This is the peace that makes friends out of former enemies.

Peace means that God is now our Friend because the reason for the hostility and the barrier between us—our sin—has been removed by Christ. And as Paul said, "If God is for us, who is against us?" (Romans 8:31). Paul went on to list a lot of things that could be against us: "tribulation, or distress, or persecution, or famine, or nakedness, or peril, or sword" (v. 35). But then he came back with the triumphant answer, "In all these things we overwhelmingly conquer through Him who loved us" (v. 37). If you have been justified, God is on your side, even when life seems to fall in on you.

Unlimited Access

Romans 5 continues with the benefits of justification, and it just keeps getting better. "Through [Christ] also we have obtained our introduction by faith into this grace in which we stand" (v. 2). This is the promise of access to God, because once you are at peace with Him and the door barring your way to Him has been opened, you are welcome to come into His presence anytime you want to come. God is ready to meet with you because you have gained access to Him through His Son.

The story is told of a man who sat crying on a bench outside the office of President Abraham Lincoln one day. He had a problem he wanted to see the president about, so he had come to the

White House hoping to see Lincoln. But the guards wouldn't let him in, so he sat there crying.

A little boy came up to the man and asked him what was wrong. The man explained his dilemma, but the boy took him by the hand and led him past the guards straight into the president's office. Nobody said anything to stop him because the boy was Lincoln's son.

Through Jesus Christ we can walk by the guards into our heavenly Father's presence. The writer of Hebrews said that since we have such a high priest, "therefore let us draw near with confidence to the throne of grace" (Hebrews 4:16). We have access to God because we have been justified by His grace.

Eternal Hope

We also have lasting hope through the salvation we have in Christ. Paul continued in Romans 5:2, "We exult in hope of the glory of God." And again, "Hope does not disappoint, because the love of God has been poured out within our hearts through the Holy Spirit who was given to us" (v. 5).

Hope means that even when it looks like it's all over, it's not all over yet. That's why the Bible says we can rejoice even in our tribulations. God is working in our hard times to produce proven character and hope in us (vv. 3–4). It's not over yet because "God causes all things to work together for good to those who love God, to those who are called according to His purpose" (Romans 8:28).

The end of our hope is the glory of God that we will see when we stand before Him as His justified saints. "Much more then, having now been justified by His blood, we shall be saved from the wrath of God through Him" (Romans 5:9). There is no wrath to come for God's saints. We are reconciled to God through Jesus Christ (see v. 11), and we are now the friends of God.

Restoration to Fellowship

When you are justified by the blood of Christ and you stand in right relationship to God, you don't need to get saved again. You will never face the penalty for your sins.

But all of us are living in a dirty world, and sometimes when you live in a dirty environment you can't help but pick up some of the dirt. When you and I sin, we can come to God on the basis of Christ's blood, confess our sin, and receive God's forgiveness, cleansing, and restoration to intimate fellowship (1 John 1:9). It's as if we come to the Lord with our clothes dirty and stained by sin, and He gives us a bath and puts new, clean clothes on us.

There is a great picture of this cleansing in Zechariah, a vision the prophet had of the high priest Joshua, who was serving at that time. In the vision Zechariah saw Joshua standing before "the angel of the Lord, and Satan standing at his right hand to accuse him" (Zechariah 3:1).

This is a picture of us as believers standing before Christ, who appeared in the Old Testament as the angel of the Lord. Satan is our accuser too (Revelation 12:10), and he often has something to work with because we still sin. Joshua stood accused, but God reminded Satan in no uncertain terms that He had already redeemed Joshua. "The Lord rebuke you, Satan! Indeed, the Lord who has chosen Jerusalem rebuke you! Is this not a brand plucked from the fire?" (Zechariah 3:2). We have already been plucked from the fire of God's wrath, for remember that Paul said there is no wrath to come for those who have been justified by Christ's blood.

Now notice Zechariah 3:3. Joshua stood before the Lord "with filthy garments." Something wasn't right, but he had come to the Lord for grace, help, and forgiveness. And God responded, "Remove the filthy garments from him. . . . See, I have taken your iniquity away from you and will clothe you with festal robes" (v. 4). Then God told Joshua, "If you will walk in My ways and if you will perform My service, then you will also govern My house and also have charge of My courts, and I will grant you free access among these who are standing here" (v. 7).

We all get dirty as we live in the world, but because we have peace and access and hope we can come to God and receive a cleansing and a new set of clothes . . . all because we have been justified as a gift of God's grace.

3
REDEMPTION: THE PAYMENT FOR SALVATION

One of the great heroes in African-American history is a woman named Harriet Tubman, a slave in Maryland who escaped to Philadelphia over the famous "underground railroad" and then became one of its most successful conductors in the years leading up to the Civil War.

Mrs. Tubman became known as "Moses" for her work in helping bring slaves to freedom. Altogether, she made nineteen trips back to Maryland and led about three hundred slaves from bondage to freedom. It was said that she worked between trips to get enough money to pay whatever it took for these slaves to reach freedom. The work of the underground railroad was a process of *redemption*, taking people out of slavery and setting them free no matter what the cost.

This story of redemption from human slavery forms an excellent backdrop for discussing the redemption that God accomplished when He sent His Son from heaven to lift us from our spiritual slavery to sin. Redemption involves paying a purchase price, and it was often used in the context of the slave market. As we will see, this is how the biblical writers used the term to describe the purchase price that Jesus Christ paid on the cross.

The people of Jesus' day readily understood references to slavery because at that time the nation of Israel itself was under the heel of its Roman conquerors, and an estimated sixty million people were living as slaves throughout the Roman Empire. These people understood slavery very well.

Most people would not appreciate being called slaves, because it's not an attractive or complimentary term. Slavery suggests being in bondage to a person or a system, with no control over your own life and no way out. But Jesus used this term on one occasion to startle His hearers with the reality of sin's bondage and their need for redemption. And not surprisingly, the people reacted with shock and disbelief.

This discussion took place in John 8, where a group of Jews came to believe in Jesus after hearing Him deal with the Pharisees (v. 30). Turning to the people around Him, Jesus said, "If you continue in My word, then you are truly disciples of Mine; and you will know the truth, and the truth will make you free" (vv. 31–32).

The suggestion that they needed to be free struck these people as a mistake, since as Jews they considered themselves to be no man's slave. So they said to Jesus, "We are Abraham's descendants and have never yet been enslaved to anyone" (v. 33). Then Jesus laid out the real deal. "Truly, truly, I say to you, everyone who commits sin is the slave of sin" (v. 34). The clear implication was that Jesus' hearers were included in this group that was enslaved to sin.

The people understood what Jesus was getting at so well that they became increasingly hostile until He finally said to them, "You are of your father the devil, and you want to do the desires of your father" (v. 44). These verses spell out the problem we all have that requires redemption, because all of us are born in slavery to sin as surely as the children of slaves on Southern plantations were born into the condition of human bondage. And as surely as the chains and shackles of slavery held their victims in an iron grip, the chains and shackles of sin hold every person in an iron grip until Jesus comes to the slave market with His precious blood and redeems us from the auction block.

This bondage to sin reveals itself in a person's attitudes and actions. Paul wrote, "For we also once were foolish ourselves, disobedient, deceived, enslaved to various lusts and pleasures, spending our life in malice and envy, hateful, hating one another" (Titus 3:3). Spiritual slavery works from the inside out, affecting the way we think and the deeds we commit.

So the biblical context of redemption is slavery. That was true in the Old Testament, where God's redemption involved bringing Israel out of slavery in Egypt and into the Promised Land. That's why God said to the people of Israel, "You shall remember that you were a slave in Egypt, and that the Lord your God redeemed you from there" (Deuteronomy 24:18). And in the New Testament, redemption is set against the backdrop of the Roman system of slavery that permeated the entire kingdom.

THE CONCEPT OF REDEMPTION

With this understanding in place we're ready to talk about the term *redeemed,* or *redemption,* and to explore the richness of its meaning in Scripture.

Making the Purchase

The Greek term for redemption means to buy or to purchase, as we saw above. A person who wanted to purchase a slave would go to the slave market and bid on slaves as they were put on the auction block and offered for sale. And depending on how much potential buyers wanted to purchase a particular slave, the bidding price could go quite high. This process is important to keep in mind as we talk about Christ's redemption and the price He paid to redeem us from slavery to sin.

Another important aspect of redemption we need to remember is that the purchaser had three options with regard to the slave he had bought. The buyer could either make that slave his own or resell him—which for the slave simply meant trading one form of bondage for another—or set the newly purchased slave free.

The Greek word usually translated redemption can also be translated "ransom," as in Matthew 20:28, where Jesus said, "The Son of Man did not come to be served, but to serve, and to give His life a ransom for many." We're familiar with the idea of paying a ransom for someone who has been kidnaped or taken prisoner and is being held in bondage until the payment that's demanded is met. Through the sin of our forefather Adam, you and I were kidnapped by sin and Satan and held in bondage until the price was paid to set us free.

Now don't get the wrong idea. We were held in bondage to sin, but the price Jesus paid to redeem us was paid to God, not to Satan. I make this clear because in the early centuries of the church, a heresy arose that said that Jesus' death on the cross was a ransom paid to Satan for our freedom. That heresy was thoroughly condemned, so let's keep the players straight in the drama of redemption. God is the offended party to whom payment for sin must be made, not the devil.

Setting the Slaves Free

The concept of a ransom helps us to understand that when Jesus redeemed us, He did so for the purpose of setting us free, not re-enslaving us. The word Jesus used in Matthew 20:28 for ransom was the redemption price for a slave. This word is closely related to the basic word for redemption, which we would expect. Emphasizing these words is important because what the New Testament writers did a number of times was take this word for redemption (*lutrosis*) and add a prepositional prefix to it (*apolutrosis*) that "super sized" it, we might say.

That is, when the Greek word for redemption is used with this prefix *(apo)*, it signifies more than that Jesus bought us from the slave market of sin. It emphasizes the fact that we have been redeemed in such a way that nobody can ever enslave us again. It means we are redeemed completely and *permanently.*

This stronger word for redemption is used in Romans 3:24, Ephesians 1:7, 14; 4:30; and Colossians 1:14, among other places. It beautifully underscores the permanence of our redemption, which is also a compelling biblical argument for the eternal security of the saved, a truth we'll get to in time.

Pushing the Goat over the Cliff

The background of redemption goes all the way back to ancient Israel as the nation observed the Day of Atonement, the most solemn day of the year, in which the high priest would offer atonement for the people's sins for another year.

According to Leviticus 16:8–26, the high priest chose two goats, one to be sacrificed and the other to be released into the wilderness symbolically bearing away the people's sins. This live goat was called the "scapegoat." The high priest laid his hands on the head of the goat and confessed the nation's sins over the goat, and then it was released in the wilderness. This ritual signified the removal of sin, thus averting the judgment of God against sin for the next year.

Now the only problem was that this goat sometimes wandered back into the Israelites' camp, which nobody wanted to see because it was like having their sins come back on them. So according to some sources, the person who led the goat into the wilderness often took the goat to a cliff and pushed it off. That's a picture of complete redemption—the removal of sin in such a way that it will never show up again.

The reason you can't lose your salvation is that your sins have been pushed off the cliff, so to speak. The scapegoat isn't going to wander back into town tomorrow. If you have trusted Jesus Christ as your Savior, the only way you can miss heaven is if heaven were to cease to exist.

There's a modern-day illustration of redemption that you'll probably remember very well if you're over forty years of age. I'm referring to the Green Stamps that our mothers used to collect at the grocery store. These stamps became a part of American culture when I was growing up.

Shoppers were given a certain number of stamps based on the amount of their purchases. The stamps were pasted into small books, which could then be exchanged for merchandise. Green Stamp catalogs showed these products and how many filled books of stamps it took to purchase each product.

This process was referred to as "redeeming" your Green Stamps. In fact, there were also special Green Stamp stores called redemption centers, where shoppers could take their filled-up stamp books and redeem them for whatever they wanted.

My generation grew up with this vivid picture of redemption woven into the fabric of our everyday lives. "Redemption center" was the right term for these stores, because when we came in with the necessary purchase price in the form of Green Stamp books, we set that merchandise free from the center and took it home so it could fulfill its intended function.

THE COST OF REDEMPTION

What was the cost Jesus had to pay to redeem us? Peter addressed this when he wrote to believers scattered across the empire. He urged them to live in the fear of the Lord, because "you were not redeemed with perishable things like silver or gold . . . but with precious blood, as of a lamb unblemished and spotless, the blood of Christ" (1 Peter 1:18–19).

Now if you're a slave on the auction block and someone wants to purchase you, your redeemer has to be able to afford the cost of your redemption. To use the illustration above, a person couldn't go into a Green Stamp redemption center with one book of stamps and expect to walk out with a major appliance. The price tag for something that valuable would be far beyond that. Sin was so costly that it required heaven's best to buy us out of the slave market, because God's judgment against sin is so severe.

Jesus Had to Shed His Blood

Blood has always been the price for sin. "Without shedding of blood there is no forgiveness" (Hebrews 9:22). Money won't do the job. We can't buy our way out of the sin mess. Peter called silver and gold "perishable things" that have no purchasing power in heaven's economy. "In Him [Christ] we have redemption through His blood" (Ephesians 1:7).

When an Israelite brought that spotless lamb to the priest as a sin offering, the priest laid his hand on the head of the lamb while the person who brought the lamb confessed his or her sin, signifying the transfer of guilt to the lamb. Then the priest cut the lamb's throat and shed its blood as the lamb died in place of the guilty person. God's price tag for redemption has always been blood.

Why blood? The Bible tells us in Deuteronomy 12:23, "The blood is the life." So the shedding of blood is another way of saying that the sacrifice had to die. Jesus had to die on the cross, not simply hang there and suffer for a while. Because He died, He was able to enter into the tabernacle in heaven to offer His blood as the payment for sin (see Hebrews 9:11–14). And what did His death purchase? "The redemption of the transgressions that were committed under the first covenant," according to Hebrews 9:15.

Jesus Had to Be Sinless

The redeemer also had to be someone who was not among the slaves himself. If you and I are both slaves, I'm not going to come to you saying, "Pay the price and set me free." If you can't set yourself free, you certainly can't buy my freedom. It's like the two men who fell into a deep ditch. One of the men panicked, turned to the other man, and said, "Get me out of here!" But the other man was in the same mess. What those men needed was someone from above the ditch reaching down to pull them out.

Whoever is going to redeem slaves has to be a free person. Transferring this to the spiritual realm, it means our Redeemer has to be sinless. Why? Because we're enslaved to the sin that we inherited from Adam and the sin we commit ourselves. Since God is perfectly holy, He will not accept payment for sin from a sinner.

That's why Jesus was born of a virgin. Sin is passed on through the father, so Jesus could not have a human father. He had to be born without sin, and He also had to live a sinless life. Peter said God's sacrifice for sin was "unblemished" and "spotless" (1 Peter 1:19), just as were the animals used for sacrifice under the Law.

The mention of a lamb as the sin sacrifice again takes us back to the Old Testament. The lambs that the Israelites brought to offer for their sins had to be without any defects. Why? Because they were a picture of the coming Redeemer who would be totally sinless and blameless, and whose death therefore would pay the redemption price God demanded.

If Jesus had the same sin problem we have, He could not be our Redeemer because He Himself would need a Redeemer. He had to be free of any blemish of sin. He had to live a perfect life and defeat the devil. He had to be perfect so He could offer His "precious blood" to redeem us out of slavery.

Jesus Had to Become a Man

Let me point out one more requirement Jesus had to fulfill to pay the cost of our redemption. The author of Hebrews made a very important statement when he said, "It is impossible for the blood of bulls and goats to take away sins" (10:4). Animal sacrifices could only cover sins until God's perfect sacrifice came. What I'm saying is that in order to be a suitable substitute for mankind, Jesus had to be a man. That's why He left heaven's glory to take on human flesh. In light of the cost that Jesus paid, anything we could offer to God as a payment for our sins would be an insult to Him.

The story is told of two boys who were swimming in the lake. One of the boys went out too far, got in trouble, and began to sink. The second boy, seeing his friend in trouble, swam out to save him. He was able to keep the first boy afloat until help arrived, but in the process became exhausted and sank beneath the water. He drowned saving his friend.

Later that day, the parents of the boy who was saved came to the parents of the boy who died saving their son and said, "All we have on us right now is a dollar and eighty-three cents. We know it isn't much, but we hope you'll accept this as our payment to you for the life of our son."

Now if you were the parents who had lost their son, how would you feel? I think you would feel terribly offended and insulted. But this is the way we appear to God when we try to offer Him our acts of human goodness as payment for our own sins. Nothing we can offer God will even begin to make up for what it cost Him to save us. Don't insult God by offering Him your dollar-eighty-three when He has given you His precious Son. The cost of our redemption is infinitely high.

THE ACCOMPLISHMENT OF REDEMPTION

What did Christ's redemption accomplish for us? In one sense, we've been answering this question throughout the chapter as we have discussed this aspect of our great salvation. But I want to give you two specifics here that are important in helping to fill out the picture of what Christ has done for us.

Jesus Freed Us from the Curse

The Bible says that we were under a curse before we came to know Jesus Christ. Paul explained the nature of the curse in Galatians 3:10: "For as many as are of the works of the Law are under a curse; for it is written, 'Cursed is everyone who does not abide by all things written in the book of the Law, to perform them.'"

This is a verse you can show your unsaved friends when they claim they're doing their best to keep the Ten Commandments and they believe this will be enough to get them to heaven. The fact is that trying to keep God's Law in your own power brings a curse, not a reward. The reason is captured in that little word *all* in the verse quoted above.

God's requirement is *perfect* obedience. A person would have to keep all of God's Law, without failure or exception, to merit His favor. Anything less than that, and the offender falls under God's curse. James put it this way: "Whoever keeps the whole law and yet stumbles in one point, he has become guilty of all" (James 2:10). In other words, the Law is not a cafeteria where you can pick out what you want and skip the rest.

Most people have a cafeteria view of the Law. "Well, I may not keep all the Ten Commandments all the time, but I keep most of them some of the time." No, no. The Law is a package deal, all or nothing.

Since we have all failed to keep God's Law, we are all under its curse. But here's the good news: "Christ redeemed us from the curse of the Law, having become a curse for us—for it is written, 'Cursed is everyone who hangs on a tree'" (Galatians 3:13). Of course, Christ hung on a tree when He died on the cross, and His death redeemed us from the Law's curse, which was the sanctions and penalties the Law imposed on those who disobeyed it.

In other words, the Law of God had consequences attached to it. That's true even in human law. Wherever you have law and the possibility of violation, you have penalties attached for those violations. God is too holy to skip the penalty for sin.

Our world operates on the same principle. Try calling your mortgage company or your bank and asking them just to skip your next house or car payment because you're a decent person and deserve a reward for being nice. It will never happen. Your creditors will demand payment, and they have the law on their side because you incurred those debts legally. The only thing your creditors want to know is whether you're going to pay your debts—and if not, who else they can go to for the money. That debt has to be paid.

That's what Christ did for us when He paid the redemption price to remove us from the Law's curse, which was physical death and ultimately spiritual death. God couldn't just look the other way and ignore His Law, because His holy demands are inextricably tied to His holy character. He can't skip the Law, but He will allow somebody else to pay the debt we owe.

That's why Jesus came. In Galatians 4:4–5, Paul made this very interesting statement about Christ: "When the fullness of time came, God sent forth His Son, born of a woman, born under the Law, so that He might redeem those who were under the Law, that we might receive the adoption as sons."

God Adopted Us into His Family

Don't hurry past that last phrase. Thanks to redemption, we're family! It's one thing to be bought off the slave market and set free. It's another thing entirely to be taken into the home of the person who freed you and given full status and inheritance as a member of the family.

That's what adoption meant in Paul's day. It was entirely different from adoption as we know it. Instead of adopting infants or children, families in those days took a child in and raised him to adulthood before adopting him. The adoptee became not only a full member of the family, but an heir of the estate.

When Christ redeemed us, He brought us into His Father's house and gave us all the rights and privileges that come with being members of God's family.

We Are Set Free from Fear

What do you think most people fear more than anything else? My guess is that most people fear death more than anything (see Hebrews 2:15).

There is fear to the thought of death, especially for those who don't know Christ. Death has a sting to it. "The sting of death is sin, and the power of sin is the law" (1 Corinthians 15:56). The Law reveals our sin to us, and sin results in death. Death is the curse of the Law. That's how it works, which is why you ought to be thankful every day that Christ has redeemed you from the curse of the Law.

Have you ever felt afraid of dying? Tell the truth and shame the devil! Well, let me give you some good news. Because Jesus Christ came and redeemed you from the slave market of sin, you will never experience the thing you fear most.

You say, "Wait a minute, Tony. All of us die. What about that casket that will be at the front of the church during my funeral?" Yes, the shell you used to live in will be lying in that casket. But the Bible says that for believers, "To be absent from the body [is] to be at home with the Lord" (2 Corinthians 5:8). Before the doctor has a chance to pronounce you dead, you will be immediately ushered into God's presence.

According to Luke 16:22, when the beggar Lazarus died, he "was carried away by the angels to Abraham's bosom."

In fact, as believers we have a special moment waiting for us as we approach death. When Stephen the faithful deacon was about to be stoned to death because of his witness for Christ, "he gazed intently into heaven and saw the glory of God, and Jesus standing at the right hand of God; and he said, 'Behold, I see the heavens opened up and the Son of Man standing at the right hand of God'" (Acts 7:55–56). The Jews hadn't started stoning Stephen yet, but when he said this they rushed upon him, dragged him outside of Jerusalem, and stoned him to death as he cried out, "Lord Jesus, receive my spirit!" (v. 59).

Now notice that Stephen saw Jesus *standing* at God's right hand. The Bible says that when Jesus finished His work of redemption and ascended to heaven, He *sat down* at God's right hand (Hebrews 1:3).

Why did Stephen see Jesus standing? To welcome him home. God was giving Stephen a standing ovation, a glimpse into glory so he wouldn't fear what was about to happen and wouldn't try to hang on down here on earth. So when you're in your last moments and the doctor says there is no hope, you can pray one simple prayer: "Lord,

I give all of me to all of You, and I only request that You let me see heaven open so that I want to be there more than I want to stay here." Redemption replaces the terror of death with a vision of heaven.

OUR RESPONSE TO REDEMPTION

Since Christ's redemption has done all of this for us, and much more, how should we respond to our great salvation? Let me suggest three appropriate responses.

We Should Serve Christ

We should be motivated to serve Christ for all He has done for us. Paul said of Jesus in Titus 2:14, "[He] gave Himself for us to redeem us from every lawless deed, and to purify for Himself a people for His own possession, zealous for good deeds." When someone pays an infinitely high price to buy you out of slavery and death simply because He loves you, nothing you can do for Him is too much. Peter said we've already spent too much time serving sin and following our own desires (see 1 Peter 4:3). It's time for us to serve the Lord.

I think of an old Western movie called *The Hanging Tree*. In the film, a young man gets shot and is near death as he is brought to a doctor. The doctor treats the young man and rescues him from the jaws of death. When the patient gets back on his feet, he says to the doctor, "I don't know how I can repay you for saving my life. What can I do?"

The doctor replies, "Well, you can stay here and help me in my practice." If you've been redeemed from the jaws of death by Jesus Christ, the best thing you can do is serve Him.

We Should Worship Christ

When John received the revelation of Jesus Christ on the island of Patmos, he saw a vision of the risen Christ, "Who loves us and released us from our sins by His blood . . . to Him be the glory and the dominion forever and ever" (Revelation 1:5–6). Later, the four living creatures and the twenty-four elders in heaven fell down before Christ in worship and said, "Worthy are You to take the book and to break its seals; for You were slain, and purchased for God with Your blood men from every tribe and tongue and people and nation" (5:9).

Notice that these are perfect heavenly beings who did not need redemption. Yet they're on their faces day and night worshiping the Lamb for His redemption of sinners like us. What does that tell us about the worship we owe to Christ? He deserves our worship because He paid the price to redeem us.

A boy once captured two little birds and put them in a cage. A man saw the boy carrying the cage and asked him what he was going to do with the birds. "Oh," the boy replied, "I'm going to play with them for a while and then feed them to my cat."

The man looked at the caged birds and took pity on them. "Say, I'd like to buy the cage and the birds from you. How much do you want for them?"

The boy thought for a minute and then named his price. The man paid it and the boy handed over the cage, after which the man immediately opened the cage and set the birds free.

That's what Jesus did for us. Satan had us caged and was going to feed us into the jaws of eternal death. But Jesus Christ purchased us, cage and all, and set us free. We're going to be worshiping Him for all eternity in heaven because He paid that price. We need to start practicing our worship down here. He is infinitely worthy.

We Should Proclaim Christ

Realizing the greatness of our redemption should also motivate us to proclaim Christ. Paul said, "We proclaim Him, admonishing every man and teaching every man with all wisdom" (Colossians 1:28). We have a message to proclaim: "We preach Christ crucified"

(1 Corinthians 1:23). Paul even said, "Woe is me if I do not preach the gospel" (1 Corinthians 9:16).

We have too many "secret agent" Christians in the body of Christ. He redeemed us at a great price, but too many of us can't even bow our heads in a public place to pray for fear of being embarrassed. Too many of us can't speak His name out loud because we're afraid of what people will think. But if we've been set free from slavery and we see our friends and loved ones still in chains about to be sold on the auction block, we ought to tell them how they can be free.

A boy made himself a special boat that he loved with all his heart. But one day as he was sailing it on the lake, the wind blew it away and he lost it. Sometime later, the boy was walking along the shore of the lake when he saw his boat for sale in the window of a store.

The boy went into the store and said to the owner, "Sir, that's my boat in the window. I made it, but the wind blew it away while I was sailing it."

The store owner replied, "I'm sorry, son. But I had to pay for that boat and I can only let you have it if you buy it."

So the boy went home and worked hard, earning enough money to buy back his boat. As soon as he had enough, he ran back to the store and bought his boat. He hugged it tight and said, "Little boat, now you belong to me twice. I made you, and I've bought you back."

You and I belong to Jesus Christ twice. He created us, and He paid the price to redeem us. We belong to Him body and soul. Our song should be, "Redeemed, how I love to proclaim it!"

4

PROPITIATION: THE REQUIREMENT FOR SALVATION

As I'm writing this book, a story has come out of Great Britain of two young men who are being released from a youth facility after serving nearly a decade for brutally murdering a two-year-old boy.

You may remember the case, because it grabbed international headlines at the time. The boys were only ten when they committed the senseless crime, but they were caught on videotape calmly leading the toddler away from his parents through the airport. The anger against them was so great that they had to be transported back and forth to court in an armored car.

The two were sentenced to a term in the youth prison, but it's obvious that their years behind bars have done little to satisfy the community's outrage. Officials said the hostility against the boys was still so intense that they would have to be taken somewhere else and given false identities for their own protection.

This story serves to illustrate the importance of *propitiation*, the next aspect of our great salvation that I want to consider. Propitiation is necessary because our sin has offended the holiness of God and incurred His wrath, which must be satisfied or appeased before He can accept us.

This is the key to the meaning of propitiation. To propitiate means to render one person favorably disposed toward another. It signifies the averting of wrath by the offering of a gift to appease the offended party's anger. We could summarize this great concept with the word *satisfaction*. To propitiate means to satisfy. God is dissatisfied with the human race because sin is an affront to His holy character. So something must be done to appease God's righteous anger.

All of us have done this at some level. We call it "making up." A husband who has upset his wife might bring her some flowers to say, "I'm sorry." Children who know they have messed up might sweet-talk their parents or do a household chore without being told to try to take the edge off their parents' anger and lessen the punishment.

THE PRINCIPLE OF PROPITIATION

The Bible is filled with examples of one person propitiating another. Jacob sought to propitiate his brother Esau after stealing his blessing (Genesis 33). After Abigail's foolish husband Nabal insulted David and his men, Abigail took David an offering and pleaded with him not to kill Nabal (1 Samuel 25:14–35). In 2 Kings 18:13–16, King Hezekiah propitiated Sennacherib, the king of Assyria, with gold and silver in order to keep him from invading Jerusalem.

Two Problems with Human Propitiation

There are at least two questions that arise in any human attempt at propitiation. The first is whether the gift or offering is sufficient to turn away the other person's anger. Esau could have considered Jacob's gift as inadequate payment for all the pain he believed Jacob had caused him.

The second question is whether the offended party will accept the gift, no matter how great it is. David could have been so angry at Nabal that he wouldn't have been satisfied if Abigail had given him every penny she had.

I mention these conditions because you need to know right up front that we don't have to worry about the payment for sin being adequate, or God refusing to accept it. Christ's death on the cross was a complete payment for sin, and God is completely satisfied with His Son's offering.

God's Nature Has Two Perfect Sides

This is definitely good news, but a lot of folk don't want to believe that God is all that upset with the human race. These are the people who say that God is too loving to judge sin or condemn anyone to hell, and they want to end the discussion of God's nature right there.

God *is* love, but He is also just. His response to sin is necessitated by His righteousness. The Bible teaches that there are two sides to God's character. Paul summarized them in Romans 11:22 when he wrote, "Behold then the kindness and severity of God." We could call these the polar caps of God's character. His kindness, or love, and His severity, or judgment, are in perfect harmony because they are both perfect attributes of His being.

The book of Nahum opens with a classic statement of God's goodness and severity. In Nahum 1 we read, "The Lord is avenging and wrathful" (v. 2). "The Lord will by no means leave the guilty unpunished" (v. 3). "Who can stand before His indignation? Who can endure the burning of His anger? His wrath is poured out like fire" (v. 6). But then in verse 7 the prophet declared, "The Lord is good, a stronghold in the day of trouble, and He knows those who take refuge in Him."

God is both wrathful and loving, but not in the same way that we are. We get upset with people who tick us off or get on our nerves, but our wrath may be anything but righteous. Or we show love toward people who please us or return our affection, but our love is also imperfect.

Not so with God. His intolerance toward sin is the intolerance of a surgeon who insists on sterile instruments for an operation. A surgeon's demand for a pure operating environment is not an angry, peevish reaction to the presence of bacteria, but a settled conviction that is part of what it means to be a surgeon.

Whether the surgeon's scalpel has been dipped in mud or just exposed to bacteria, the result would be contamination. None of us gets upset if our surgeon insists on absolute cleanliness in the operating room, where even a speck of dirt could lead to an infection. In fact, we insist on absolute purity under those conditions. We demand that our surgeon be completely intolerant of any impurity.

If you understand a surgeon's "wrath" against contamination in a hospital operating room, you understand God's wrath against sin. He is perfect and sinless in every detail, and His character demands that He deal with the slightest contamination of sin. God also knows that sin leads to total corruption and infection, so for these reasons He must judge sin. As we read in Nahum, He will not let the guilty go unpunished.

God has already passed judgment on the world and declared all of us guilty because "all have sinned" (Romans 3:23). He has also pronounced the sentence against sin: "The wages of sin is death" (Romans 6:23). Therefore, we must either bear the full brunt of God's wrath against our sin, or someone must come in between us and God and provide an offering that is adequate to satisfy His demands so that we can go free.

THE PROVISION OF PROPITIATION

This brings us to a question. What do we give someone who already has everything? What can we offer to propitiate a Being whose only acceptable standard is perfection? When it comes to propitiation, we are in trouble on our own because whatever pitiful offering we could make is so far below what God requires that the only way He could accept it would be to compromise His holy character. And that is never going to happen.

That's why human good works and attempts to live a good life will never please God on their own. Our sin is such an outrage against God that it is an insult to offer Him mere human effort. So we have a problem, because the penalty for our sin is eternal punishment and separation from God in hell. When you commit a crime against an eternal Being, there are eternal consequences. Hell is where God's eternal justice will be exacted against sinners.

God Paid the Price Himself

I don't want to pay that price, and neither does anyone else in his right mind. So what do we do? We have no gift costly enough or perfect enough to propitiate or satisfy God. The prophet Micah asked, "With what shall I come to the Lord and bow myself before the God on high?" (Micah 6:6).

This is the dilemma for every person, but there is good news. Knowing that we had nothing in ourselves with which to satisfy Him, God decided to take the initiative and provide His own sacrifice of propitiation. We ought to stop right here and have a praise service! Think about what that means for you and me. Paul put it this way: "For while we were still helpless, at the right time Christ died for the ungodly" (Romans 5:6).

We have a wonderful biblical example of this principle in the offering of Isaac by his father Abraham. As Abraham and Isaac were heading up the mountain where Abraham was going to offer Isaac in obedience to God, Isaac asked a very fundamental question. "Behold, the fire and the wood, but where is the lamb for the burnt offering?" (Genesis 22:7).

Abraham's answer summarized the heart of what God has done for us. "God will provide for Himself the lamb for the burnt offering" (v. 8). God Himself absorbed the awful cost to provide a sacrifice that would satisfy His righteous demands.

When my wife, Lois, and I came to Dallas Theological Seminary in 1972, we were as poor as poor could be. The fundamental question we faced was how in the world we were going to satisfy the seminary's economic requirements. How were we going to pay for school and still have anything left to live on?

The people at Dallas Seminary did not say to me, "Tony, since you chose our school out of all the schools you could have attended, we are going to cut your tuition in half." The folks at DTS were very caring and concerned about their students' needs, and they still are. But when I enrolled, I was given a bill to pay.

So Lois and I both got jobs, but then our oldest daughter, Crystal, got sick, and Lois had to stop working. I could only work part-time, so it soon became obvious that we were not going to be able to satisfy the "righteous" economic demands of Dallas Seminary. The school was perfectly justified in presenting us with a bill, but we did not have the wherewithal to satisfy the payments required.

That meant that Dallas Seminary either had to overlook our bill, which it couldn't do and still meet its own bills, or I had to drop out of school. But while the Evanses were still financially helpless, the propitiation was made. Someone must have looked in our checkbook, because I went to my campus mailbox one day and found a letter that said that Dallas Seminary had awarded me a full scholarship for the cost of my education.

In other words, the school was paying its own bill—providing its own propitiation, if you will. I'm glad they did, because my meager offerings would have never satisfied that bill! The scholarship so completely satisfied the financial charges that were posted against my account that from then on, the school was free to charge me nothing and yet continue to provide me with the full benefits of a seminary education.

God Turned His Wrath on His Son

You get the idea. God looked into our bankrupt spiritual account and saw that we had nothing with which to pay the bill of sin. So in the Person of Jesus Christ, God made Himself the answer to our problem. Since we could not satisfy God's wrath against sin, He decided to satisfy His wrath by turning it on His own Son.

The story is told of a king who made a law that anybody in his kingdom who committed a certain crime would have an eye put out by a hot poker. One day a young man committed that crime, and as the poker was being prepared he was brought before the king. But when the king saw the young offender, he cried out in shock and sadness because the young man was his son.

The law had to be satisfied, however, so the king took the poker and put out his own eye. The law demanding an eye for this crime was satisfied, but in order to save his son, and as an act of love, the king absorbed the pain and the punishment in his own body. The king's son was thus set free.

God's judgment against sin had to be applied, but His love moved Him to devise a plan whereby the guilty would go free and His innocent Son would be punished. We could say that God drew on His love to pay His wrath—a divine transaction that we had no part whatsoever in helping to bring about.

God was propitiated by the offering of a sacrifice. In the Old Testament system, the place of propitiation for sin was the "mercy seat" that formed the lid on the ark of the covenant (Hebrews 9:1–5). The high priest entered the Holy of Holies, the inner sanctum of the tabernacle and later the temple, once a year to offer the blood of the sacrificial lamb on the mercy seat. If God accepted the sacrifice, the sins of the people of Israel were covered for another year.

We know that this sacrifice was an act of propitiation because the word translated "mercy seat" in Hebrews 9:5 is a form of the word for propitiation. The mercy seat was the place of propitiation.

This is significant because later in Hebrews 9 the writer said that Jesus Christ entered the Holy Place of the true temple in heaven as a once-for-all sacrifice for sin (vv. 24–28). He did this "by the sacrifice of Himself" (v. 26), offering His own blood on the mercy seat. Through Christ's death, God has been propitiated forever toward sinners, and the way of salvation is open. That's why when Christ comes back the second time, He will appear "for salvation" and not to offer another sin offering (v. 28). Because of Christ's provision, we have moved from being the objects of God's eternal wrath to the objects of His eternal favor.

THE POWER OF PROPITIATION

This aspect of our great salvation called propitiation was accomplished two thousand years ago on the Cross. But it doesn't end there, because Jesus Christ is active today in heaven as our Great High Priest. The Bible says, "He is able also to save forever those who draw near to God through Him, since He always lives to make intercession for them" (Hebrews 7:25).

Christ needs to intercede for us today because we still sin even as believers. The apostle John spelled out the power of Christ's propitiation to deal with our sin and keep our salvation secure. What we have already learned about His work is sweet, but this gets even sweeter:

> My little children, I am writing these things to you so that you may not sin. And if anyone sins, we have an Advocate with the Father, Jesus Christ the righteous; and He Himself is the propitiation for our sins; and not for ours only, but also for those of the whole world. (1 John 2:1–2)

Our Defense Attorney in Heaven

Jesus Christ is called our "Advocate," or defense attorney, who appears before the Father on our behalf. Why do we need a defense attorney? Because Satan, "the accuser of [the] brethren" (Revelation 12:10), is constantly bringing our sins before God, knowing that God cannot overlook sin and must respond to it. Satan is looking to get a judgment against us.

You see, Satan understands the wrath of God because he has experienced it. He was banished from heaven, and will spend eternity in hell, because of God's righteous wrath against sin. What Satan wants to do is take us down with him.

But he will never succeed, because our Advocate is Jesus Christ, who has forever satisfied God's demands. The setting in 1 John 2 is a courtroom. God is the Judge, and we are the defendants who have sinned and broken fellowship with Him. The prosecutor is Satan, who wants the Judge to throw the book at us for our sin.

But then our Advocate steps forward and says, "Father, I object. While the accuser is correct on the sin, what has not been brought forth is the fact that I have already paid for this sin and satisfied Your demands through the blood I shed on the cross. And My blood will continue to pay for sin because the accused is one of those I have redeemed." Case dismissed.

This is what John had said earlier in his letter: "If we walk in the light as He Himself is in the light . . . the blood of Jesus His Son cleanses us from all sin" (1 John 1:7). You have a defense attorney who is related to the judge, so make sure you use your attorney when you sin. When you confess your sins to God (1 John 1:9), your Advocate speaks up for you. Attorneys cost too much not to use them, and your attorney, Jesus Christ, paid too high a price not to call on Him!

Notice that John called Jesus Christ "the righteous" in 1 John 2:1. In other words, He's qualified to speak in the courtroom because He doesn't have the sin problem of those whom He is representing. Jesus is the only Person who is qualified to be our heavenly Advocate.

We need such an Advocate because Satan is looking to chew us up. On the night of Jesus' arrest, Christ said to Peter, "Simon, Simon, behold, Satan has demanded permission to sift you like wheat; but I have prayed for you, that your faith may not fail" (Luke 22:31–32). Peter came back with a cocky assurance that He would stand with Jesus even to death, but Jesus predicted Peter's betrayal. Peter failed, but Jesus was praying for him.

You are not the only person praying for you. When you call on God "in Jesus' name," you are tapping into the power of God. This is not just a magical catchphrase to throw in at the end of a prayer. When you pray "in Jesus' name," you are saying to the Father, "Lord, I have laid all of these things before you. But since I'm not qualified for Your grace, I come in the authority of Your Son and ask You to do this for His sake, because I know You won't refuse Your Son."

God's Only Program for Sin

This is our Advocate, Jesus Christ, who Himself is the propitiation for our sins. Later in his epistle, John used this term again to describe Jesus when he wrote, "In this is love, not that we loved God, but that He loved us and sent His Son to be the propitiation for our sins" (1 John 4:10).

God only has one program to deal with sin, and that program is His beloved Son. God the Father is completely satisfied with Jesus' sacrifice for sin, which is why He doesn't want to hear about our plans for trying to make ourselves acceptable to Him. Let's make sure we are clear on this point. The only thing that satisfies God is His Son, so for us to be talking about our goodness and our works is not only irrelevant to the discussion, it is an insult to grace.

You see, God doesn't want to know what you are going to do with your sin. He wants to know what you are going to do with His Son. God will talk to you about your good works *after* you have been to the Cross and applied the blood of Jesus to your sins. Until then, anything you try to do for Him is not satisfactory, because only Jesus can satisfy God.

THE EXTENT OF PROPITIATION

I didn't deal with the last phrase of 1 John 2:2 earlier because I wanted to save it for special study as we close this chapter. John said that Jesus was not only the propitiation for our sins, meaning that of believers, "but also for those of the whole world." We need to find out what John meant by this, because at first reading it sounds like everyone is going to be saved.

But we know that the Bible does *not* teach universal salvation, so it's important to understand in what sense Jesus has made propitiation for the sins of every person. This raises the issue of the extent of Christ's atonement, a vital biblical doctrine that we will deal with at several points throughout this book. Let's begin by examining some key Scriptures on the subject.

The Reality of God's Love

According to Romans 5:8–9, "God demonstrates His own love toward us, in that while we were yet sinners, Christ died for us. Much more then, having now been justified by His blood, we shall be saved from the wrath of God through Him." Notice several things about the Bible's teaching concerning salvation.

First, we read that God demonstrated His love. He didn't just talk about it. We often talk a better game than we play when it comes to love, but God put His love on the line by giving His Son for our sin.

How do you know God loves you? Because of Calvary. The proof of God's love is what Jesus suffered on the cross of Calvary when He took our place and suffered God's full wrath against sin to satisfy God's righteous demands.

Second, notice also that God's love in salvation is unconditional. God gave us His Son while we were still sinners in rebellion against Him. He didn't ask us to get better first, or clean up our act before Jesus would receive us. Jesus died for you and me when we weren't even thinking about our act, much less cleaning it up. Salvation comes without preconditions.

Third, the Bible also says that salvation is permanent. We're going to spend part of this book studying the doctrine of our security in Christ, but let me give you a taste now. Paul asked, "Who will separate us from the love of Christ?" (Romans 8:35). Answer: No one and nothing! He gives a long list of possibilities, then, in case he missed anything, he adds, "nor any other created thing, will be able to separate us from the love of God, which is in Christ Jesus our Lord" (v. 39). Once you truly receive salvation, you can never lose it.

Fourth, the salvation God provided in Christ Jesus extends to all people. This is what John was saying in 1 John 2:2. The atonement of Christ is unlimited, in other words. The question is how the atonement is applied to believers and unbelievers, since the Bible also clearly teaches that many people will be lost for eternity despite the fact that sufficient provision has been made for their salvation if they will turn to Christ.

The Outworking of God's Love

There is a lot of debate in the church about the extent of Christ's atonement. The Bible is clear that Christ died for every man, woman, boy, and girl who was, is, and ever will be born. Jesus is the Savior of the whole world (see John 1:29; 3:16).

Paul made this important statement: "While we were still helpless, at the right time Christ died for the ungodly" (Romans 5:6). How many people are ungodly? Everybody. The Bible says Jesus "gave Himself as a ransom for all" (1 Timothy 2:6). We could multiply biblical examples that show that Christ died for every person.

In 1 Timothy 4:10, Paul wrote to Timothy, "We have fixed our hope on the living God, who is the Savior of all men, especially of believers." Please notice that the apostle was careful to distinguish believers from the rest of the world as he spoke of Christ's salvation. In what sense is Christ the Savior of all people?

The answer is that Christ's salvation has a two-pronged effect. We saw in chapter 1 that because Adam was acting as our representative when he sinned in the Garden, his sin was charged to the account of the human race. "Through one man sin entered into the world" (Romans 5:12).

We could use a sports analogy and say that when Adam sinned the whole team was penalized. This is very important to understanding the extent of salvation, so let's read on in Romans 5, because here Paul compared the work of Christ to the sin of Adam, and compared the extent of salvation with the extent of Adam's sin.

"For if by the transgression of the one the many died, much more did . . . the gift by the grace of the one Man, Jesus Christ, abound to the many" (v. 15). The key phrase here is "the many." In relation to Adam's sin, "the many" are those who inherited his sin and the spiritual death it brought, which is every person. Paul said this same group has been given the gift of grace in Jesus Christ. As the apostle wrote in 1 Corinthians 15:22, "For as in Adam all die, so also in Christ all will be made alive."

The question is, Does this teach universal salvation? After all, John said that Jesus accomplished the work of propitiation for the whole world. I use the word *accomplished* for a reason, because the Bible teaches that Christ did not simply offer or make possible salvation for all. He *accomplished* salvation for all.

Some people see a conflict between this fact and the undeniable reality that not all people are saved. One group tries to get around this by saying that Christ died only for the elect. But that doesn't work, because Hebrews 2:9 clearly says that Jesus tasted death for every person.

Another group tries to solve the problem by arguing that Christ merely provided or offered salvation to everybody. But this weakens the power of salvation's offer because according to Romans 5:18, from Christ's "one act of righteousness there resulted justification of life to all men." This says that the work necessary for salvation has been accomplished, not just offered or made possible.

Why Not Everyone Is Saved

So if all of this is true, why are not all people saved? We need to look at one more verse in Romans 5, and then we'll put all of this together. "For if by the transgression of the one, death reigned through the one, much more those who receive the abundance of grace and of the gift of righteousness will reign in life through the One, Jesus Christ" (v. 17). Here is the key to what the Bible means when it says that all those who inherited Adam's sin have been brought under the saving death of Christ.

The answer is quite simple. Take note of the word *receive* in the middle of verse 17. Christ has accomplished salvation for all people regarding Adam's sin, but His atonement is effective for personal sin only for those who receive it. You didn't have a choice about inheriting Adam's sin, but you do have a choice to receive or reject God's grace in Christ for the sins you have committed. If you refuse Jesus as the propitiation for your sins, you are left with the impossible task of trying to satisfy God through your own merits and good works.

You see, two things must happen before we can be saved. First, God's holy and righteous wrath against sin must be satisfied by the shedding of blood, which is the act of propitiation we have been talking about. Because God is propitiated by the death of His Son, He is now free to forgive and save sinners.

But you and I need something else to get us into heaven. We not only need God's judgment against sin to be satisfied, we must have perfect righteousness to stand before Him because God is perfect. When we trust Christ, His righteousness is credited to our account, just the way Adam's sin was charged to our account. This wonderful transaction is called imputation, meaning that Christ imputed or transferred His righteousness to us, canceling out the sin that was charged against us from Adam.

To sum it all up, the work of Christ accomplished salvation for sin. That includes both our individual sins and the contamination of our sin nature that Adam passed on to the human race when he sinned. According to Romans 5:15, the atonement that Christ provided on the cross caused God's grace to "flow" to the same people who were dead spiritually because of Adam's sin. Paul was teaching that Adam's sin was a different case because he was acting as the head of the human race when he sinned. That's why one man's sin could bring condemnation on the whole race (v. 16). So God applied Christ's death to Adam's sin to reverse its effect on all of us, but God only applies Christ's atonement to your personal sin when you believe in Christ as your personal Savior. The sins of every person have been completely paid for, but people can reject that payment.

The implications of this are staggering. This answers the objection of those who say they don't think it's fair that they should die for Adam's sin. No one has to worry about that, because the fact is that nobody will go to hell for Adam's sin. Adam's sin was paid for in Christ's death for the whole human race. The sin for which people will have to answer is their own sin, not the sin nature they inherited from Adam.

This explains, for example, why babies go to heaven when they die. Babies are born with a sin nature inherited from Adam, but they have no personal sin to account for because they have not reached the age at which they can be held accountable. Babies go to heaven because what Jesus did on the cross took care of Adam's sin, that is, original sin.

So make no mistake. People will go to hell because they sinned, not because Adam sinned. The effects of his sin are still with us, to be sure. But Christ's death canceled the penalty of Adam's sin. Jesus said in John 3:18 that people are condemned because "[they have] not believed in the name of the only begotten Son of God." Jesus has done everything necessary for salvation. All we need to do is place our faith in His finished work and He applies His righteousness to us.

No wonder Paul cried out, "'O death, where is your victory? O death, where is your sting?' The sting of death is sin, and the power of sin is the law; but thanks be to God, who gives us the victory through our Lord Jesus Christ" (1 Corinthians 15:55–57). Jesus took the sting out of sin on the cross.

A Prayer We Don't Have to Pray

Jesus gave us a wonderful picture of the difference between those who trust in God's propitiation and those who are trusting in their own goodness to please Him. In Luke 18:10–14, Jesus told about two men who went to the temple in Jerusalem to pray. One was a proud, self-righteous Pharisee and the other was a tax collector, at the bottom of the religious ladder.

Jesus said that the Pharisee "was praying this to himself" (v. 11). Why does it say he was praying to himself? Because nobody else was listening, least of all God. That's because this man prayed, "God, I thank You that I am not like other people: swindlers, unjust, adulterers, or even like this tax collector. I fast twice a week; I pay tithes of all that I get" (vv. 11–12). As far as this Pharisee was concerned, he and God were already tight.

But the tax collector knew where he stood before God—not because of his profession, but because he understood that he was a sinner who needed someone to satisfy God's wrath against his sin. This man also knew he didn't have what it took, which is why he beat on his chest as a sign of contrition and prayed, "God, be merciful to me, the sinner!" (v. 13). The word translated "merciful" here is really the word for propitiation. The tax collector was praying, "God, be propitiated toward me, the sinner."

Now look at Jesus' conclusion. "I tell you, this man went to his house justified rather than the other; for everyone who exalts himself will be humbled, but he who humbles himself will be exalted" (v. 14).

The tax collector knew he had a problem he couldn't solve. But he also knew that God had taken the initiative to propitiate Himself, and he was trusting in God's provision. Coming as it did before Jesus had died, this man's prayer was answered in Israel's sacrificial system that allowed sinners to offer an animal in place of themselves.

But for us on this side of Calvary, there is no need to ask God to be propitiated toward us in regard to sin and salvation. He is perfectly satisfied, forever, by the death of His Son. We don't have to try to please God by the filthy rags of our own righteousness. *Propitiation* may be a hard word to pronounce, but it ought to be music in our ears.

⑤
RECONCILIATION: THE RELATIONSHIP OF SALVATION

The story is told that Britain's Queen Victoria and her husband, Prince Albert, had a spat not long after they were married. Albert went away and angrily locked himself in their private residence at the palace.

The queen pounded furiously on the door, and when Albert asked who was there, the answer was, "The Queen of England, who demands admittance." But the door did not open.

Victoria knocked again, and again Prince Albert asked who was there. The answer was the same: "The Queen of England." But the prince would not open the door.

Finally, the story goes, Victoria knocked in a more restrained way, and when asked who was there, responded, "Your wife, Albert." The door opened immediately and the royal couple was reconciled.

This illustrates the basic concept of *reconciliation*, another great transaction that took place when we were totally saved by the grace of God. Reconciliation has to do with the removal of hostility and the restoration of harmony in a relationship. It means that the wall separating the hostile parties has been broken down; the breach between them has been healed.

God took the initiative to reach out to sinners through the sacrifice of Jesus Christ. One of the things that Christ's death provided for us was the healing of the broken relationship between God and mankind that occurred in the Garden when Adam sinned. As we will see, we have been reconciled to God through the death of His Son. I want to consider four aspects of this divine work by which sinners can be at peace with a holy God.

THE NECESSITY OF RECONCILIATION

We've already given a basic definition of reconciliation. Here's a theological definition of the term: Reconciliation is that work of God, made possible through the death of Christ, by which sinners are brought from hostility toward God into a state of spiritual fellowship and harmony with Him. It is a movement from alienation to restoration.

Sin Alienated Us from God

The alienation that Adam's sin created in his relationship with God is evident in what happened immediately afterward. Whereas Adam and Eve had enjoyed intimate fellowship with God in Eden, they hid from the Lord after they sinned because they knew something was wrong (see Genesis 3:8–10).

In fact, we could say that when Adam sinned, he declared war on God, because sin is rebellion and rebellion is like war. What had been a relationship of harmony became a relationship of hostility, and the human race has been alienated from God ever since because all of us have sinned.

In Romans 5, the apostle Paul described our alienation as spiritual helplessness, a total inability to rectify the problem of our separation from God. Paul began this chapter by discussing what God has done to provide our great salvation, and then he proceeded to describe our situation that makes this salvation so great. "For while we were still helpless, at the right time Christ died for the ungodly" (v. 6). To be helpless means you can't do anything about your situation. To be ungodly means to be totally unlike God. We lacked any resources or merit to win His favor or overcome the barrier of hostility that sin had built between us and Him.

More than that, "we were yet sinners" (Romans 5:8). We stood guilty before a holy God, and that's not the end of the bad news. Paul said we were also God's "enemies" (v. 10), a term that graphically points out our need for reconciliation.

God Reached Out to Meet Our Need

Romans 5:10 is one of those Bible verses where we can be grateful the writer didn't stop too soon. It was when we were helpless, ungodly sinners and enemies of God that "we were reconciled to God through the death of His Son." By the way, the word *if* at the beginning of the verse doesn't imply any doubt or uncertainty about God's work. It could just as accurately be translated "since."

Reconciliation is God's work and His initiative all the way. Christ's death brought our sin account into balance, so to speak, so that we no longer owe a debt of sin we can't pay. Although this isn't necessarily the focus of Romans 5:10, the term *reconciliation* is often used in this accounting sense. We talk about reconciling our bank statement with our checkbook to make sure the two figures agree and we aren't bouncing checks all over the place. The damage of an unreconciled bank account is obvious, as is the damage of an unreconciled relationship in which there has been broken fellowship.

God has done all that is necessary for people to be reconciled to Him, so the only thing that can prevent this healing is sin. One of the things I love in pastoral ministry is to see married couples who are estranged become reconciled and reconnected. There's nothing more satisfying than seeing hostility turn into harmony, and turmoil turn into peace. What a great message we have for sinners. God wants to restore fellowship with them!

THE DIMENSIONS OF RECONCILIATION

God's work of reconciliation is so complete that it reaches to every corner of creation and touches every relationship you will ever have. There are at least three crucial relationships that were restored when God reconciled the world to Himself.

Our Relationship with God Is Restored

We've established the fact that reconciliation involves a change in our relationship with God, which is where all true reconciliation begins. Paul gave this truth its classic statement when he wrote, "Now all these things are from God, who reconciled us to Himself through Christ" (2 Corinthians 5:18).

Our individual reconciliation with God as believers is a glorious reality, but notice that Paul also went on to say in verse 19, "God was in Christ reconciling the world to Himself." Verse 18 is addressed to believers, those who have received God's offer of forgiveness and peace. But the reconciliation Christ achieved is bigger than us. Paul said the world has been reconciled to God, so we need to ask in what way this is true.

This takes us back to a biblical doctrine we've encountered before and will encounter again. Christ's death on the cross was so completely sufficient for sin that it paid the penalty for the original sin of all people and your personal sin. Christ's death rendered the world savable. Some people do not benefit from Christ's payment because they refuse His offer of salvation, but that doesn't diminish the sufficiency of His work.

If you offend another person, or are offended by a person, and try to make it right, the fact that the other person may refuse your offer of peace doesn't mean the offer is not legitimate. So it is that

God has reconciled the whole world to Himself. His offer of reconciliation is universal, but it is only actual to those who trust Christ.

From God's standpoint, the chasm that separates sinful mankind from Him has been bridged by the Cross. The only issue now is whether people will put their faith in Christ and be reconciled to God. That's why, as we will see in a moment, we are charged with the task of inviting sinners to be reconciled to God.

The results of this are awesome. Christ's death canceled the sin and rebellion of Adam. This means that the sin that was the original cause of our alienation from God has been removed—so that what God is upset about now, if I can use this term, is the fact that people refuse to believe and accept the message of reconciliation.

No person can say, "My sin is too great for God to forgive me. I want to come to Christ, but my sin keeps me from Him." No, if you don't come to Christ it's because you refuse to come. Sin is a dead issue at the Cross.

After Adam sinned, he tried to sew fig leaves together and cover himself, and human beings have been trying to fashion their own covering ever since. Religion without the cross and the blood is merely putting on the fig leaves of human effort.

Adam had his little "fig leaf" program, but God killed an animal and provided His own covering for Adam. It was only on this basis that God could have fellowship with His sinful creatures. If Adam had refused God's plan and insisted on wearing his fig leaves, there would have been no reconciliation, because God's only plan to deal with sin is through the shedding of blood.

Our Relationship with Others Is Restored

When we are reconciled with God, we are in position to be reconciled with others. There is an important horizontal dimension to reconciliation, and this is where things get very interesting.

People talk a lot about reconciliation between races, between nations, between husbands and wives, or between generations. But the problem with most attempts to bring harmony and peace is that there will be no true and lasting horizontal reconciliation without a proper understanding of vertical reconciliation between man and God.

The ancient world had a huge racial divide between Jews and Gentiles. The church at Ephesus felt the impact of this problem, so Paul addressed it straight on:

> Therefore remember that formerly you, the Gentiles in the flesh, who are called "Uncircumcision" by the so-called "Circumcision," which is performed in the flesh by human hands—remember that you were at that time separate from Christ, excluded from the commonwealth of Israel, and strangers to the covenants of promise, having no hope and without God in the world. But now in Christ Jesus you who formerly were far off have been brought near by the blood of Christ. For He Himself is our peace, who made both groups into one and broke down the barrier of the dividing wall. (Ephesians 2:11–14)

This dividing wall was a literal partition, part of the Jewish temple in Jerusalem that kept the Gentiles walled off in an outer area of the temple so they couldn't worship with the Jews. A Gentile who tried to go beyond this barrier invited a death sentence.

This wall symbolized the Gentiles' alienation from God and from the Jews, so Paul used it to teach that Christ broke down the walls between Jew and Gentile. He did it "by abolishing in His flesh the enmity, which is the Law of commandments contained in ordinances, so that in Himself He might make the two into one new man, thus establishing peace" (Ephesians 2:15).

Therefore, according to verse 16, God is now at work removing the hostility between Jews and Gentiles and reconciling both groups into one body in Christ. That's why Paul said of Christ, "He came and preached peace to you who were far away, and peace to those who were near" (v. 17).

The biblical principle is that peace between people must be predicated on what God did for us in Christ. This means that since the world is lacking the basis of true peace we shouldn't be surprised if most peace efforts ultimately fail, whether on the individual or the national level.

But let's talk about horizontal reconciliation in the body of Christ today, because we're not doing such a great job here ourselves. Christians who dislike or reject others because of their skin color, financial status, or any other superficial reason show that they have no real understanding of their salvation.

There's a good reason that Paul said "remember" in Ephesians 2:11–12. We tend to keep forgetting. We forget the pit from which Christ lifted us, so we forget how we should relate to other redeemed sinners.

One of the problems that people who grew up in the ghetto can have is that once they start doing better and leave, they forget where they came from. Then they start looking down on people in the ghetto, failing to remember that it is only by God's goodness that they are no longer there.

As a pastor, one of my jobs is to remind God's people that we are all sinners saved by grace. I tell the people at our church in Dallas that once we walk through the door on Sunday, the only thing special about us is that we've been bought with the blood of Christ. Neither the cars we drive nor the houses we live in matter when it comes to relating to one another. The ground is still level at the Cross.

God has accepted the poor along with the rich, which is why the apostle James told the church, in so many words, "How dare you treat the poor man who comes into your assembly with contempt? You have forgotten who you are" (see James 2:1–13). The Bible consistently condemns racism and classism and cuturalism, because our faith has an important horizontal dimension.

When a husband and wife are at each other's throats, they are actually dealing with a spiritual issue in a verbal or physical way. And until they revisit their conflict from the vantage point of their vertical relationship to Christ, they will never come to a lasting horizontal reconciliation.

Peter explained how disruptions in a believing couple's horizontal relationship have vertical repercussions. He urged husbands to live with their wives "in an understanding way" and grant them honor, "so that your prayers will not be hindered" (1 Peter 3:7). So husband, if you're not treating your wife this way, don't bother to pray. If your most important horizontal relationship is messed up, God is not going to pay attention to your pleas. Reconciliation with God has to make a difference in your human relationships.

John stated this in the form of a penetrating principle. "If someone says, 'I love God,' and hates his brother, he is a liar; for the one who does not love his brother whom he has seen, cannot love God whom he has not seen" (1 John 4:20). Your closeness to the invisible God can legitimately be measured by the way you relate to visible people.

Show me a person who enjoys sowing discord in a marriage, a family, or a church, or who is comfortable with the body of Christ being divided by racism, classism, and culturalism, and I'll show you a person who has no spiritual life to speak of. The reconciliation that reached all the way from heaven to touch us must reach out between people to bring horizontal healing.

Our Relationship with Creation Is Restored

Reconciliation also has a cosmic dimension. That is, the salvation Christ purchased at Calvary has implications for all of creation.

Sin was so devastating that it not only ruptured mankind's relationship to God; sin also marred the whole universe's relationship to God. Adam lived in a perfect paradise until he sinned, and then all of a sudden the ground began producing thorns and thistles. Life became a struggle to survive in a sometimes harsh and hostile environment.

When God created the universe He pronounced every part of it good, but sin threw the entire world out of order. Creation feels the alienation of sin and is waiting anxiously for the day of redemption (see Romans 8:19). Paul went on to say that the world is waiting in hope for the time when "the creation itself also will be set free from its slavery to corruption into the freedom of the glory of the children of God" (v. 21).

That's in the future, but for the present the reality is that "the whole creation groans and suffers the pains of childbirth together until now" (Romans 8:22). Creation is groaning from the burden of sin and the alienation it brought between God and His creation. Every time an earthquake occurs, we are witnessing the restless groaning of creation. Hurricanes are a result of creation groaning for the day when it will be reconciled with God. Nature is aching to be delivered from its bondage to the corruption of sin.

Who and what is going to reconcile nature once and for all? The answer is in Colossians 1:15–20, one of the greatest passages in Scripture about the deity and the redeeming work of Jesus Christ. His life, death, and resurrection have the power to reconcile the entire creation to God.

We can see the cosmic impact of Jesus' redemption in the fact that when He returns, nature will be revolutionized. According to the book of Revelation, the earth will undergo tremendous changes in its topography in judgment on earth's rebels and in preparation for the Lord's return (see Revelation 6:12–14; 21:1). The work of Christ is designed to bring the entire universe back into right relationship with God.

Jesus has this power because "He is the image of the invisible God, the firstborn of all creation. For by Him all things were created. . . . He is before all things, and in Him all things hold together" (Colossians 1:15–17). Jesus Christ was the active agent in the original creation, and the only thing keeping the molecules of this universe from flying apart is His eternal power. Therefore, His death and resurrection could not help but affect the creation.

Now let's read on in Colossians 1, because it gets even better:

He is also head of the body, the church; and He is the beginning, the firstborn from the dead, so that He Himself will come to have first place in everything. For it was the Father's good pleasure for all the fullness [of deity] to dwell in Him, and through Him to reconcile all things to Himself, having made peace through the blood of His cross; through Him, I say, whether things on earth or things in heaven. (Colossians 1:18–20)

That's as complete a statement of the extent of Christ's reconciliation as you will read anywhere in Scripture. How many things did Christ reconcile to God? All things.

Now let's put this great truth to work. If everything in the universe is held together by Jesus Christ, then that includes your life. So if your life is coming apart at the seams, if the stars and planets of your universe are flying out of their orbits, if your financial or marital or family world is spinning in chaos, then the cosmic reconciliation Christ accomplished on the cross has something to say to you.

Now you may be wondering, *If Jesus Christ has reconciled all of creation to Himself, why isn't the universe reconciled today? Why is there still chaos in nature?* Because as we read in Romans 8, nature won't be fully reconciled until Christ returns and the universe bows before Him as the One who has first place in everything. The universe has not yet recognized the "first-placeness" of Jesus Christ.

But the Bible says that Christ's "first-placeness" also includes the church. That's you and me. The natural world may not yet have Christ in His rightful place, but there's no reason that He should not be enthroned as Number One in our hearts.

Do you see what I'm saying? If your universe is in chaos, the reason could be that Christ has somehow been pushed into second, third, or fourth place in your life. He's somewhere down the line in your priorities instead of in the place of absolute preeminence.

But it's only as He is first in *everything* that you enjoy the fullness of the reconciliation He has paid for. If you're tired of the thorns and thistles that are choking your spiritual growth and the earthquakes and hurricanes that are throwing you around and splitting your world apart, put Christ back in the place He deserves, which is "first place in everything."

THE BLESSING OF RECONCILIATION

We're getting a great picture of all that God has done to reconcile us. Let me summarize quickly the truths we have covered, not only in this chapter but in the previous chapters as we have been learning what it means to be totally saved.

The death of Christ gave God the legal grounds to declare us justified, not guilty, freed from the charges that were posted against us. At the same time, we were redeemed or bought back from the slave market of sin by Christ's precious shed blood, which also propitiated God's wrath against sin so completely that He was free to reach out and end our rebellion and hostility against Him by reconciling us. Our justification provided propitiation, which made possible reconciliation.

Those are a lot of big words, but then God has done a lot of big things for us! Every aspect of the doctrine of reconciliation is a blessing, but there is one particular blessing or benefit that I don't want you to miss. It may be less obvious on a casual reading of Scripture, but it is powerful and important nonetheless.

We Are Saved by Christ's Life

For this we need to go back to Romans 5:10, especially the last phrase of the verse. After explaining all that Christ did in His death to reconcile us while we were His enemies and helpless to help ourselves, Paul added, "We shall be saved by His life."

This definitely broadens our understanding of salvation. We were reconciled to God by Christ's death, but Christ is now alive and sitting at the right hand of the Father in heaven (see Hebrews 1:3). There He is serving as our "great high priest who has passed through the heavens" (Hebrews 4:14), and He "always lives to make intercession for [us]" (Hebrews 7:25).

In other words, the idea behind Romans 5:10 is that if you put your trust in Christ's death to save you, now that He's risen from the dead you haven't seen anything yet.

If Christ can save you and reconcile you to God by His blood, wait until you see what He has in store for you now that He is alive forevermore. If He can take you from hell to heaven by dying, what more can He do for you by rising from the dead? If He can forgive you for all your sins and deliver you from judgment by His death, imagine the power that is at work on your behalf now that He lives!

As our Great High Priest, Jesus Christ is presently, at this very moment, interceding for us with the Father. We talked about this earlier in terms of a courtroom in which we are being accused by Satan but Jesus is our Defender.

But there's more to Jesus' present intercession than this. He also interprets our situation and our needs to His Father, which Christ can do because He has been where we are. The Bible says that Christ "has been tempted in all things as we are, yet without sin" (Hebrews 4:15).

Jesus Christ Is Our "Umpire"

The suffering patriarch Job made a very interesting statement as he was being harassed by his accusers. "For He [God] is not a man as I am that I may answer Him, that we may go to court together. There is no umpire between us, who may lay his hand upon us both" (Job 9:32–33).

Job knew that he was in no position to plead his case before God because God was so high and transcendent and he was merely a man. Job said he needed an "umpire," someone who could listen impartially to both God and him and make a ruling. But Job wound up disappointed because he knew of no one who could fill this role.

The umpire Job wished for would have had to understand Job so well that he could accurately represent him before God, and yet be as great as God Himself in order to accurately represent God. The umpire Job longed for, a mediator who could stand between us and God and represent each side perfectly, became flesh in the person of Jesus Christ. He is God Himself, yet He also knows the human condition intimately because He took on human flesh and experienced everything we have experienced.

God the Father knows everything because He is God. But He does not know *experientially* what it is like, for instance, to be tempted by the devil, to have the Enemy on your back and feel like you can't shake him off. But Jesus knows what it feels like to be tempted by the devil, and He understands and sympathizes with us when we cry out to Him (see Hebrews 4:15).

God the Father also doesn't know what it feels like to suffer, or to face death. God cannot die because He is pure spirit. No one can torment God by pressing a crown of thorns down onto His brow or beat Him until He is near death. God the Father does not know what it's like to cry and sweat drops that are like blood running down His face.

But Jesus suffered all of that when He became a man. In the greatest event this universe has ever witnessed, "the Word became flesh, and dwelt among us" (John 1:14). What's more, it is Jesus Christ's job to explain the Father to us (see v. 18).

In other words, Jesus Christ can reach out to God because He is God, and He can reach out to us because He is a man. Jesus brings the two together, explaining to the Father what we are experiencing, and explaining the otherwise invisible and unreachable God to us. And Christ is doing this now and every day as our High Priest who is alive forever! He is our Umpire, our arbiter, bringing God and man together.

Without the reconciling work of Christ, we would be where Job was. Before expressing his wish for an umpire, Job said that no matter how much he tried to clean up to appear before God, the verdict would be "guilty," because Job knew himself to be a sinner (see Job 9:28–30). In fact, he knew what would happen if he came before a holy God: "You would plunge me into the pit" (v. 31).

In other words, Job knew he had no hope of God's mercy on his own. He was like a worm before God. Since I live in Texas, let me change the imagery to a roach. When was the last time you showed mercy to a roach? Anytime you let a roach live it's mercy, because in your eyes—and mine too—roaches deserve to die.

But instead of stomping on "roachy" sinners like us, God decided to save us by His grace. Do you feel like praising Him right now? Go ahead . . . I'll wait for you!

THE DUTY OF RECONCILIATION

The Bible's teaching on reconciliation is exciting stuff, but as always we are called to do something more with the truth than merely sit on it and keep the good news to ourselves. The God who has reconciled the whole world to Himself has called us to be His ambassadors, taking this message to every corner of the earth. This is what I call the duty of reconciliation.

We Are God's Mouthpieces

Our charge is found in 2 Corinthians 5:18–20. Paul began by saying that God "gave us the ministry of reconciliation" (v. 18), which is the message that God has taken the initiative to end our hostility toward Him by charging our sins to Christ and making peace with us through His blood.

Therefore, since God has "committed to us the word of reconciliation" (v. 19), our duty is clear. "We are ambassadors for Christ, as though God were making an appeal through us; we beg you on behalf of Christ, be reconciled to God" (v. 20). The duty of reconciliation is that we speak to others on God's behalf, telling them that they don't have to be alienated from Him any longer. An ambassador speaks for another, and we are to speak as if God were speaking through us.

We have the great duty and delight of telling sinners that in Christ God's anger has been appeased, and that if they will come to Him the war will be over and they will find peace. We can say to sinners, "God told me to tell you that if you will believe in His Son, you will be safe from His judgment." What a great message for people who are at war with God!

So when someone says, "Yes, but you don't know what I've

done," or, "You don't know the kind of person I've been," we can say, "But God told me to tell you that He wants you to be reconciled to Him, and He's already done everything necessary to make it happen." There is no greater message you can bring than that.

Now let me pause here and say a word about our duty to deliver the message of reconciliation. A nonwitnessing Christian is a carnal Christian, because this is one reason God saved us. He saved us to be His ambassadors, His mouthpieces to a lost world.

You may say, "Well, evangelism isn't my gift."

This is not about your gift. This is about your responsibility. If your neighbor's house is on fire, you are not going to say, "Well, I don't really believe my gift is to yell 'Fire!' because I don't think anyone will listen to me."

When people you care about are facing impending doom, you will find a way to get the message to them. If we have friends and family members who are facing the fires of hell and need to know that God is not unapproachable anymore, we need to be getting the message of reconciliation to them because we are God's ambassadors, His mouthpieces to share the good news.

Restoring What Has Been Disrupted

Reconciliation implies that something has been disrupted and divided and it needs to be brought back together. Satan is the great alienator and the great divider. His only agenda is to tear families and marriages and churches and individuals apart so that they and others will fail to see God's power of reconciliation.

Jesus is the great Reconciler who wants to bring things together. But in order to accomplish His work of reconciliation in our lives, He must be at the center.

When I taught this at our church, I used a husband and wife to illustrate my point. I stood underneath a light at the center of the podium and had them come up and join me. I pointed out the light above to them, and then had them turn their backs to each other as if they were alienated and angry and couldn't stand the sight of each other. Then I explained to the congregation that what we had here were two people with a serious breach in their relationship.

So with this couple standing with their backs to each other, I asked them to turn around—but to look at the light rather than at each other. I told them to keep their eyes on the light and start walking toward it until they were underneath it. I urged them not to lose sight of the light above them.

As this husband and wife started looking up, they automatically began coming closer together as they walked toward the light. It was a simple visual illustration, but it really drove home the point. If we can get our eyes focused on Christ and get our relationship with Him in order, we will draw closer to one another. This is the message of reconciliation.

Elizabeth Barrett was a Victorian-era poet whose father violently objected to her marriage to fellow poet Robert Browning. For ten years, Elizabeth wrote to her parents, asking them to reconcile with her. She never got a response.

But finally, Elizabeth got a box in the mail. She opened it to find all of the letters she had written to her parents, not one of which had been opened. Her father never knew the depth of her love and her desire to be reconciled.

God has written the world a letter telling people of His love for them and His desire to have them reconciled to Him. It's our duty to open this letter, the Word of God, and help lost people understand how far God has gone to bring them back to Himself. Otherwise, if the message of His letter never gets through to those who need it the most, there will be no reconciliation. Let's make sure we are fulfilling our duty as ambassadors who have a great message to tell.

6

REGENERATION: THE MIRACLE OF SALVATION

Even though leprosy can be successfully treated today and is rarely fatal, just the mention of the word has struck fear in people's hearts for thousands of years.

We know why leprosy is so feared. In extreme cases, the nerve endings to the face, arms, and legs are so severely damaged that patients lose feeling and can injure or burn themselves very badly. Many leprosy victims lose parts of their fingers or toes from such damage. Another form of leprosy can cause fingers and toes to become paralyzed and curl inward.

If the damaged nerve endings and destroyed flesh of a leprosy patient suddenly began regenerating themselves on their own with no medical treatment or explanation, to the point that the patient's body was completely restored, we would call it a miracle. Regeneration, the act of making new, restoring, or being reborn, does not ordinarily happen in such cases.

Leprosy is a good illustration of the damage that sin has done to the spiritual nervous system of the human race and, in some cases, to the bodies of its victims. It is a disease that has deadened and destroyed our spiritual nerve endings and tissue so completely that the Bible says that unsaved people are born spiritually dead. Sin has disrupted our ability to have fellowship with the God who made us and who seeks to have a relationship with us.

The leprosy of sin first afflicted the race in Eden when Adam and Eve disobeyed God, and the infection was passed on to all of their descendants. The cure for the problem of deadened and destroyed spiritual tissue is regeneration, which I call the miracle of salvation because only God can bring new life where there is death. Regeneration is another of the great truths that help us appreciate what it means to be totally saved.

THE MEANING OF REGENERATION

It's always helpful to begin with a definition of our terms, so let's talk about the meaning of the term *regeneration*. We can define it as the process by which God implants new spiritual life, His very life, in the heart of a sinner who believes on Jesus Christ for salvation.

Regeneration Is a New Birth

The Bible uses at least three figures to describe the process of regeneration. The first is the new birth, which we are most familiar with under the term "born again." Jesus gave a very well-known treatment of this concept when He told Nicodemus that he needed to be born again (John 3).

We're going to deal with this passage in detail below, so I just want to mention it here. When a new birth occurs, it means that there is life where life did not exist before. The moment a sinner places his or her faith in Christ, that person is born anew as the life of God is imparted to the new believer.

Regeneration Is a Spiritual Resurrection

The Bible also describes regeneration as spiritual resurrection. Paul said that just as Jesus Christ was raised from the dead, "so we too might walk in newness of life. For if we have become united with Him in the likeness of His death, certainly we shall also be in the likeness of His resurrection" (Romans 6:4–5).

Later he added, "Do not go on presenting the members of your body to sin as instruments of unrighteousness; but present yourselves to God as those alive from the dead, and your members as instruments of righteousness to God" (Romans 6:13). If you were dead and you are now alive, that means a resurrection has occurred.

Regeneration Is a New Creation

A third important biblical figure for regeneration is a new creation. We have seen the apostle Paul's powerful statement in 2 Corinthians 5:17: "If anyone is in Christ, he is a new creature [or creation]; the old things passed away; behold, new things have come."

Salvation not only brings such a complete change that we are born again spiritually and raised from the dead, but we are completely remade people. It's as if God started the process of our creation all over again and re-created us into such totally different people that all the things we knew or cared about before are gone, and everything is new.

THE NECESSITY OF REGENERATION

The truths we have just reviewed describe radical changes of heart and life, because regeneration is a radical process. Nothing less will do the job when it comes to bringing life out of death.

We Are Born Spiritually Dead

The Bible declares that we are made up of three realities: body, soul, and spirit. Our bodies give us the ability to communicate with our environment through the five senses. Our souls are the source of our self-awareness and our ability to communicate with others and to process the information we receive from our senses so that we can understand our world. Our spirits are designed to enable us to communicate with God, and it is here that the problem occurs.

When God told Adam, "In the day that you eat from [the forbidden tree] you will surely die" (Genesis 2:17), He was speaking of spiritual death. Of course, the human body also suffered from the effects of sin because all of us will eventually die physically. But our first parents died spiritually the day they disobeyed God, and every member of the human race is born dead in "trespasses and sins" (Ephesians 2:1).

The reality of mankind's spiritual death means that we lost our ability to communicate with God. Not that people don't try, and try hard. On one of our recent ministry trips to Israel, we visited the mosque on the Temple Mount in Jerusalem.

When we got to the temple area, we had to take off our shoes to go into the mosque. A husband and wife were holding hands. As they were about to go in, the Muslims quickly separated them. There is no touching between the sexes, married or not, when you are in the area of the mosque.

At one point we were turned away because it was time for one of the five daily prayer times that Muslims observe, bowing toward Mecca to pray in an attempt to communicate with their god and seek his favor.

But no matter what we do with our bodies, and even our souls, the only way we can make contact with God is when our spirits that are dead in sin are made alive again. And that only happens when a person comes to Jesus Christ and trusts Him alone for salvation.

We Are in Need of Eternal Life

Regeneration occurs when God imparts to us His very life, which the Bible calls eternal life. Jesus described this life in His great prayer the night before His crucifixion. Speaking of His followers, Jesus said, "This is eternal life, that they may know You, the only true God, and Jesus Christ whom You have sent" (John 17:3).

It's important to see that Jesus did not define eternal life solely in terms of its length. Eternal life certainly means that we are going to live forever; that's why it's also called everlasting life. But there's much more to it than that. Even the lost will exist forever in hell. The eternal life that God gives is a *quality* of life that Jesus defined as knowing God the Father and Himself.

This is personal, intimate knowledge, not just a body of data, and it begins not when we arrive in heaven but the moment we trust Christ. Once we have been regenerated or made new by the power of the Holy Spirit, we can enjoy intimate, face-to-face fellowship with God because we have His life within us. And we will continue to have this relationship with Him for eternity. Heaven will be the uninterrupted knowledge of God, and we will never reach the end of that knowledge because God is infinite.

What we're talking about here is a far cry from just knowing about God. Just as it is possible for people to desire to communicate with God even though their spirits are dead, it is also possible for people to know about God without truly knowing Him.

This was also made abundantly clear to me during this same trip to Israel I mentioned earlier. If you've ever traveled to the Holy Land, you know how knowledgeable the Israeli tour guides are. Our guides on this trip knew more about the people, the events, and the geography of the Bible than seemed possible. They could go through the history of the Old Testament and move on to the events of Jesus' life on earth without missing a beat.

One of the people from our church who was on the trip with us listened to all of this and said, "These men must be Christians.

Nobody can know this much about God and Jesus and the Bible and not be a Christian."

So one day our people asked the tour guide if he was a Christian. "Oh, no," he said. "I'm a Jew." The point is that it's possible to know a lot about God and yet not know Him, because although salvation is "to the Jew first" (Romans 1:16), the Bible is clear that there is no salvation in anyone but Jesus Christ (Acts 4:12).

Regeneration results in new life, not just new knowledge. The apostle Peter called it "becom[ing] partakers of the divine nature" (2 Peter 1:4).

THE MEANS OF REGENERATION

Regeneration occurs by a sovereign work of God in the heart of the believing sinner. It could not be any other way, for salvation is God's initiative from beginning to end.

In fact, the entire Trinity is involved in the work of regeneration. According to James 1:18, God the Father brought us forth to new life through His Word, while John 5:21 says that God the Son gives life to whomever He wishes. Regeneration is also attributed to the Holy Spirit, whose work in salvation is to renew us to the point of salvation (see Titus 3:5).

What, then, is the means by which God regenerates us? We have hints of it in James 1:18 and John 5:21, where the words "brought us forth" and "gives life" suggest that a new birth is the means by which we pass "out of death into life" (1 John 3:14). This is exactly what Jesus taught in John 3, a seminal passage on the new birth that I want to unfold in depth.

Since we are going to talk about the birth process, let's review some basic physiology. Conception takes place when the father's sperm unites with the mother's egg in her body to generate a new life. Both elements must be present for life to begin and a birth to eventually result.

So it is in the spiritual realm when the Spirit of God unites with the Word of God in the "womb" or heart of a believing sinner. The power of God the Spirit to give life results in the new birth. And even though the process of physical conception and birth can fail or be interrupted at various points, the new birth that God produces can never fail or be aborted.

Spiritual conception always leads to new spiritual life. When a lost person hears the gospel and the Holy Spirit opens that person's heart to receive the truth, the convergence of the Word and the Spirit produces new life.

Jesus Announces the New Birth

Now we're ready to look at John 3. It's a story we know well, the night that a man named Nicodemus visited Jesus to find out what this Man and His teaching were all about.

John identified Nicodemus as "a man of the Pharisees . . . a ruler of the Jews" (v. 1). We could call Nicodemus a model person of his day, which is important because Jesus was about to tell Nick that his religion and his goodness weren't enough to enter heaven.

Being a Pharisee meant that Nicodemus was religious to the core, part of the group that set the standard for Israel. Nick was also a ruler, a term used of those who were members of the Sanhedrin, the Jewish ruling body of the day.

And that's not all. Nicodemus was a Greek name, indicating that this man probably grew up in a Greek neighborhood, went to Greek schools, and partook of Greek culture. In other words, Nicodemus was religious, cultured, and well-connected—a man to be admired and emulated. If correct religion could save a person and produce new life, Nicodemus would have been fine just as he was.

But Nicodemus wasn't fine just as he was, and he sensed that. This is the real reason he came to Jesus at night. It wasn't because Nicodemus was too busy during the day to break away and see Jesus. Nicodemus came at night so his religious buddies wouldn't see him, perhaps out of fear that he would be ridiculed if he was discovered seeking out Jesus. But I think there was another reason too.

Nicodemus realized that even though he was religious and cultured and powerful, something was missing in his life. As he was about to learn, that something was regeneration or the new birth.

Apparently Nicodemus was too uncomfortable to start with the real issue, so he began by paying Jesus a compliment. "Rabbi, we know that You have come from God as a teacher; for no one can do these signs that You do unless God is with him" (John 3:2).

Jesus' response in verse 3 is interesting, because the Bible says that He answered Nicodemus, "Truly, truly, I say to you, unless one is born again he cannot see the kingdom of God." I find this interesting because Nicodemus didn't ask a question for Jesus to answer. What Jesus did was get to the heart of the issue by answering the unspoken question on Nicodemus's heart.

In other words, Jesus knew that Nicodemus did not go to all that trouble just to compliment Him. Jesus could see the hole in Nick's heart. The Lord knew that in spite of all Nicodemus's religious stature and cultural sophistication, something was missing in his life.

This important leader may have been exemplary in his religion, and he may have been in the temple all of his life, but he still didn't know how to get to heaven or how to have a relationship with God. Jesus was saying, "Nicodemus, I know what you came to talk to Me about, so here is the truth about how to get to heaven. You must be born again."

Before we go any further, let me mention that the Greek term Jesus used for "born again" can also be translated "born from above," which points to the source of regeneration and the new life that it brings.

Religion Is Not the New Birth

Nicodemus was mystified by Jesus' answer, which is why he asked, "How can a man be born when he is old? He cannot enter a second time into his mother's womb and be born, can he?" (John 3:4). Now Nicodemus was ready to get down to the real deal. He forgot about his opening statement and pursued the discussion Jesus had begun.

When Jesus said that Nicodemus needed to be born again, that got Nick thinking about obstetrics. This was fine, because Jesus wanted to discuss obstetrics too—except that Jesus was talking about spiritual birth. The Lord moved the conversation along when He answered Nicodemus's question. "Truly, truly, I say to you, unless one is born of water and the Spirit he cannot enter into the kingdom of God" (v. 5).

There is some confusion about Jesus' use of "water" in connection with the new birth. A lot of people believe this is referring to the water of baptism. But the context here is birth and a mother's womb, not the rite of baptism. I believe Jesus is referring to the water that is released from a mother's womb at the start of the birth process, using the term "water" as a synonym for physical birth.

Many fathers have had the experience of their wife sitting up in bed in the middle of the night (these things always seem to happen in the middle of the night) and announcing, "Honey, my water just broke."

This happened to us at the birth of Jonathan, our youngest child. Lois and I were sound asleep about midnight when I heard this sound and a voice out of the darkness, "My water just broke." A couple of hours later, Jonathan was born.

Jesus was telling Nicodemus that he needed to be born twice, not once, to enter the kingdom of God. Physical birth is not enough—even birth into the best family and the most dedicated religion and the highest culture. We must be born again because physical birth does not give us a relationship with God. It gives us a relationship with our environment and with ourselves because we have a body and a soul. But to relate to God we need to be made alive in our spirits, which only comes through spiritual birth.

Jesus made this clear by His next statement to Nicodemus. "That which is born of the flesh is flesh, and that which is born of the Spirit is spirit" (John 3:6). Flesh can only give birth to flesh. It cannot give birth to spirit. Only spirit can replicate spirit, which is why Jesus told Nicodemus, "Do not be amazed that I said to you, 'You must be born again'" (v. 7). Flesh and spirit reproduce after their own kind.

This is the problem with religion that does not call for regeneration. Religion can make you a better person, but only Christ can make you alive when your spirit is dead in sin. A religious person may prove to be kinder, more charitable, and more ethical than a pagan, but even if so, it's not enough. That's because even on its best day, man-made religion is only flesh producing flesh. The life of God can only come from a spiritual source.

Salvation Is from God Alone

Jesus then perplexed Nicodemus even more by using another analogy to illustrate the mysterious, sovereign nature of salvation. Nick was still trying to grasp the idea that God didn't operate according to the set rules of established religion when Jesus added, "The wind blows where it wishes and you hear the sound of it, but do not know where it comes from and where it is going; so is everyone who is born of the Spirit" (v. 8).

We can be pretty sure that by this point, Nicodemus's head must have been spinning. His response in John 3:9 reveals that. "How can these things be?"

The wind is one of the most unpredictable and uncontrollable forces of nature. The TV weather reporters can observe and report on the wind and show its effects, but they can't direct it. In the same way, salvation is from God alone. It is not something we conjure up, and it is not a process we can control by setting various religious rules.

Nicodemus thought that all he had to do was scrupulously follow the religion of his ancestors and he was home free. He knew nothing about the need for the new birth of regeneration. He didn't even realize he was dead and needed to be reborn, although as we said he did sense that something serious was wrong in his life.

We've Been Bitten by Sin

So the means of regeneration is the new life. I like the illustration Jesus used in John 3:14–15, a story from the Old Testament that

Nicodemus would have known. "As Moses lifted up the serpent in the wilderness, even so must the Son of Man be lifted up; so that whoever believes will in Him have eternal life."

On this occasion the people of Israel grumbled against Moses and against God, and God sent serpents into the camp to bite them. God told Moses to erect a bronze serpent on a pole so that anyone who was bitten and looked to the serpent would live.

All of us have been bitten by the snake of sin and will die spiritually unless something is done. Jesus was lifted up on the cross to pay for those sins, and anyone who looks to Him will not die, but will receive new life.

THE MANIFESTATION OF REGENERATION

Regeneration is such a powerful spiritual reality that we should expect to see manifestations, or evidences, of its effect in a believer's life. Let me explain what I mean by borrowing once again from the analogy of human development and birth.

Our New Life Will "Show"

When a woman is pregnant and the new life within her begins to grow the way it was designed to grow, after a while she will begin to exhibit definite signs of her pregnancy. We say she is "beginning to show" as the baby grows in her womb.

More than that, the new life within a mother will affect her own life in unmistakable ways. She will start to dress differently to allow for more growth. Her appetite will change as she begins to desire foods she didn't desire before. The new life within her will even begin to make the mother uncomfortable in her "old life" to the point that she begins to change her daily routine and her sleeping habits.

Do you see where I'm going with this? If you are born again by the Spirit of God and the life of God is in you, there should be manifestations of that life that are unmistakably obvious both to you and to those around you.

How can you help ensure that your daily walk with Christ is marked by these manifestations? Paul gave us the key in Galatians 5:16–17: "But I say, walk by the Spirit, and you will not carry out the desire of the flesh. For the flesh sets its desire against the Spirit, and the Spirit against the flesh; for these are in opposition to one another, so that you may not do the things that you please."

If you want the new life that God placed within you at salvation to grow and produce the changes that God wants, you need to feed the Spirit while starving your sinful flesh. If you want to see God change your tastes so that sin doesn't taste as good as it used to taste; if you want to see God give you a love for the right kind of spiritual food; and if you want to see God reverse some things in your life, you have to grow in grace by chomping down on nourishing spiritual food such as prayer, study of God's Word, regular fellowship with other believers, and service to the Lord.

We Will Resemble Our Father

Another way that regeneration manifests itself is by virtue of the fact that a child bears the characteristics of its parents. That's true in physical and spiritual birth. We have seen that when God saved us, He put His own nature within us.

With that in mind, I want to show you a characteristic of your heavenly Father you bear that may startle you. "No one who is born of God practices sin, because His seed abides in him; and he cannot sin, because he is born of God" (1 John 3:9).

Now this verse will throw you. It may make you wonder if you are saved, because John states clearly that the one who is born of God cannot sin. He's talking about you and me. John said the reason we cannot sin is that we have God's seed within us, and that seed "abides" or remains in us. John was also using birth language here, the seed being likened to a baby in a mother's womb that is alive and growing.

Now if you're like me, you have to admit that what John is talking about is not our experience. We sin every day in thought, word, and deed. But the new life or seed that we have from God is not the part of us doing the sinning. We know this because this new life is the very life of God Himself, and God is wholly perfect and utterly separate from sin.

While you're letting this settle in your mind, let me remind you that Peter said we became "partakers of the divine nature" when we were saved (2 Peter 1:4). We have a divine nature that is perfect and complete in every detail, for Paul said in Colossians 2:10 that we have been "made complete" in Christ. In other words, every Christian is born again perfectly. There are no spiritual defects in our new life.

But this raises a question. If we have the perfect life of God within us, why do we still have imperfect thoughts, and say and do imperfect things?

The answer is that the life of God resident in our spirits exists in a body and soul that still bear the damage of sin. This is the principle of sin that Paul called the "sin which dwells in me" (Romans 7:20).

The Bible calls this old part of us the flesh, the soul that has been contaminated by the principle of sin that uses the body as the vehicle through which to express itself. The flesh is totally unlike God and completely opposed to God. The flesh wants to sin. The flesh does not want God.

Now our flesh or old nature is a burden and a drag that seeks to pull us downward, and it is going to be discarded when we get our new bodies in heaven. But since we're stuck with this flesh as long as we are in this life, how can we know that we are beginning to resemble our heavenly Father, who gave us new birth and wants us to reflect His nature?

Here's one important way: You'll know you are becoming more like your Father when you reflect His attitude toward sin. In other words, when you're saved you may do the same sin you did before you were saved. But you won't do that sin the same way you did it when you were unsaved, because now you will run into a brick wall of resistance every time you sin. That brick wall is the presence of the Holy Spirit within you.

Someone explained the difference this way: Before we were saved we leaped into sin and loved it, but now we lapse into sin and loathe it. We used to sin without even thinking about it. But now the presence of sin in our lives causes us great distress and discomfort because we know it grieves our Father.

So don't misunderstand. Believers are still capable of sin, even terrible sin. But they have to climb over a wall of opposition to sin, and when they do, it is never their new divine nature that is doing the sin.

If you have been regenerated by the Spirit of God, you have the life of God within you. So the challenge is to make sure that the new you is growing so that the flesh can't dominate the scene. The way to do this is to feed the new you, the new life or seed that is within you from God, so that it grows to the point where you show!

7

GRACE:
THE GIFT
OF
SALVATION

One day the great Christian apologist and author C. S. Lewis walked into a room where a group of men was debating what makes Christianity unique among all the world's religions.

The question was posed to Lewis, who answered right away, "That's easy. It's grace." Then he went on to explain that no other religion teaches the concept of a God who takes the initiative to respond with undeserved favor to sinners.

C. S. Lewis was right, of course. Every other religion is founded on the premise that mankind must do something to reach and to please God. The various religions may have different names, but at the core of their belief is a system of human effort to try to appease the gods, pay whatever penance the gods demand, and win their favor.

But the heart of Christianity is the good news of what God has done to bridge the gap of sin and make it possible for sinful human beings to have forgiveness and fellowship with Him. Grace is the unbridgeable divide between the Christian faith and every other religion, and it is a large part of what makes our salvation so great.

THE CONCEPT OF GRACE

Theologians have developed a classic definition of this great concept called grace. They define it as God's unmerited, or undeserved, favor toward sinners. I define grace as the inexhaustible supply of God's goodness whereby He does for us what we could never do for ourselves. Grace has to do with the work of God whereby He breaks into history to solve a problem that we could never solve by ourselves. Grace is "the gift of God" (Ephesians 2:8).

Now if God wants to give us something that we desperately need and could never earn for ourselves, we would be foolish to try to earn it. And since all of God's dealings with us are anchored in His grace, to live apart from grace is to miss God's activity in history. By the way, that's true for our Christian lives as well as our salvation. We are saved by grace, and the only way we grow as Christians is by grace, as we'll see later.

No study of grace can proceed very far without taking us to Paul's great letter to the Ephesians, a part of your Bible that should become worn and dog-eared by the time we finish this book. Ephesians highlights many aspects of God's grace. Paul used the word itself twelve times in this letter, beginning with his trademark salutation, "Grace to you" (1:2).

Then the apostle said, "[God] predestined us to adoption as sons through Jesus Christ to Himself, according to the kind intention of His will, to the praise of the glory of His grace, which He freely bestowed on us in the Beloved" (1:5–6). Notice that God poured out His grace lavishly on those who are His elect in Christ (we'll discuss the doctrine of election in detail later). The only motivation for this outpouring of grace is God's kindness, which is why we will be praising God throughout eternity for the glory of His grace.

Paul knew whereof he wrote. He told Timothy that God called

him into His service although Paul had been "a blasphemer and a persecutor and a violent aggressor" (1 Timothy 1:13). Despite this, "The grace of our Lord was more than abundant" to the apostle (v. 14). Grace overflowed to Paul. It came in waves. Elsewhere he described the flow this way: "Where sin increased, grace abounded all the more" (Romans 5:20).

Our concern here is God's grace in salvation, but we need to note that God is gracious to all people, including the lost. This is called "common grace," or God's kindness to all of His creatures. Jesus said of His Father, "He causes His sun to rise on the evil and the good, and sends rain on the righteous and the unrighteous" (Matthew 5:45). Paul said that the appearance of God's grace has brought salvation "to all men" (Titus 2:11), meaning that Christ's death is sufficient for the salvation of all people.

In other words, your unsaved neighbor enjoys the same sunshine and rain that make your grass grow because God is gracious to all people. But only those who place their faith in the finished work of Christ for salvation experience God's special or saving grace. Let's look deeper into God's grace as it relates to our great salvation.

THE NEED FOR GRACE

In order to appreciate grace to the full, we have to understand how badly we need it. The best way to do this is to contrast grace with its opposite, which Paul did in Ephesians 2. This chapter begins with our problem. "And you were dead in your trespasses and sins" (v. 1). We were "sons of disobedience . . . indulging the desires of the flesh and of the mind, and were by nature children of *wrath*" (vv. 2–3, italics added). God's wrath is the only alternative for those who reject His grace.

Grace is necessary because of sin, which is a big problem because sin is an offense against a perfect God. Someone may say, "But I just told a little lie." That may be the perspective on earth, but when that lie hits the courtroom of God in heaven, it's a capital offense. Adam and Eve were banished from Eden for the disobedient act of eating forbidden fruit. Most people wouldn't classify this as a terrible sin, but it is when measured against the law of God.

When the Bible says people are dead in sin, it doesn't mean they are incapable of doing good things. It means that none of their good deeds can raise them from spiritual death to spiritual life, because those deeds are done apart from a relationship with God. A corpse is a dead body no matter whether it's still dressed up and presentable or badly decomposed.

Sin created such a huge chasm between man and God that there is nothing we can do to bridge it. Jesus pictured this chasm in Luke 16 as He told the story of Lazarus and the rich man. Lazarus died and went to Abraham's bosom, while the rich man went to hell.

In the flames of suffering the rich man begged for mercy, but Abraham told him, "Between us and you there is a great chasm fixed, so that those who wish to come over from here to you will not be able, and that none may cross over from there to us" (Luke 16:26). The Bible says that our sins have hidden God's face from us (see Isaiah 59:2). The prophet Habakkuk said to God, "Your eyes are too pure to approve evil" (1:13). The chasm between God and sinful people is a yawning hole that reaches into eternity for those who don't know Him.

God's intolerance of sin is a foreign concept to the world, and too often to believers, because we accommodate sin. People can go to a hotel and get smoking or nonsmoking accommodations, but there are no "sin accommodations" in heaven. Grace is so sweet because God's wrath is so awful.

THE PROCESS OF GRACE

Now we're ready to look at the process by which God reaches down to sinful people and showers them with His grace. Romans 11:32 says, "God has shut up all in disobedience so that He may show mercy to all." All people are shut up in this container called sin, with no way out. The only way the container will be opened is if the One who shut it opens it.

God Has Two Great Words of Grace

Grace is when God opened the container of sin in which we were shut up. Ephesians 2:4 begins with two of the most merciful, grace-filled words we will ever read. After establishing that we were sons of disobedience and children of wrath, Paul wrote, "But God . . ." In other words, God did not leave us in this mess.

"But God, being rich in mercy, because of His great love with which He loved us, even when we were dead in our transgressions, made us alive together with Christ (by grace you have been saved)" (Ephesians 2:4–5). According to Paul, two attributes of God came together when He revealed His grace to us. Grace is the marriage of God's love and His mercy.

Some people confuse the concepts of grace and mercy. Mercy can be defined as God *not* giving us what we deserve, which is judgment and eternity in hell. Grace is God giving us what we don't deserve, our great salvation and eternity in heaven. Because God is rich in mercy, He withheld His wrath and gave us His grace instead.

Someone illustrated the difference this way. If a person murdered your son and was condemned to death, and you let the law take its course, that is justice. If you pled for the murderer's life to be spared, that would be mercy. But if you took the murderer of your son out of prison, brought him into your home, adopted him as your son, and gave him all the love and privileges and inheritance that you would have given your own son, that's grace!

The Bible also says that God acted because of His great love for us. Biblical love is an act of self-giving on behalf of the one who is loved. It is more of a decision than a feeling. Feelings come and go, but God's love is an irreversible decision to love those who were not deserving of His love. God removed the misery of sin by His mercy when He dealt with the problem of sin by His grace. It all adds up to the greatness of His grace.

God's Grace Will Unfold for Eternity

Just how great is God's grace? According to Paul, it's so great that it will continue to unfold throughout eternity. God saved us by grace "so that in the ages to come He might show the surpassing riches of His grace in kindness toward us in Christ Jesus" (Ephesians 2:7). God's supply of grace is so immense that it will take the ceaseless ages of eternity for you to grasp all that He has in store for you.

And the most amazing thing of all is that grace is a *gift*. Let's continue reading in Ephesians 2. "For by grace you have been saved through faith; and that not of yourselves, it is the gift of God; not as a result of works, so that no one may boast" (vv. 8–9).

This is important because it means that God alone gets the credit for grace. Verse 7 said that the spotlight of eternity will be on the richness of God's grace, not anything we have done to deserve it. When you and I get to heaven, we'll be singing one song: "To God be the glory, great things He has done." Heaven will be a celebration of grace.

God's Grace Is Complete

When our children were small, it seemed as if every toy we bought them for Christmas or a birthday contained these discouraging words on the box: "Batteries not included." That was always frustrating to me because I wanted to ask the toymaker, "Why are you selling me this thing without selling me the power to make it work?" I wanted the toy or whatever to work without having to buy something else.

If you too are tired of having to buy batteries, I have good news for you. When God saved you, the batteries were included! Your great salvation is complete. Grace not only provides you with the "gift" of salvation, but with the power to make the gift perform. Grace is a complete package. "Blessed be the God and Father of our Lord Jesus Christ, who has blessed us with *every* spiritual blessing in the heavenly places in Christ" (Ephesians 1:3, italics added).

James 4:6 tells us that God also gives "a greater grace." One writer calls it "more and more abundant grace." In other words, grace keeps on coming when we are committed to living the way God wants us to live, which is the context of James 4.

Whenever I read this, I think of those cans of orange juice concentrate that make an entire pitcher of juice. When you were saved, you got "grace concentrate." This thing can expand and grow to meet any need you may have. You haven't seen everything God has for you. He always has more grace.

THE MECHANISM OF GRACE

Now that we've laid some foundation for the understanding of God's grace, I want to tackle a complex and important doctrine that belongs under the heading of grace because it is the essence of God's grace in action. This doctrine is election, which I call the mechanism by which God's grace operates to save sinners. Election is also the guarantee of grace, because no one whom He has chosen will be lost.

Election Raises Important Issues

Let's acknowledge right up front that election is a difficult doctrine and that we are not going to solve all the issues involved in a few pages. But I want to spend some extra time here because the subject is so important to a proper view of grace.

One problem with the Bible's teaching on election is that it flies in the face of what we think is fair and right from our perspective. For example, how is it fair that God has elected some sinners to salvation while passing over others? And how is it fair that these nonelect sinners are held accountable for not being saved? If God so loves the world, how can He choose some sinners and not others?

The Bible says that God chose or elected us in Christ "before the foundation of the world" (Ephesians 1:4). Thus, before anyone was born, the Trinity in council with each other elected some to salvation. In other words, election is based on God's eternal purposes and His prerogative to choose, not on our behavior.

Paul confirmed this in Romans 9 as he discussed God's choice of Jacob and rejection of Esau. "Though the twins were not yet born and had not done anything good or bad, *so that God's purpose according to His choice would stand,* not because of works but because of Him who calls, it was said to her, 'The older will serve the younger'" (vv. 11–12, italics added).

Some people think the fact that election is not based on human behavior or response to God is a problem, since it appears to make His choice arbitrary. But in reality, locating the motive for election in God's eternal, unchanging plan rather than in man's temporal, changing actions removes it from the category of arbitrary. Remember too that all have sinned and are deserving of God's wrath, so the fact that He chose to rescue some is an act of grace in the first place.

God Has a Gracious Purpose in Election

What was God's purpose in election? To demonstrate His grace by reaching down into the mass of lost humanity and redeeming a people for His name's sake, a people who will be trophies of His grace and bring Him glory for eternity. Paul told Titus that God's grace "has appeared" so that He might "purify for Himself a people for His own possession, zealous for good deeds" (Titus 2:11, 14).

To get deeper into our subject I want to return to Ephesians 1, which contains a comprehensive statement on the electing work of God. I quoted verse 3 earlier, but let me start there again for the context. "Blessed be the God and Father of our Lord Jesus Christ, who has blessed us with every spiritual blessing in the heavenly places *in Christ,* just as He chose us *in Him* before the foundation of the world, that we would be holy and blameless before Him" (vv. 3–4, italics added).

The key that unlocks the doctrine of election is found in the phrases I emphasized. The words "in Christ," "in Him," or "in the

Beloved" occur in verses 1, 3, 4, 6, 7, 9, 10 (twice), 12, 13 (twice). The centrality of the truth that we are chosen "in Christ" is too often overlooked in the discussion of election. God's electing purpose is centered in the life, death, and resurrection of Jesus Christ and His present ministry in heaven as our High Priest.

The point is that God has not elected believers in the abstract. He is not sitting in heaven deciding whom He loves and whom He does not love. The Bible says God loved the world (see John 3:16). The book of Hebrews says that Jesus tasted death for every person (see Hebrews 2:9). And Peter wrote that God does not want anyone to perish, "but for all to come to repentance" (2 Peter 3:9).

The Bible is unmistakably clear that God loves all people. And we have learned that the Cross of Christ was so powerful that it dealt with the sin of Adam and rendered the whole world savable so that anybody who believes in Christ will be saved. The doctrine of election must not be made to detract from God's love for all sinners or the lengths He went to in order to save every lost person.

But at the same time, we know that not everybody is saved. And we read in Scripture that God elected some in Christ before the world was created, and that those who are not saved will be judged and condemned for their sin.

God's purpose to call out a people who are "in Christ" is the key, because when it comes to mankind's condition there are only two people as far as God is concerned: the first and last Adam (1 Corinthians 15:45). (It's amazing how often we come back to this biblical contrast.) In God's mind all people are either still in Adam—that is, in their sin—or in Christ. Those who are in Adam are lost and condemned, while those in Christ are elected to salvation.

The difference between being in Adam and being in Christ is all-important because God imputed or charged Adam's sin to all of mankind. So we are born in sin, and we commit sin ourselves. Thus the whole world is shut up in sin, and God owes us nothing but judgment.

But because God is gracious, He chose to provide a bridge whereby sinful people could cross over from being in Adam to being in Christ. The bridge is the cross, and the offer of salvation is made to everyone on earth.

There Is Mystery in Election

Now this is where some of the mystery of God's work in election manifests itself. God's offer of salvation is valid to all, and yet those who respond do so because they are the elect of God before the foundation of the world was laid. And those who do not come to Christ are blameworthy because the Bible never says that people are lost because they are non-elect. The lost are lost because they refuse to believe.

These two truths may appear to us to be mutually exclusive, but the Bible teaches both and holds both in perfect balance. In Acts 13 Paul and Barnabas preached the gospel to the people of Pisidian Antioch on the first missionary journey. When they had finished their message, the Bible clearly says, "As many as had been appointed to eternal life believed" (Acts 13:48).

But Jesus said concerning Himself, "He who believes in Him [the Son of God] is not judged; he who does not believe has been judged already, because he has not believed in the name of the only begotten Son of God" (John 3:18).

Now someone may argue, "The unfair thing about election and God condemning the lost is that the non-elect don't really have the capacity to believe." That's not what Jesus said. Let's read on in John 3: "This is the judgment, that the Light has come into the world, and men loved the darkness rather than the Light, for their deeds were evil" (v. 19). The unsaved are judged because they see the light of Christ and yet fail to believe in Him but choose instead to follow their evil hearts.

We could sum it all up in these statements. God elects some to salvation for His own sovereign purposes and because He is gracious. The invitation to salvation is generously open for all, and "whoever will" may still come. All people are responsible for their response to Jesus Christ, and yet those who come can never take the glory for their salvation. We as believers are responsible to go and share the gospel with the world so that lost sinners will hear the good news and turn to Christ for forgiveness from their sin.

God Has Adopted Us

God's grace in election has a wonderful goal or end to it as far as we are concerned. "He predestined us to adoption as sons through Jesus Christ to Himself, according to the kind intention of His will" (Ephesians 1:5).

In other words, God determined that our destiny was to become His adopted children. *Adoption* is a rich term in the New Testament because it means to be a fully privileged son or daughter. Adoption in the ancient world usually didn't happen until the adopted person was grown. At that time the adoptee was given the same rights, privileges, and inheritance as a birth child who grew up in the home.

The adopted child also had full access to his or her inheritance. For us as God's elect and His adopted children, this inheritance includes "every spiritual blessing in the heavenly places in Christ" (Ephesians 1:3).

Adopted children in that world had to grow up to realize all they had. As Christians, too many of us are still living in the spiritual ghetto even though our Daddy owns it all. We've not grown up to discover all of our rights and privileges in Christ.

Paul said that God did all of this "according to the kind attention of His will" (Ephesians 1:5). What is God's will? "To the praise of the glory of His grace, which He freely bestowed on us in the Beloved," who is Christ (v. 6). Election is another aspect of God's grace that results in salvation for those who believe and will bring Him eternal glory.

Grace Is Available to Everyone

There's an illustration of election that I have used over the years to help explain this doctrine. You may find it helpful, so allow me to share it with you. Imagine that I have invited five hundred people to an auditorium for an event. It's hot outside and the air conditioner isn't working very well, so to be gracious I buy everyone in the auditorium a cold drink because I want them to have a thirst quencher. I order five hundred cold drinks at a cost of one dollar each.

It costs me everything I have to buy these drinks, but I love the people in that auditorium so much that I'm not willing that any of them should thirst. And by the way, there are no water fountains and no one else has any money to purchase drinks, so if I don't pay the price no one will have a drink.

So I set these cold drinks before the five hundred people and issue the invitation: "Whoever will, come and drink freely. I have paid the price already."

But now suppose that different people say, "I want a diet drink," "I don't really feel that thirsty," "That's not my favorite flavor," and they all give reasons for refusing my invitation to take a cold drink that I paid everything to purchase for them. So all the people get up and go out into the hallway without their cold drinks.

The problem isn't that the drinks aren't paid for. I didn't have to buy them, but I paid for them out of love and grace because I care for these hot, thirsty people. And because of the cost I paid, I am not about to let these five hundred cold drinks simply go to waste.

So I step out into the hall and "elect" or choose twenty people to whom I say, "Can I speak to you for a minute? You know, these cold drinks cost me too much to let them go to waste. I paid too high a price to give you refreshment. Won't you come back in and enjoy what I have purchased for you? I still have cold drinks inside for each one of you who will quench your thirst, and they are still free."

These twenty people decide to accept my offer; and you are one of them, and you realize that you are really thirsty. You recognize that I am being gracious, so by an act of your free will you accept my offer, come back into the auditorium, and enjoy a cold drink. I chose you for this opportunity, and if I hadn't chosen you, you would not have had a cold drink. But you made the decision to drink, because I didn't coerce you. So you come back in, enjoy your drink, and praise me because I bought you this drink.

What about the other 480 people in the hall that I didn't speak to in this special way? I have not been unfair to them because I already offered them a drink. Not only that, but they can still come back in and drink if they change their minds because the door is open, the cold drinks are there, and the price has been paid. In fact, those who decide to accept my offer and come back now demonstrate that they are members of the elect without negating the importance of their making a choice. The others who go away thirsty do so because they refuse my offer, not because I didn't come out and get them. The ones who miss out can't blame me, and the ones who get a drink can't thank anyone but me because they didn't do anything to earn their cold drink.

In the end, many of the five hundred people may refuse my offer, but in election I have guaranteed that at least twenty people will enjoy my gracious offer.

Calvary cost God far too much for everybody to turn down His offer of salvation. So He made sure that some are saved, and He did it in a way that whoever will may still come. If they don't come it's because they didn't want to come, not because God is blocking the door. And He gets the glory and the praise in everything.

So while there is mystery to election because God cannot be fully explained, the Bible is clear that God offers the opportunity for salvation to all people while guaranteeing the salvation of His elect.

Here's one final thought on God's goal in election. Paul wrote, "For those whom he foreknew, He also predestined to become conformed to the image of His Son" (Romans 8:29). God the Father loves His Son so much that He wants Him to have look-alikes. Through election we have been let in on the love relationship between the Father and the Son. So our calling is clear. We are to become so much like Jesus Christ that the world will be irresistibly attracted to Him.

OUR RESPONSE TO GRACE

The grace of God calls for a commensurate response on our part—not to try to pay for what we have, but out of overflowing gratitude for what God has done for us.

We Are Made for Good Works

One way we are called to respond to grace is by our works. Ephesians 2:8–9, the classic statement of salvation by grace alone, is followed by this statement: "For we are His workmanship, created in Christ Jesus for good works, which God prepared beforehand so that we would walk in them" (v. 10). The service we do for Christ is done out of gratitude for grace, not as our attempt to replace grace with works.

One of these works is daily self-sacrifice to the Person and the will of God. "Therefore I urge you, brethren, by the mercies of God, to present your bodies a living and holy sacrifice, acceptable to God, which is your spiritual service of worship. And do not be conformed to this world, but be transformed by the renewing of your mind, so that you may prove what the will of God is, that which is good and acceptable and perfect" (Romans 12:1–2).

We've talked a lot about the blessings of salvation by grace, and rightfully so. But we also have a responsibility to live by grace. Consider Paul and the tremendous life of service, self-sacrifice, and even suffering that he led.

Now listen to Paul's own commentary on his life: "By the grace of God I am what I am, and His grace toward me did not prove vain; but I labored even more than all of them, yet not I, but the grace of God with me" (1 Corinthians 15:10). Paul would be the first to tell you he was saved by the unmerited grace of God alone. But he didn't just sit and soak up God's goodness.

We Must Grow in Grace

If a great man's last words are some of his most important, then 2 Peter 3:18 is a very important verse. It contains Peter's last recorded words to the church: "Grow in the grace and knowledge of our Lord and Savior Jesus Christ. To Him be the glory, both now and to the day of eternity. Amen."

Peter said grow in your understanding of grace, because the better you understand grace the better you will live the Christian life. And to grow in your understanding of grace means to grow in your knowledge of Jesus Christ, for grace is not an abstract concept but a Person.

John said of Jesus, "We saw His glory, glory as of the only begotten from the Father, full of grace and truth" (John 1:14). God's entire deposit of grace is found in the Person of His Son, so therefore the way we grow in grace is by coming to know Jesus more intimately and surrendering to Him more fully. And that brings us back full circle to Romans 12:1–2 and the daily surrender of our will to Christ. The better you know Jesus Christ, the more you will experience His grace.

We Must Draw on the Grace We Have

This may sound obvious at first, but we have to recognize that it's possible for us to have the limitless grace of God at our disposal and fail to use it. Think about what we do so often when we're in a time of need. We go running to everyone but the Person who can actually do something about our problem. Let me show you what I mean.

It's encouraging to read about how we can confidently approach Jesus Christ, our Great High Priest in heaven, in our time of need to "receive mercy" and "find grace to help in time of need" (Hebrews 4:16; note vv. 14–15). But did you know that this great passage is set in a context of unbelief and failure to enter into everything that God has for us? Read Hebrews 4:1–13 and you'll understand this word of admonition: "Let us hold fast our confession" (v. 14). Our response to grace is to hold fast to our Lord and partake of His grace.

And what an invitation this is. The writer of Hebrews called it "the *throne* of grace" (italics added). A king sits on a throne, and Jesus is a King who has all authority in heaven and on earth (see Matthew 28:18). So when you come to Christ, you are coming to the final authority in the universe.

This is a tremendous promise, but don't miss the order in Hebrews 4:16. God is ready to dispense all the grace we need when we need it, but it begins with our drawing near. You can't have a casual, long-distance relationship with the Savior and expect to find grace in your time of need.

But make no mistake about it. When we know the Lord and are growing in His grace, He dispenses His grace in an ever-flowing, ever-growing stream. I was reminded of this one day several years ago when my family and I were eating lunch in a local restaurant after church.

We were finishing our meal when the waiter came over and said, "Sir, that gentleman over there has already taken care of your meal." He pointed to another table, and I recognized one of the members of our church. He smiled and nodded, and I smiled back in gratitude.

Then I said to the waiter, "Well, we were going to order dessert," thinking I would go ahead and pay for that myself.

"Oh," he said, "that's taken care of too. The gentleman already told me to add whatever dessert you want to the bill and he will pay for it."

So we enjoyed dessert, and then I reached for my wallet to put down the tip. But before I could do anything, the waiter was there again. "The gentleman is covering the tip, too."

I went into the restaurant thinking that I had to pay it all. But someone else had already picked up the tab, simply as an act of grace. And my benefactor's grace kept flowing, covering more and more of my need. And the more grace flowed, the more I appreciated the goodness of the grace-giver. I didn't know the fullness of the grace that awaited me, but I learned more and more about it as the meal progressed.

Let grace be your instructor, and you will grow in grace and become more like Christ. "The grace of God has appeared, bringing salvation to all men, *instructing* us to deny ungodliness and worldly desires and to live sensibly, righteously and godly in the present age" (Titus 2:11–12, italics added).

As we understand and respond to grace, we will find grace to be a wise teacher. The challenge of our great salvation is to become acquainted with the grace of God that saved us and the God of grace who saved us. Then we will experience the multiplying power of grace. "Grace and peace be multiplied to you" (2 Peter 1:2).

⑧
SANCTIFICATION: THE PROGRESS OF SALVATION

Several years ago a well-known Christian leader made a disturbing observation about the state of Christianity in our culture. He described American Christianity as three thousand miles wide and half an inch deep.

Unfortunately, we would have to say that to a large degree this assessment is still true today. With the people and the resources that the church in America possesses, we should be turning the world upside down for Jesus Christ. The reason we are not might lie in the fact that too many of us Christians don't understand who we are in Christ and the abundant life that He has designed for us.

The result is that too many Christians are on the right side of pardon, but the wrong side of power. They are on the right side of forgiveness, but the wrong side of fellowship. They have come out of Egypt, but they haven't made it to the Promised Land.

This is definitely not the way God wants the Christian life to be lived. Christians have been forgiven and are indwelt by the Holy Spirit, and God intends for us to progress in our faith from infancy to maturity, and from spiritual defeat to spiritual victory.

Translating these truths into daily life has become a challenge and a trauma for many Christians—even sincere believers who want their lives to make an impact for God. My thesis is that we need to understand what the Bible teaches about sanctification, another great word that opens up more of the depths of our great salvation.

Sanctification is an important biblical word that we don't hear used much anymore. Older believers would often say, "I'm saved and sanctified." That is a true statement because anyone who is saved is sanctified. But a more accurate statement might be, "I was sanctified the moment I was saved, I am being sanctified today, and one day I will be fully sanctified."

I say that because sanctification refers to the three tenses of salvation: past, present, and future. It deals with the progress that God wants us to make in our Christian lives from the moment we trust Christ until we are with Him in heaven.

You see, salvation is progressive. You were saved when you put your faith in Christ. You are being saved today and every day as you walk with Him and grow in grace, and someday you will be saved when you step into God's presence. Sanctification is the term the Bible uses for this progression that encompasses what it means to be totally saved. It's a good place to wrap up this first section of the book, because sanctification ends in the glory of heaven.

THE MEANING OF SANCTIFICATION

It always helps to begin by defining our terms. The word *sanctification* means "to be set apart." The concept isn't hard to grasp because all of us have utensils in our homes that are set apart, or dedicated, for a particular use. If you ever used your mother's good sewing scissors, or her best kitchen knife, to cut cardboard or for some other "unsanctified" use, you probably learned very fast what it means for a utensil to be set apart!

Now I want to lay a common misconception to rest before we go any further. In some circles, being sanctified was more or less equated with "being holy" in the sense of being a "super-saint." That is, sanctified people looked and acted different than ordinary saints. Among some groups, sanctified people were those who experienced a further work or baptism of the Holy Spirit in their lives subsequent to salvation. And then there is the branch of Christendom that reserves the title of saint for people who reach a certain exalted status and are even said to be responsible for miracles.

But none of this is what the Bible means by sanctification. Sanctification is the normal experience of every Christian. God set us apart for Himself the moment Christ redeemed us. In fact, anyone who isn't sanctified isn't saved. And every believer is a saint, a "holy one." So don't let anyone tell you that sanctification is a spiritual experience that we must seek after salvation, or a holy status only achieved by the elite.

Set Apart from, and Set Apart to

Both the Hebrew and Greek terms for sanctification are at the root of words and phrases such as *holy, holiness, set apart, saint, consecrate,* and others that appear many times in the Bible.

Sanctification is a two-sided truth that includes being set apart *from* something and set apart *to* something else. As Christians we have been set apart from sin and to God. We are no longer to give ourselves over to evil to please our own flesh, but to give ourselves over to God to please Him.

Before our salvation we ran away from God and toward sin. After salvation we are supposed to be running away from sin and toward God. Which direction you are heading today in your spiritual life has a lot to do with the degree of spiritual victory or defeat you are currently experiencing.

The most frequent use of *sanctification* in Scripture is to set something apart from a common or secular usage to a holy purpose for the service and glory of God. Ordinary people and ordinary things became sanctified when they were dedicated to God. Our modern practice of dedicating babies to the Lord, or dedicating a home or business to the Lord, reflects the biblical concept of setting someone or something apart for the Lord.

After the death of Egypt's firstborn and Israel's Exodus from Egypt, the Lord said to Moses, "Sanctify to Me every firstborn, the first offspring of every womb among the sons of Israel, both of man and beast; it belongs to Me" (Exodus 13:2). From that point forward, the Israelites were to consider every firstborn male as set apart for God (see Numbers 8:17). They were special and holy unto Him. And since a sanctified person or article belonged wholly to the Lord, He could do whatever He chose with them.

In other words, sanctification is a way of acknowledging that God is to hold first place in the lives of His people. He had redeemed Israel, and the nation belonged to Him. We are called to the same consecration today: "Sanctify Christ as Lord in your hearts" (1 Peter 3:15). If your heart is set apart for Jesus, there is no room for any other lord.

God's Special Purpose for Us

God's holiness, His total "apartness" from anything unholy, demanded that anything that belonged to Him be holy. We see this later in Israel as God prepared to give the nation His law:

> The Lord said to Moses, "Behold, I will come to you in a thick cloud, so that the people may hear when I speak with you. . . . Go to the people and consecrate them today and tomorrow, and let them wash their garments; and let them be ready for the third day, for on the third day the Lord will come down on Mount Sinai in the sight of all the people." (Exodus 19:9–11)

God also told Moses to have the priests consecrate themselves, and even to consecrate Mount Sinai by setting boundaries around it so the people would not touch the mountain and die (vv. 21–24).

"Consecrate" in these verses is the same word usually translated "sanctify." Sanctification involved a separation of holy things and holy people to God for a special purpose. With the Israelites at Sinai, the separation was visible in the form of the boundaries around the mountain. Our sanctification also has a specific purpose, as well as a definite beginning and a definite ending point.

THE THREE PHASES OF SANCTIFICATION

God's ultimate goal in our sanctification is stated for us in Romans 8:29, "Whom He foreknew, He also predestined to become conformed to the image of His Son, so that He would be the first-born among many brethren." God has saved us and sanctified us—and is presently sanctifying us—so that we become more and more like Christ. And then in eternity, we will be like Him forever.

These are the three phases of sanctification. We have a past, a present, and a future as believers in Jesus Christ. It also helps to think of our sanctification as positional, progressive, and perfect. These are the three headings under which I want to discuss the heart of this great doctrine.

Our Sanctification Is Positional

Positional sanctification sounds like one of those heavy theological subjects that aren't very relevant to our everyday lives. But far from it. The Bible teaches that we have an exalted position in Christ, which we received at salvation and which is absolutely crucial to knowing who we are as Christians. That's why theologians have coined the term *positional* to describe this phase of sanctification.

What is the spiritual position we were given at salvation? We are seated with Christ "in the heavenly places" (Ephesians 2:6). We're already there spiritually, and someday we'll be there in person. This is an accomplished fact that occurred at salvation and is something we will never lose, so we can think of our position as the past tense of our sanctification. It happened at a definite moment in the past, and is still in effect. From this standpoint, we are already sanctified.

This is why Paul could give this greeting to the Corinthians: "To the church of God which is at Corinth, to those who have been sanctified in Christ Jesus, saints by calling" (1 Corinthians 1:2).

Now these folk were carnal, cantankerous, and prideful believers who needed more rebuke and correction than any other collection of people in the early church. And yet, they were sanctified people whose job description was being saints. The Corinthians were not functioning in a sanctified way, but they were still sanctified by position and therefore saints.

As we said above, saints are not people who are deified by the church and have added a title to their names. Every believer is a saint, because every believer is positionally sanctified in Christ Jesus. Paul spoke of the Corinthians' sanctification as a settled reality, although he had a lot to say about their behavior as saints.

So you are a saint by position. God sees you as set apart to Him, which means that you must begin to see yourself as God sees you. This is important because the way you see yourself will lay the foundation for victory or defeat in your spiritual life. If you want victory in your day-to-day Christian experience, you must first of all have victory in your thinking. You must begin to think of yourself as a saint.

That does not mean everything is perfect, but it means that you know who you are. You have the position you need to gain victory over any sin or habit or thought pattern that is keeping you in bondage.

Our Sanctification Is Progressive

Remember 1 Peter 3:15? "Sanctify Christ as Lord in your hearts." You are sanctified, but now you are told to do what you are. This is the essence of progressive sanctification, which involves acting in accordance with your position. This is the present tense of sanctification, relating to the day-to-day conduct of our Christian lives.

This is why I believe that one of the most important doctrines Christians can learn is their identity in Christ. Second Corinthians 7:1 says, "Therefore, having these promises, beloved, let us cleanse ourselves from all defilement of flesh and spirit, perfecting holiness in the fear of God." This is another way of saying, "Keep becoming more sanctified in your behavior as is fitting for those who reverence God."

What's interesting is that these are the same people whom Paul referred to as sanctified saints in his previous letter. The idea is that as believers who still retain the principle of indwelling sin, we are not there yet. We are holy in position, but not always in practice. We can't improve on our position. It doesn't get any better than being seated with Christ. But we can definitely improve on our practice. In fact, the goal is to bring our practice in line with our position.

The way we do this is by cleansing ourselves. This refers to breaking sin's power over us. When we were saved, we were delivered from sin's *penalty*. Now we are in the process of being delivered from sin's *power*. And when we reach heaven, we will be delivered from sin's *presence*. Progressive sanctification means that we are now telling sin what to do and where to get off instead of sin bossing us around.

When the future Queen Victoria learned at the age of eleven that she was next in line for the British throne, she burst into tears, then got hold of herself and said solemnly, "I will be good." In other words, she was aware of her need to act the way a queen should act. She had begun thinking like the royalty she already was.

One reason that doctrine is so important to Christian living is that correct doctrine helps you to get your thinking and your doing on the same wavelength.

Our Sanctification Will Be Perfect

Our sanctification is not only positional and progressive, but someday it will be perfected. We're on our way to an eternal destination, and it's going to be glorious. The completion of our sanctification will be the completion of our salvation. When we leave this earth and these corrupt bodies behind and are ushered into the presence of Jesus Christ, we will finally be just like Him. And we will be delivered from the presence of sin forever.

We saw earlier that all believers are guaranteed sanctification. It's impossible for there to be unsanctified believers because if you are unsanctified, you are unsaved. All believers are guaranteed sanctification, and every believer who is sanctified is guaranteed to be glorified, another term for the moment when we leave earth for heaven.

This is what Paul said in Romans 8:30. We read verse 29, which takes us up to our maturity in Christ. Paul continued the thought in verse 30 with an inseparable argument that ends this way: "And these whom He justified, He also glorified." No one who starts out with Christ in true salvation will be lost along the way. There is no such thing as a believer who is unsanctified or a justified person who is unglorified. Our great salvation ends in glory for every child of God.

God is able to pull this off. Just ask the apostle Jude, Jesus' half-brother. Jude closed his short letter with a benediction of praise "to Him who is able to keep you from stumbling, and to make you stand in the presence of His glory blameless with great joy" (v. 24).

How does the process of trading our sin-scarred bodies for new bodies take place? How do we leave behind these earthly lives of progressive sanctification for the perfection of heaven when we are with the Lord?

It will happen immediately at death when our perfect spirits—the new nature we received at salvation that is like God—deliver our blemished souls into His presence. John gave us a glimpse into how this will come about. "Beloved, now we are children of God, and it has not appeared as yet what we will be. We know that when He appears, we will be like Him, because we will see Him just as He is" (1 John 3:2).

John was referring to Christ's second coming, at which point all dead believers will be instantly raised and given new bodies, and all living believers will be transformed faster than the eye can twinkle. But until that day, every Christian who dies is immediately in the Lord's presence. We believe because of Paul's word of comfort and hope: "We are of good courage, I say, and prefer rather to be absent from the body and to be at home with the Lord" (2 Corinthians 5:8).

It's impossible to shoehorn any intermediate stages between death and glory into that verse. That may seem obvious to you, but there are entire segments of official Christendom that teach either an intermediate state called purgatory or a doctrine called soul sleep, which basically posits that the soul is still in the grave with the body, awaiting the resurrection. Thus, according to this teaching, there will be no conscious existence after death until Jesus comes.

Neither of these ideas is biblical. Paul's hope and expectation was that death meant being with Christ. He told the Philippians, "For to me, to live is Christ and to die is gain. But if I am to live on in the flesh, this will mean fruitful labor for me; and I do not know which to choose. But I am hard-pressed from both directions, having the desire to depart and be with Christ, for that is very much better" (1:21–23).

Paul's longing for heaven makes little sense if he knew that he would have to spend a thousand years in purgatory paying penance for his sins, or slumbering unconscious in the grave. Jesus told the dying thief on the cross, "Today you shall be with Me in paradise" (Luke 23:43). That was a promise of immediate glory in God's presence.

Stephen's experience as he was being stoned also proves that glory awaits us when our lives on earth are over. Just before he died, Stephen saw heaven open up with Jesus standing at God's right hand (see Acts 7:55–56). Stephen was getting a standing ovation in heaven as he became the church's first martyr and was with the Lord just minutes later.

If you know your Bible, its teachings on heaven and the future awaiting us with Christ are a real comfort. We have a tremendous advantage because we have God's complete Word before us. But the early church didn't have this benefit, and in the church at Thessalonica there was great concern and even a sense of hopeless grief over believers who had died.

These believers wondered if they would ever see their loved ones again, so Paul answered their question in his first letter to the Thessalonian church. And in doing so, he gave us one of the great passages about our future hope: "But we do not want you to be uninformed, brethren, about those who are asleep, so that you will not grieve as do the rest who have no hope. For if we believe that Jesus died and rose again, even so God will bring with Him those who have fallen asleep in Jesus" (1 Thessalonians 4:13–14).

This may be a very familiar passage to you and me, but imagine what these words meant to people who were hearing this particular teaching for the first time. The Thessalonians would have known that those who were asleep in Jesus were their dead loved ones and fellow believers. Paul assured them that when Jesus returned, these dead saints would come back with Him.

You can't bring people back with you unless they are already with you when you leave wherever it is you are. Jesus is in heaven, which means that those who are coming with Him must also be coming from heaven. We know from other passages that these saints are returning in their perfect spiritual state to receive their perfect bodies, which will rise from the grave when Jesus comes "with a shout, with the voice of the archangel and with the trumpet of God" (1 Thessalonians 4:16). What a comfort this must have been to these worried believers in Thessalonica.

God's promise is a great comfort to us too. If we are among the glorified believers who return with Jesus in the rapture to catch away His church, we will receive our new bodies first (see v. 16). And until then, to be absent from the body in death is to be present with the Lord. And if we are still alive when Jesus comes back, we will get our new bodies on the way up! Either way, our sanctification will be complete.

And by the way, when you are ushered into the presence of God, you won't be alone. You'll be in a vast company of other perfectly sanctified and glorified people who have also run their race and completed their course. The author of Hebrews contrasted Israel's experience at Mount Sinai with the experience of the saints in the heavenly Mount Zion:

For you have not come to a mountain that can be touched and to a blazing fire, and to darkness and gloom and whirlwind, and to the blast of a trumpet and the sound of words which sound was such that those who heard begged that no further word be spoken to them. ... But you have come to Mount Zion and to the city of the living God, to the heavenly Jerusalem, and to myriads of angels, to the general assembly and church of the firstborn who are enrolled in heaven, and to God, the Judge of all, and to the spirits of the righteous made perfect, and to Jesus, the mediator of a new covenant. (Hebrews 12:18–19, 22–24)

When your worship is transferred to heaven, it's going to be unlike anything you can even imagine. Your redeemed loved ones in heaven will be part of the glorified. You'll be surrounded by countless numbers of angels, and the Old Testament saints will be there too—"the spirits of the righteous made perfect." And best of all, God the Father, God the Son, and God the Holy Spirit will be there.

The saints in heaven are in their spirits and souls because the resurrection of the body has not yet occurred. So they are looking forward to the day when Jesus returns, because they will also receive their glorified bodies, which will be the perfect "house" for their spirits. They have shed their sin-contaminated bodies, and we must do the same, because we can't take them to heaven, and we wouldn't want to.

If you have an old, torn, or worn-out piece of paper money, you can take it to a federal reserve bank and they must exchange it because they made that bill and they stand behind it. When these worn-out bodies are presented to God in the resurrection, He will exchange them for brand-new bodies that will allow us to function in the new environment of heaven.

So don't worry if you have to go to the undertaker before you go to the "upper-taker." It won't matter where your body is or what condition it is in, because when God calls you home, you'll be raised as a perfectly sanctified, glorified saint fitted for heaven.

THE DYNAMIC OF DAILY SANCTIFICATION

There's another question I want to address in this matter of sanctification, because I know many believers are asking it even if not out loud. It's wonderful to know that nothing can unseat us from our position in heaven with Christ, and it's great to think about the glories of heaven.

But the question many believers are asking today is, "How can I get victorious sanctification working in my life right now?" This is an issue for all of us, because every Christian has ingrained habits and sin patterns that need to be broken and a mind that needs to be re-educated.

God and You Are Working Together

I want to start with an important principle that will keep you from going off either end of an extreme when it comes to daily sanctification or Christian growth.

The principle is that your growth in Christ is a cooperative effort between you and God. One extreme of this teaching is that the Christian life is all of God. Our only job is to "let go and let God." The other extreme says that the Christian life is basically a matter of self-effort, pulling yourself up by your own bootstraps. These are the "power of positive thinking" people.

But neither extreme gets at the truth of Scripture. Consider Romans 8:13, where we read, "If you are living according to the flesh, you must die; but if by the Spirit you are putting to death the deeds of the body, you will live."

Do you see the cooperative effort there? You are to put to death the sinful deeds of the body, but you do so by the power of the Holy Spirit. Don't misunderstand my use of the word "cooperative." I don't mean a 50/50 partnership in which you put in your half and God puts in His half. The power is all His, but He does not act without our cooperation. The Holy Spirit will not levitate you to church if you decide you don't want to get up next Sunday.

But we can't miss the clear teaching of Scripture that the Christian life is a cooperative effort. Paul said of himself, "For this purpose also I labor, striving according to His power, which mightily works within me" (Colossians 1:29). Elsewhere the apostle declared, "I can do all things through Him who strengthens me" (Philippians 4:13). And just so we won't feel left out, here's a word for us: "So then, my beloved, just as you have always obeyed, not as in my presence only, but now much more in my absence, work out your salvation with fear and trembling; for it is God who is at work in you, both to will and to work for His good pleasure" (Philippians 2:12–13).

You can't work out that which God hasn't first worked into you, so again this is not a matter of you and God playing equal roles. But the Bible never lets us get away with sitting back and expecting God to do something with us by osmosis.

The Trinity Is at Work in You

Exodus 31:13 calls God "the Lord who sanctifies you." Jesus prayed to His Father, "Sanctify them in the truth; Your word is truth" (John 17:17). God the Father uses the Word to bring cleansing in the Christian's life. He is also "the God of all grace" (1 Peter 5:10). He supplies us with all the grace we will ever need to live as the sanctified people we are.

God also disciplines us (see Hebrews 12:3–13) and brings conviction of sin to correct us. After David's sin with Bathsheba, which he refused to face for about a year, he said of God's conviction, "Day and night Your hand was heavy upon me" (Psalm 32:4). God the Father sends difficulties into our lives to get our attention (see 1 Corinthians 11:30–32). And He is working in our trials and temptations to make sure we always have a way out (see 1 Corinthians 10:13).

In fact, when God allows you to be oppressed with a situation, give thanks that it is not what it could have been. In His grace, God limits our trials. You say, "Well, what I'm going through right now is pretty bad." But you didn't see what God headed off and refused to let Satan do. If Satan could do everything to us he wants to do, we couldn't stand, because his goal is to kill us (John 10:10). Satan wanted to take Job's life, but God said no (see Job 2:6). God's objective was to purify and sanctify Job, not take him out.

God the Son is also involved in our sanctification. He provides our cleansing, as John explained: "If we walk in the light as [God] Himself is in the Light, we have fellowship with one another, and the blood of Jesus His Son cleanses us from all sin" (1 John 1:7). And even when we fall into sin, the blood of Christ continues to cleanse us, as verse 9 promises: "If we confess our sins, He is faithful and righteous to forgive us our sins and to cleanse us from all unrighteousness."

Jesus Christ is our Cleanser and Sanctifier because even on our most sanctified day, dirt still shows up. So we come into His presence each day for what I call general cleansing, which is the cleansing effect of the Word and prayer as we spend time with the Lord in our personal devotions, learning from Him what He wants us to do.

But we also need specific cleansing for specific sins. This is the cleansing addressed in 1 John 1:9. Confession of sin is vital to sanctification and fellowship with Christ.

God the Holy Spirit has a transforming role to play in our sanctification. "But we all, with unveiled face, beholding as in a mirror the glory of the Lord, are being transformed into the same image from glory to glory, just as from the Lord, the Spirit" (2 Corinthians 3:18). We have seen that the goal of sanctification is to make us more and more Christlike. Now we learn that the Spirit provides the dynamic for this transformation.

The Holy Spirit also regenerates us (Titus 3:5), baptizes us into the body of Christ (1 Corinthians 12:13), and seals us in Christ (Ephesians 1:13). All of this happens at salvation, and then on a daily basis the Spirit holds the mirror of the Word before us so we can see how much we are looking like Christ and reflecting Him to the world.

You Have a Role in Your Sanctification

Someone may say, "Tony, it's great that I have God the Father, Son, and Holy Spirit at work within me. But the truth is that I am not being transformed. I'm experiencing more defeats than victories in my Christian life."

Maybe the problem in this case is what we're giving God to work with. This is a cooperative work, and God will always be faithful to do His work. But again, He won't drag us kicking and screaming into holiness. The Holy Spirit won't drive us toward spiritual maturity. We have a role to play in working out our salvation, as Paul instructed us in Philippians 2:12.

Now let me remind you that the Bible tells us to work out our own salvation. In other words, I can't work out your salvation for you, or vice versa. We can encourage and pray for each other and be faithful in teaching the Word, but this is an individual process.

This is an important word because of all the Christian television, books, seminars, and other resources available to the average believer today. It's easy to develop a secondhand faith reading about other believers' experiences or watching people shout and jump and claim miracles on TV. But the Christian life is a walk, not a piggyback ride.

With that in mind, let me suggest several steps you can take each day to help work out your salvation and grow in grace. First, walk by faith and not by sight; second, deny yourself; and third, abide in Christ.

Paul said that walking or living by faith is the norm for Christians (see 2 Corinthians 5:7). My life's verse is Galatians 2:20: "I have been crucified with Christ; and it is no longer I who live, but Christ lives in me; and the life which I now live in the flesh I live by faith in the Son of God, who loved me and gave Himself up for me."

Walking by faith means living based on what God has said in His Word, not on what we can see or the way we may feel at the moment.

God told Abraham to go to a place that He would later show him (see Hebrews 11:8). Abraham obeyed without even knowing exactly where he was going. He didn't know his destination until he got up and left his home in Ur. If you want victory in your Christian life, you are going to have to learn to go when God says so, if even you can't always see where you are going.

A second step toward spiritual victory is self-denial. Jesus was crystal clear on this. "If anyone wishes to come after Me, he must deny himself, and take up his cross and follow Me" (Mark 8:34). Denying yourself means laying down your life to follow Christ, even if there's a cross at the end of the line. But the glory of it is this: "Whoever loses his life for My sake and the gospel's will save it" (v. 35).

A third daily discipline or step for spiritual victory is abiding in Christ. Jesus said, "I am the vine, you are the branches; he who abides in Me and I in him, he bears much fruit, for apart from Me you can do nothing" (John 15:5). Abiding in Christ has to do with the focus of our lives.

For too many believers, the focus is on avoiding this or that sin, or on what they can't do. These things are important, but they are not the essence of the Christian life. The essence of being a Christian is "trying to learn what is pleasing to the Lord" (Ephesians 5:10). If the focus of your life and the passion of your heart is to please God, you won't have to spend all of your time trying to make sure you don't go over the cliff.

For instance, a lot of us try very hard to avoid doing wrong. But if our desire is to please God, not doing wrong things will be a result of seeking His smile of approval.

Here is a principle that may encourage you as you work out your salvation and seek to live as the sanctified person you already are. The principle is that rate multiplied by time equals distance.

What I mean is that you can control your own rate of spiritual growth. You can speed it up by devoting the time and energy and commitment it takes to obey Christ and walk with Him in holiness. If you want to accelerate the rate of your growth in grace, give God all of your time, talents, and treasures. Make each day count for Him. All of us are growing older physically, but are we growing up spiritually?

THE ASSURANCE OF SALVATION

9

ASSURANCE AND CERTAINTY

A great spiritual malady permeates the church of Jesus Christ today. If I were to give it a name, I would call it ADD: Assurance Deficit Disorder.

The proportions of this spiritual affliction are gigantic. One veteran Christian broadcaster who has counseled with thousands of callers over the years said that the number one issue his listeners wrestle with is the assurance of their salvation. The problem affects millions of sincere Christians who have put their faith in Christ for salvation and are faithful in church attendance, read their Bibles almost every day, and pray regularly.

And yet, these people have little or no assurance that their eternal destiny is secure in Christ. When asked if they are on their way to heaven, they might answer if they're being honest, "I think so," or "I certainly hope so." But they would stutter to say, "I know so."

The symptoms of Assurance Deficit Disorder include an inordinate fear of death and hell, a questioning of God's love or of the believer's worthiness to be His child, a sense of real insecurity concerning eternity, and—not surprisingly—a lack of spiritual victory in daily Christian living.

Assurance of salvation is not a minor issue, for several reasons. First, it's important because the Bible addresses it in a number of places and, therefore, assurance is a vital part of Christian doctrine and teaching. It must have been important to Jesus, because His last words to His disciples included this statement: "Peace I leave with you; My peace I give to you; not as the world gives do I give to you. Do not let your heart be troubled, nor let it be fearful" (John 14:27).

The issue of assurance is also important because if you are shaky about your eternal destiny, this lack of solid footing will hinder you in standing firm and will undermine your spiritual growth. It will turn you into a spiritual schizophrenic and work against many of the things that God wants to accomplish in your life.

We are going to devote this section to the subject of assurance, approaching it from a number of biblical perspectives. My goal is really twofold. I want to help true believers who are trusting Christ alone to gain absolute assurance of their salvation and give them a solid foundation for Christian living. The greatest blessing of assurance is that it sets us free to enjoy and grow in the Christian life. If you aren't even sure you are going to heaven, you probably won't enjoy the trip there.

But at the same time, I hope these studies shake up the security of those who are trusting in baptism, church membership, good works, or anything else for their ticket to heaven. Eternity is too long for any of us to gamble with our souls or miss out on heaven. God wants us to be absolutely certain of our eternal destiny.

THE PROBLEM OF ASSURANCE

There are many reasons that people lack assurance of salvation. Some people are simply chronic doubters. If you told them the sun came up this morning, they wouldn't believe it until they saw it for themselves. They are so used to doubting that they are willing to doubt the clear teaching of God's Word before they are willing to doubt their doubts.

Other people have unconfessed sin in their lives, which will always undercut assurance. Ask a child who is in deep trouble with his parents how comfortable he is in their presence, or how confident he feels in asking them for something he needs.

Still other believers suffer from Assurance Deficit Disorder when they are undergoing the stress of trials. This is chronic among believers in our culture because we have this persistent idea that if we were really God's children, we wouldn't be going through these things.

And then there are those Christians who, because they can't remember the exact day and hour they were saved, often doubt the reality of their salvation. Again, this is often a problem in our culture due to our fixation with knowing exactly when, where, and how something happened.

Faulty Theology That Erodes Assurance

The reasons for a lack of assurance may vary, but unfortunately bad Bible teaching is a leading cause of this malady. A faulty understanding of the gospel of God's grace will play havoc with a believer's confidence in the power and promises of God.

We are not the first generation of believers to experience this problem. The Christians at Thessalonica were shaken and uncertain because they feared they would never see their dead loved ones again. Paul wrote to assure them with the truth of the church's rapture (see 1 Thessalonians 4:13–18).

But the most common reason for a lack of certainty among those early Christians was the presence of false teachers who followed the apostles around to the various churches, upsetting some people's faith and undermining their assurance. The writings of Paul, Peter, and John contain many references to these deceivers (see Romans 16:17–18; 2 Corinthians 11:13; Galatians 1:6–7; Ephesians 4:14; 2 Peter 2:1; 1 John 3:7). Jude changed the purpose of his letter to warn the church of false teachers (Jude 3–4).

Those who fell victim to the deceivers were deeply distressed. If you believe in an eternal heaven and an eternal hell, and if you aren't sure you are going to make heaven and miss hell, that will ruin some good nights' sleep.

John had to deal with false teachers among the believers to whom he addressed his first epistle. In 1 John 2:22, the apostle asked and answered an important question. "Who is the liar but the one who denies that Jesus is the Christ? This is the antichrist, the one who denies the Father and the Son." The false teachers were attacking the deity of Christ and challenging the people's faith in Him as the sufficient ground of salvation. John offered the antidote later in his epistle, as we'll see later.

Two Extremes Today

The early church dealt with false teachers, and so do we today. But even within the church there are at least two extreme systems of teaching that undermine the assurance of salvation God wants us to enjoy. Although these groups certainly do not deny Christ's deity and do not intend to mislead believers, their teachings have the effect of denying that we can be certain of our salvation and have assurance of eternal life.

The first extreme is that our salvation is only as good as our present level of experience. In other words, we can only be sure we're saved as long as we are obeying God and walking with Him. In this view, sin leads to a loss of salvation. So we can be saved today and lost tomorrow. This "He loves me, He loves me not" theology shreds any real certainty. There is no ultimate assurance, only present assurance.

Another extreme teaching focuses not on sin and the danger of losing salvation, but on the importance of good works as the ultimate proof of salvation. Those who take this position would not take issue with the doctrine of security, but they argue that the only way we can know we are truly saved is if we persevere to the end in a life of good works.

The problem with using perseverance as the basis of assurance is that we can't know for sure we're going to make it to heaven until we get there. It also raises the problem of how many good works we have to perform to please God and prove we are saved. Perseverance in good works as a standard of assurance really is no standard at all, because there is no way to measure when it has been achieved.

THE PREMISE OF ASSURANCE

The common element in these things that rob Christians of assurance is that they are man-centered. When we try to anchor assurance in our feelings, or in the things we either do or avoid doing, we're building on the wrong foundation. If you want a building that won't sway with every wind that comes along, you'd better be careful how you lay the foundation.

Your Assurance—Found in Christ

So if assurance isn't based on anything in us or around us, where is it to be found? The answer is so simple that I believe it passes right by most of us because we're looking for some complex theological solution. The answer to the question is this: Our assurance is found in Christ. In other words, we don't look to Christ for salvation and then look elsewhere for the certainty of that salvation.

My premise for saying this, the proof of which I want to demonstrate from 1 John 5:6–13, is that assurance is bound up in the promise of the gospel. It's part of the total package we receive from God at the moment of salvation. Assurance is not an afterthought or a separate issue.

John, whom we could call the apostle of assurance, built a powerful case for this doctrine:

This is the One who came by water and blood, Jesus Christ; not with the water only, but with the water and with the blood. It is the Spirit who testifies, because the Spirit is the truth. . . . If we receive the testimony of men, the testimony of God is greater; for the testimony of God is this, that He has testified concerning His Son. . . . And the testimony is this, that God has given us eternal life, and this life is in His Son. He who has the Son has the life; he who does not have the Son of God does not have the life. (1 John 5:6, 9, 11–12)

With these verses as background, let me give you the climactic verse of this passage and then we'll put it all together: "These things I have written to you who believe in the name of the Son of God, so that you may know that you have eternal life" (v. 13).

A lot of us memorized this verse when we first became believers. It has been used for years as part of evangelistic presentations. But even if you can recite the verse from memory, step back mentally for just a minute and read it again as if you've never heard it before. When you do that, the certainty of this promise leaps out at you.

Notice how salvation and assurance are woven together in this passage. God not only gives us eternal life in Jesus Christ, He also gives us the knowledge or certainty of that eternal life. The offer of the gospel includes assurance. The two cannot be separated. The God who saves us through His Son is the God who secures us and testifies of our assurance through the Holy Spirit. All three persons of the Godhead are involved in ministering assurance to believers.

Curing a Split Personality

The fact that salvation and assurance are located in the same place explains why so many genuine Christians lack certainty even in the face of God's promise. These people have a split spiritual personality.

For instance, most people who really understand the doctrine of salvation and are trusting Christ alone would deny that they are relying on their feelings, their works, or the reassurances of other people for their salvation. But the fact is that when it comes to knowing they have eternal life, many believers are actually relying on these very things. No wonder their sense of security is only as good as their mood or their actions at any given moment. These things may give relative and temporary assurance, but complete and lasting assurance is found only in God and the promises of His Word.

Paul told the Colossians, "Therefore as you have received Christ Jesus the Lord, so walk in Him" (2:6). We received Christ by faith, and we live by faith. The same principle is true for assurance. We could paraphrase Paul by saying, "Just as you have received Christ alone as your Savior, find your assurance in Him alone as well."

So assurance in found in Christ and the offer of the gospel that God makes through Him. This also suggests that assurance is as immediate and as complete as salvation itself. God does not parcel out assurance to us on the installment plan.

If someone came into your church and taught that God saves people a little bit at a time, and only after they have proved themselves, you'd recognize that was heresy. But too many of us live as if God's intention is to save us now, but then let us thrash around in doubt and uncertainty until some later point when we're finally ready to receive His assurance.

Now don't misunderstand. There is a sense in which we grow in our understanding and appreciation of what it means to be secure in Christ, just as we learn and grow in other areas of the Christian life. But this experiential, subjective growth is different from the unchanging, objective truth that God wants us to know for sure that we have eternal life.

God's Testimony to Us

If our certainty is located in God's objective promise and not in our subjective experience, then what does John mean by the statement, "The one who believes in the Son of God has the testimony in himself" (1 John 5:10)? This sounds subjective.

But notice that the testimony we have within us as believers is not just a warm, fuzzy feeling or a sense of security that we have to work up within ourselves by self-talk. The testimony we have internally is "the testimony of God" (v. 9) about who Jesus is and what He has done. This truth may generate good feelings of assurance and joy—and it should. But the feelings are not what John is talking about here.

We also know that this internal testimony is not just self-talk because of Romans 8:16. "The Spirit Himself testifies with our spirit that we are children of God." This is the Holy Spirit, whose job it is to inform your human spirit of the certainty of your salvation. But the Holy Spirit only informs your spirit based on what you have done with the testimony of God about His Son—that is, whether you have received or rejected Jesus Christ as your Savior.

Therefore, anyone who claims to be sure of heaven apart from faith in Christ alone is a victim of false assurance, whose source is the devil. Don't be too surprised by the cultists who come to your door with false doctrine and yet seem so serene and at peace and so sure of heaven. The devil will give people deceptive assurance if it will keep them from true faith.

For some true Christians, the issue is not only that they are looking in all the wrong places for assurance, but that they simply can't believe real certainty is possible. As far as they're concerned, expecting to have certainty about things we can't see and feel and measure is just too much to ask.

John met this objection when he said, "If we receive the testimony of men, the testimony of God is greater" (1 John 5:9). The argument is from the lesser to the greater. We believe other people all the time about all kinds of things we can't see or measure for ourselves. So why should we have such a hard time believing what God tells us is true?

It's easy to demonstrate this. Suppose my wife tells me that she will meet me for dinner one evening at a certain restaurant at 8:00 P.M. Since I know and trust her, I have inner confidence that this dinner is going to happen, so I can go at the appointed hour without any doubt or hesitation. I do this not because I have a warm "eight o'clock" kind of feeling inside my soul, but because I believe the "testimony" of my wife.

The Bible says the testimony of God is greater than any human testimony, and it is completely trustworthy. Jesus' experience with Martha and Mary at the death of their brother Lazarus is a classic example of this truth in action.

Lazarus had been dead for several days when Jesus arrived in Bethany. When Martha came out to Him, Jesus told her, "I am the resurrection and the life; he who believes in Me will live even if he dies, and everyone who lives and believes in Me will never die" (John 11:25–26).

This is a great word of assurance because it means that Jesus has the power both to bring the dead back to life and then to give them eternal life so that they will never die again. That's a no-lose deal.

Now as soon as He made this great declaration, Jesus asked Martha a very important question. "Do you believe this?" (v. 26). In other words, "Martha, do you believe that I am the Source of life for those who have died, and the Source of eternal life for all who come to Me?" That's the question we need to answer too. Do we believe the testimony of God concerning His Son, that Jesus is the Source and Guarantor of eternal life?

Martha answered Jesus in the affirmative. "Yes, Lord; I have believed that You are the Christ, the Son of God, even He who comes into the world" (John 11:27). This was far more than the average person's answer to the question, "Do you believe in God?" The majority of people will say they do, but it's clear that Martha had not only believed Christ's testimony about Himself, but had put her faith in Him. In the context of Jesus' question, she believed that He was the Source of life for all who come to Him.

God's Completely Reliable Testimony

In John 5:24 Jesus said, "Truly, truly, I say to you, He who hears My word, and believes Him who sent Me, has eternal life, and does not come into judgment, but has passed out of death into life." Notice the certainty of this. You hear, you believe, and you have eternal life. Jesus did not add any qualifiers to His promise. There is no "may have" or "might have" here. Jesus never brought anyone from spiritual death to eternal life only to let that person fall back under God's judgment.

This is a tremendous word of assurance to all believers, but the key is to look to Christ both for salvation and the guarantee or assurance of salvation. He told Martha that the person who believes in Him would never die. And in John 5 it is His word that brings and secures salvation. I am certain that I am going to heaven because Christ not only gave me eternal life, but He also gave me His warranty with it. My salvation is guaranteed by the Person and power of Jesus Christ.

So we come back to the issue of the reliability and the trustworthiness of the person making the promise. Every year we celebrate Presidents' Day in the United States, honoring the birthdays of George Washington and Abraham Lincoln, because we believe that the history books are reliable when they tell us these two men were the first and sixteenth presidents.

None of us has ever seen George Washington, but because we believe the historians we're willing to teach our children about Washington, celebrate his birthday, and honor his achievements.

I think you get the idea. The testimony of God to the certainty of our salvation is reliable because the One making the promise is eternal Truth. God the Father testified that Jesus is His Son. Jesus guaranteed eternal life to all who believe in Him. And God the Holy Spirit testifies to our human spirit that we are the children of God. So if you are in doubt about your salvation today, don't look anywhere but to Christ for assurance. He who gave you life is able to guarantee the life that He gave to you.

THE PROMISE OF ASSURANCE

We've come full circle back to 1 John 5 and that great verse of promise and assurance that we read earlier. "These things I have written to you who believe in the name of the Son of God, so that you may know that you have eternal life" (v. 13). This is a summary statement encompassing all that John had written to this point in his letter, and in particular the immediately preceding verses.

The bottom line of this verse is so clear and simple. You can know that you have eternal life. Did you get that? You can *know* that you have eternal life. If you know Jesus Christ as your Savior, you are as certain of heaven today as if you had already been there ten thousand years.

Many of the things that we do or plan to do are matters of probability or only relative certainty. I may go here or there tomorrow, but then again I may change my mind and not go. Or something may come up that alters my plans.

I can deal with probability when it comes to the things of earth, but I don't want to say that I am probably going to heaven. I can handle relative certainty about life's plans, but not about my eternal destiny. Praise God that His promise is sure and certain.

If you're like a lot of people, it helps to believe something if you know that other reliable and credible people whom you can trust believe the same thing. So if you're looking for some good company when it comes to having confidence in God's promise, let me point you to a few key passages of Scripture.

One of the greatest believers in the certainty of salvation was Paul. Believers have quoted and even sung about his great declaration of confidence in God: "I know whom I have believed and I am convinced that He is able to guard what I have entrusted to Him until that day" (2 Timothy 1:12). In another place, Paul said that for him, departing this life meant being with Christ (see Philippians 1:23). He also spoke with confidence to the Philippian jailer who was about to kill himself: "Believe in the Lord Jesus, and you will be saved" (Acts 16:31).

Jesus' half-brother Jude also left us a ringing statement of God's ability to keep His own unto the end. Jude closed his one-chapter letter with a benediction "to Him who is able to keep you from stumbling, and to make you stand in the presence of His glory blameless with great joy" (Jude 24).

And of course, Jesus Himself spoke with certainty to His disciples when He told them, "Rejoice that your names are recorded in heaven" (Luke 10:20). It would be hard to rejoice if you had to worry about doing something that could cause your name to be erased from the Book of Life in heaven.

Jesus also assured His people, "My sheep hear My voice, and I know them, and they follow Me; and I give eternal life to them, and they will never perish; and no one will snatch them out of My hand" (John 10:27–28). And then as if to add even greater certainty to His promise, the Lord added, "My Father, who has given them to Me, is greater than all; and no one is able to snatch them out of the Father's hand" (v. 29). You don't have to worry about holding on to Christ. He's holding on to you.

THE BLESSINGS OF ASSURANCE

There are so many practical ways that the biblical doctrine of assurance informs and impacts our daily Christian lives. Doctrine is designed to make a difference in the way we live, not just in the way we think.

One blessing of assurance we ought to be thankful for is the fact that it lifts a heavy weight from our shoulders. If you really believe that it's up to you to keep your salvation intact, and that your failures could cause God to open His hand and let you fall from His grace, you have just assumed an impossible burden. Too often the result of this kind of thinking is service to God that is driven by fear and doubt over losing your salvation and an inordinate sense of guilt. Securing your own salvation is a responsibility you were never meant to bear.

On the other side, when you realize that God is holding you firmly in His grip, and that no power on or under the earth can snatch you from your Father's hand, you are free to serve Him out of gratitude and love. In the words of 1 John 4:19, "We love, because He first loved us."

I'm not saying that Christians who don't believe it's possible to have complete assurance of their salvation are incapable of serving God with the right motives. The problem is a nagging cloud of uncertainty that they can never come out from under. It can't help but affect their daily fellowship and intimacy with Christ.

I liken it to marriage. Imagine a married couple trying to carry on the normal daily routines of life together—to say nothing of marital intimacy—even though they are uncertain about the current status and legitimacy of their marriage. It would be impossible for those two people to simply ignore the doubt over whether their union is intact. Uncertainty in their relationship would produce even greater uncertainty in their fellowship.

The same is true for the Christian. But when you can say you know whom you have believed, and you are convinced that He is able to keep you until the day He comes for you, then you are free to serve God as never before. The issue becomes not how you can avoid messing up and losing your salvation, but how you can serve a Savior who did so much to save and secure you.

One day an elderly woman who had never traveled much went to a large and busy train station to board a train for St. Louis. There were so many trains that she became afraid she would get on the wrong one, so she asked a passerby for help. The person tried to be of service, but he didn't seem very sure about things and only succeeded in making the woman even more apprehensive.

She didn't know what to do, so she went over to the platform that she hoped was the right one. There she saw a man sitting very calmly, waiting for the train. He smiled at her, and she sat down next to him. As the train pulled up, she turned to him and asked nervously, "Is this the train to St. Louis?"

"Yes, it is," he answered confidently.

"How can you be so sure?"

"Because St. Louis is my home. I've just come from there to take care of some business, and now I'm on my way back home. Just come with me and you'll have nothing to worry about. I'll make sure you get to St. Louis." The woman boarded the train with her new friend and slept like a baby all the way to St. Louis.

There are going to be times when you don't feel saved. There are going to be times of doubt and confusion when you wonder if you are on the right train. And there are going to be times when you have sinned and failed and don't even feel worthy to be on the train. But when Jesus says, "Come with Me and I will take you home," you can rest in that promise because He has been to heaven and back and He knows the way.

10

ASSURANCE AND GRACE

One episode of the classic 1960s television series *The Andy Griffith Show* involved a threat that a local tough guy made against Sheriff Andy Taylor's timid deputy, Barney Fife.

Barney had given the man a parking ticket, which infuriated him. He appeared before the sheriff and paid his fine, but he told both Andy and Barney in no uncertain terms that if he ever caught Barney on the streets out of uniform, he was going to beat him up. The rest of the program revolved around Barney's reaction to this threat.

Of course, Barney was famous for being nervous and fearful and easily intimidated, and he definitely was no match for this bully. So he decided not to change out of his uniform, no matter what. That got to be a problem as situations came up in which people didn't expect to see Barney in uniform. He was too ashamed to admit that he was afraid of the other man, so in typical Barney-like style he bluffed his way through the week.

But the issue came to a head when Barney insisted on going to the big Saturday night dance in uniform. No one knew what was really going on except Andy, and he didn't want to embarrass his deputy and friend by telling on him.

But with Andy's urging, Barney finally realized he couldn't hide behind his uniform and decided to face the issue. He changed into a suit and, sure enough, met the bully face-to-face on the street. Barney was shaking in his shoes, but he rose to the occasion with a stirring speech about the authority that his badge and uniform represented, and the importance of upholding the law. The intimidator was undone by Barney's newfound assurance and left without carrying out his threat.

I'm afraid that when it comes to the Christian life, and especially the issue of assurance, too many of us adopt the Barney Fife approach. That is, we let the enemy bully us into believing that we're only safe as long as we're wearing our Christian "uniform." These are the outward actions and symbols of faith that, while they may be valuable, were never meant to serve as the basis for the assurance of our salvation.

The solution for us is the same as it was for Barney. Once we come to understand that our security and protection are not in the "badge" of faith that we wear, but in the grace and power of Christ behind the badge, we can walk in confidence and not fear that the Enemy is going to take us out.

This is why we need to understand the relationship of saving grace to the doctrine of assurance. We dealt with grace's role in salvation, and I would urge you to review that chapter if you need to refresh yourself on the way grace operates.

My purpose in the present discussion is not to repeat what was said there, but to develop a twofold thesis. First, the grace of God that saves us totally apart from any merit of our own is the same grace that keeps us saved, totally apart from any merit of our own. Second, the God who saves us by His grace totally apart from anything we can do to earn it is the same God who guarantees the uninterrupted flow of that grace, totally apart from anything we can do to earn or keep it.

THE CONFUSION THAT SURROUNDS GRACE

As Christians we often tend to get our Bible doctrines confused and start mixing truths that were never meant to be mixed. The relationship between grace and works is Exhibit A of this tendency. If the truth about salvation is compromised, our assurance will also be compromised.

Compromising Our Assurance

One reason for this confusion is that grace simply sounds too good to be true. Human nature being what it is, if you told me you were going to give me one dollar with no strings attached, I probably wouldn't question the gift too much. But if you told me you wanted to give me one hundred dollars with no obligation, I'd have to think about it for a minute before accepting. And if you upped your gift offer to one million dollars, no strings attached, I would really wonder what was going on, because I know I haven't done anything to even *begin* to deserve such a lavish gift. And if I did accept your gift, I would probably feel obligated to do something for you in return.

Now if I did something nice for you in an attempt to pay you back for your kindness, I would be confusing grace and works. If it's any comfort, the early church also became confused about the nature of grace even though they heard the truth straight from the apostles themselves. The Christians in Galatia got sidetracked because a group of people called the Judaizers had confused them about the relationship between the gospel of grace and the works of the law.

When Paul learned that the Galatians had been infected with a faulty theology of grace and works, he knew he had to deal with that mess right away, because trying to substitute works for grace always undercuts grace. Galatians is not one of the letters you read by the fireplace when you just want to feel better about being a Christian. It has some sting to it because Paul had contended too hard for the truth of salvation by grace to let it be undermined.

Paul brought the issue to the floor right at the beginning of the letter.

> I am amazed that you are so quickly deserting Him who called you by the grace of Christ, for a different gospel; which is really not another; only there are some who are disturbing you and want to distort the gospel of Christ. But even if we, or an angel from heaven, should preach to you a gospel contrary to what we have preached to you, he is to be accursed! (Galatians 1:6–8)

This was a serious issue to Paul. Even if he, or the angel Gabriel himself, showed up in Galatia with a message other than the gospel of grace, the Galatians were to show the person or angel the door. This was a reference to the Judaizers and their message that people needed to add law-keeping to grace to truly be saved and sanctified.

Paul summarized the problem this way: "I do not nullify the grace of God, for if righteousness comes through the Law, then Christ died needlessly" (Galatians 2:21). To try to win salvation by the works of the Law ruins grace. Law and grace are an unholy mixture. That's why Paul called his readers "foolish Galatians" (3:1) for thinking they could begin the Christian life by grace and then progress in it by works (see v. 3).

This kind of mixed-up thinking takes a huge toll on a believer's assurance of salvation. You can hardly expect to have peace about your relationship with Christ when you're doing all kinds of things to try to hang on to something that God has already given you as a gift.

Confusion's Road to Trouble

How confused can people become concerning the proper relationship between grace and law or works? The answer to that is in Galatians 5:

> It was for freedom that Christ set us free; therefore keep standing firm and do not be subject again to a yoke of slavery. Behold I, Paul,

say to you that if you receive circumcision, Christ will be of no benefit to you. And I testify again to every man who receives circumcision,
that he is under obligation to keep the whole Law. You have been
severed from Christ, you who are seeking to be justified by law; you
have fallen from grace. (vv. 1–4)

One of the Law's requirements that the Judaizers insisted on was
that Gentile believers become circumcised. But Paul warned that if
the Galatians submitted to this rite as a means of seeking God's favor,
then they were assuming the obligation to keep the whole Law, which
is what God demands and yet is impossible for anyone to do.

More than that, those who sought to be justified by law-keeping cut themselves off from Christ. Phrases like "severed from Christ"
and "fallen from grace" (Galatians 5:4) sound like it is possible for
believers to lose their salvation, which if true would fly in the face
of everything the Bible says about our security in Christ. So let's find
out what Paul meant by these severe warnings.

The first thing to remember is the context of Galatians 5:1–4. The
teachings of the Judaizers had thrown these believers into such confusion that at least some of them were ready to take a giant step back-
ward and place themselves under an impossible burden. Paul spared no
severity or sternness in warning them against making this mistake.

This had become personal for Paul because he had to rebuke
Peter for allowing these Jewish teachers to influence him and giving Gentile Christians the wrong idea that there was some saving
merit in law-keeping. You won't find a clearer statement of salvation
by faith alone than what Paul said to Peter on that occasion (see Galatians 2:15–16).

So the very nature of the gospel as a gift of God's grace was at
stake in this Galatian controversy. Those who were on the verge of
"seeking to be justified by law" (5:4) were setting themselves up to
be severed from a connection they had and to fall from a height
they had reached. Did Paul mean that these believers would lose
their salvation and fall back under God's judgment if they submitted to circumcision?

No, for at least two reasons. First, loss of salvation is not the subject under discussion here. Second, the Bible is clear that those who belong to Christ are kept by Him forever. If you or the devil or anyone else could remove you from Christ's hand, then that entity would be greater than Christ and the eternal life He gave you would not be eternal at all. That's an impossible equation.

The issue Paul was addressing in Galatians 5 was not the loss of salvation for those who have believed in Christ, but the ground or basis upon which a person is saved. In other words, we can choose either "works of the law" righteousness or "by grace through faith" righteousness to be acceptable to God. But the Bible wants us to understand that these two paths are so mutually exclusive that the person who chooses to try to work his own way to heaven is cut off from the grace of Christ. It has to be either/or, not both/and.

Confusion's Great Cost

But what about those believers in Galatia who had begun with Christ by grace through faith in Him alone, but were now in danger of putting themselves under the Law's obligation? The severing from Christ and falling from grace that they would undergo did not mean they would lose their salvation.

Instead, these people would be placing themselves on a different footing in relation to Christ and lose not their salvation itself but the benefits and blessings of salvation. And one of those benefits is the peace that comes when the Holy Spirit ministers the assurance of our salvation to our hearts. So don't be surprised if you have no assurance when you let go of grace and start putting yourself on a performance basis to maintain your relationship with Christ.

Someone may say, "Tony, that doesn't sound serious enough to warrant the kind of strong warning language that Paul used here." I beg to differ. To exchange grace for law is to trade a life of peace, joy, spiritual power, love, and confident assurance for one of guilt, frustration, exhausting effort, spiritual ineffectiveness, and restless uncertainty. A believer who decides to live like this in a misguided attempt to please God will still make it to heaven, but he won't enjoy the trip.

The Bible says in Colossians 2:6, "Therefore as you have received Christ Jesus the Lord, so walk in Him." How did we receive Christ? The Bible answers that for us. "For by grace you have been saved through faith; and that not of yourselves, it is the gift of God" (Ephesians 2:8). So how does God want us to live our Christian lives? By grace.

In fact, God has something special for us as believers when it comes to His grace. The apostle John said of Christ, "Of His fullness we have all received, and grace upon grace" (John 1:16). I call this "super grace." Christ is so completely sufficient that His grace overflows to meet whatever need you may have. That's why the Bible says, "In Him you have been made complete" (Colossians 2:10). Paul found his sufficiency in Christ.

By the way, John went on to make an interesting statement in John 1:17: "The Law was given through Moses; grace and truth were realized through Jesus Christ." In other words, the Law cannot supply what you and I need. It condemns us, whereas the grace that comes to us through Christ saves us.

I seriously doubt if there are any false teachers in your church trying to put you under the Law of Moses. But we can allow our walk with Christ, including our assurance, to be compromised when we lose sight of grace.

God's grace is a package deal that we will still be learning about throughout eternity. It reminds me of the car I bought several years ago. I didn't bother to read the owner's manual, so I wasn't aware of all the accessories that came with the car.

One of these handy devices is a button up front that opens the trunk. Before I discovered this button I spent an unknown amount of time turning off the ignition, grabbing the keys, jumping out of the car, running around to the back, opening the trunk with the key, then jumping back in the car and starting the engine again every time someone wanted to put something in the trunk.

I would have been better off learning what was included with my car when I first got it. Our challenge is to learn and to use all that

God has given us in His grace package instead of trying to do it all ourselves. And when we open the "owner's manual" to the Christian life, we'll discover that God's grace includes this assurance: "He who began a good work in you will perfect it until the day of Christ Jesus" (Philippians 1:6).

The Cost of Grace

God's grace is incredibly costly because He had to give His only Son to save us. But what does the cost of grace have to do with the issue of assurance?

It has everything to do with it, because when God gives us His complete package of grace in Christ and says, "This is My gift to you; it is free of charge, and I will never take it back," we can react in one of two ways. We can receive the gift with gratitude, thank the Giver, and rest in His promise that the gift really is ours forever. Or we can insist on trying to pay for that gift despite the Giver's assurance it already belongs to us.

The Impossibility of Paying for a Gift

Suppose a friend of mine shows up at my next birthday party with a huge box, beautifully wrapped with a big bow on top and a gift tag saying, "Happy birthday Tony, from your friend Joe." I open the box and find something that I have always wanted but was not able to afford.

Now suppose I say, "Joe, this is way too much. I can't allow myself to accept a gift like this. I don't deserve it. You really shouldn't have. I've just got to do something to try to pay you back for this magnificent gift. How much did this cost you?"

Of course, this kind of question is inappropriate when receiving a gift, but stay with me for the sake of illustration. Let's imagine that I badger Joe for the price of the gift until he finally says, "OK, if you must know, it cost me two thousand dollars." I gasp in disbelief, then open my wallet and offer my good friend two dollars.

At this point Joe may have several reactions. First, he will probably be offended by the fact that I basically called him a liar by refusing to believe what he wrote on the gift tag. And second, he will probably feel insulted by my weak attempt to repay a two-thousand-dollar gift with two bucks.

I would never insult a friend like that, and neither would you. But this is exactly what we do to God when we say to Him, in effect, "Lord, I believe Your grace is enough to save me, but not enough to keep me saved. Thank You for the gift of my salvation, but now I'm going to work hard for You and try to do everything right so You'll be satisfied with me and I won't lose my salvation." That's an insult to God (see Hebrews 10:29).

The point is that if God went to all of that trouble and paid such a dear price to save us, why should we think that it's too hard for Him to guarantee the eternal life He gave us? Paul asked the question this way: "He who did not spare His own Son, but delivered Him over for us all, how will He not also with Him freely give us all things?" (Romans 8:32). Assurance is part of the "all things" of the gospel.

I'm aware that many people get jittery when the subject turns to assurance and security because they're afraid that some will abuse grace and use it as permission to live in sin without having to worry about missing their trip to heaven. Paul anticipated that problem, and answered it with an exclamation point. "Are we to continue in sin so that grace might increase? May it never be! How shall we who died to sin still live in it?" (Romans 6:1–2). Next question.

So anytime you hear someone say, "You mean I can get saved and then live any old way I want because nothing can separate me from Christ?" you know that this person either is not a believer at all or is seriously misinformed. Anybody who is thinking like that is on the wrong track already.

Many of us find it hard to accept God's grace for the same reason we find it hard to accept gifts from other people. We've been taught that we have to work for what we get, that nothing worth having comes without effort, that we need to stand on our own two feet and do it ourselves. And we're part of a culture in which more often than not, "free" doesn't really mean free.

Like a lot of other people, I learned about the world's definition of grace the hard way some years ago when we got one of those "free gift" offers in the mail. All we had to do was drive to this place and receive our gift, which was either a new car, a television, or a secret special gift. I must have felt like taking a drive at the time, because I talked my wife into driving there with me.

It took a couple of hours to get there, so I was already out the cost of a tank of gas to pick up my free gift. Then we had to sit down and watch a video about the condominiums this organization was planning to build on the property.

They wanted us to buy a parcel of land, of course, so after the video we had to endure a high-pressured sales presentation. I had to keep saying no before they gave up and gave us our gift. Trust me that it wasn't the car or the television. I would have remembered that. The gift was something I can't even recall except for the fact that it wasn't as costly as the tank of gas or our time to get there.

Too often the world's gifts aren't really gifts. A "buy one, get one free" sale is a discount, not a gift. A gift would be "get one free," period.

Our "Thank-You Note" to God

Now if our salvation and assurance rest solely in Christ and what He has done for us, where do our good works fit into the picture? After all, immediately after saying that salvation is a gift, Paul added, "For we are His workmanship, created in Christ Jesus for good works, which God prepared beforehand so that we would walk in them" (Ephesians 2:10).

In other words, the answer is quite simple. Grace inspires and empowers works while at the same time being distinct from works (see Romans 11:6).

Following the analogy of the birthday gift I used above, we could say that works are our thank-You note of gratitude to God for what

He has given us. We serve the Lord not to get saved or make sure we stay saved, but in appreciation for His grace and because He has promised to reward us for the things that we do in His name and for His glory.

When somebody gives you an expensive gift that you've always wanted, and then asks you for a drink of water, you would be more than happy to honor that request. It's not a payback for the gift, but a way of showing your appreciation for such a wonderful and costly gift and for the person who gave it.

Some Christians may be looking to their good works as their source of assurance, but the service Christ has called us to perform was never meant to fill that need. It's much more liberating to serve God as a child who is secure in the Father's love than it is to serve as a way of trying to maintain the Father's love.

It's true that a believer whose works get burned up at Christ's judgment seat "will suffer loss" (1 Corinthians 3:15). But this is referring to rewards and blessing in heaven, not salvation. Paul was even careful to add, "But he himself will be saved, yet so as through fire." Even the Christian who has very little of lasting value to present to Christ will discover that his salvation is secure. This is true because of the wonderful grace of God, which should be our primary motivation for serving Him.

So if you're clinging to works to ensure your salvation, let go of them and look to Christ and His grace. And for those who object that the doctrine of God's grace in assurance kills a believer's motivation to work hard and faithfully for Christ, let me offer several observations.

First, the fact that all of us are going to appear before Christ to give an account of our Christian lives ought to be enough to motivate anybody (see 2 Corinthians 5:10–11). Even though our salvation is not in question, it would be an awful thing to see all of our works burned up and miss Christ's commendation, "Well done, good and faithful servant."

Here's another truth to keep in mind: Far from killing motivation for Christian service, grace is the source of our enablement for ministry. Paul said that the grace that God showed him was not in vain. Why? Because "I labored even more than all of them, yet not I, but the grace of God with me" (1 Corinthians 15:10). Without the power of God's grace working in us, our labor for Him would produce nothing of eternal value. Once you get your eyes on Christ alone for your assurance, your Christian life will soar, not crash.

THE COMFORT OF GRACE

When you understand all that God has done both to save you and to keep you until He delivers you to His Son in heaven, then you're ready to appreciate and enjoy the comfort that the truth of assurance brings.

The best place to see this comfort in action is in the last part of Romans 8 where Paul summarized a tremendous section on the Christian life. In Romans 8 Paul linked together truth after truth and fact after fact until he had built an unbreakable chain of Christian assurance.

No One Will Be Left Behind

I want to begin with verse 29 of Romans 8, which begins with God's choice of us in eternity past. From there until the end of verse 30 we see a progression that takes us from foreknowledge and predestination in eternity past to glorification in heaven in eternity future. Along the way God doesn't lose one person who is in the process of being called, saved, and glorified. Everybody who gets saved also gets glorified—that is, arrives in heaven with a new, glorified body.

Once you grasp the exciting truth of Romans 8:29–30, you might react by saying, "Wow, think what all this means!" Well, you're not alone if you feel that way. Paul said essentially the same thing in verse 31: "What then shall we say to these things? If God is for us, who is against us?" This verse begins a series of rhetorical questions that keep piling up reasons for our security in Christ until the evidence is absolutely overwhelming.

For instance, "Who will bring a charge against God's elect?" (Romans 8:33). Who is going to come before God and try to convince Him that you are not really saved? Satan can accuse us, but as soon as he does our defense attorney, Jesus Christ, comes to defend us. So the question is not what your accuser says about you, but what God says about you. No charge against us can stick because Jesus paid it all, and He paid it all for all time—past, present, and future (see Hebrews 10:10, 14, 17).

Verse 34 of Romans 8 asks another question: "Who is the one who condemns?" Answer: No one can condemn us. Why? Because Jesus, the only Person who has the authority to condemn us, is the same Person who died for us. More than that, He was also raised from the dead and is standing at the Father's right hand as our Intercessor and Advocate.

Verse 35 begins with a question that is especially relevant to our discussion on assurance. "Who will separate us from the love of Christ?" To get the full answer, you have to work your way to the end of Romans 8, where Paul triumphantly declared that none of these things "will be able to separate us from the love of God, which is in Christ Jesus our Lord" (v. 39).

Notice that in this most victorious of all declarations of our assurance, Paul brought us back to Christ. I know that I am saved because my Savior always finishes what He starts.

We Will Make It Because of Jesus

In sports they talk about athletes who are finishers. Anyone can start a marathon and look good for a while, but it's another thing to finish a long race. Jesus is "the author and finisher of our faith" (Hebrews 12:2 KJV). He never did anything halfway. I'm going to heaven not because I'm a finisher, but because Jesus began and finished my salvation. That way, He gets all the glory because He is the only One deserving of the glory.

⓫
ASSURANCE
AND
FAITH

Ⓘn the classic film *Lilies of the Field,* the traveling handyman played by Sidney Poitier is building a place of worship for some local nuns when he approaches a businessman in the town for a donation to help with the church. The man turns him down at first, but then has a change of heart. He not only contributes to the building project, but he even gets up on the roof to help out himself.

The handyman sees the man on the roof and asks him why he is helping build the church, to which the businessman replies, "I want to cover myself just in case."

That's the way a lot of people approach the subject of religion. They're not sure that there are such things as life after death and heaven and hell. But just in case all of it proves to be true, they want to hedge their bets and get on the good side of whatever god they may meet in the afterlife. They're like the ancient Athenians who had an altar to the unknown god in case they overlooked any deity (see Acts 17:23). These are the kind of people who would have no problem wearing a cross or a crucifix, a Star of David, and the Islamic crescent, and carrying a rabbit's foot in their pocket all at the same time, just to make sure they had all their bases covered.

I'm confident that this is not the way genuine believers in Jesus Christ would practice their faith. But when it comes to the issue of how they can know they are saved and secure for eternity, far too many Christians have a "cover all the bases" approach. That is, they look to their emotions, their Christian activities, their level of commitment, their fellow believers, and many other things for confirmation of their faith. They hope that if they get everything just right, they will finally find the peace that comes with knowing where they stand with God.

I call this "mutual fund" faith. A mutual fund is simply a pool of money put together by a lot of people so they can invest in a number of different stocks and have more chances of making a profit. Mutual funds also spread out the investment risk because the investors' money is not all in one place in case one segment of the market starts falling.

Multiplying your investments in the hope that some of them will pay off may be a good idea for an investment house, but it doesn't work that way in God's house. He doesn't save you by grace through faith plus nothing, then put you on a performance basis so that you never know for sure which "investment" will pay off in terms of bringing you assurance. Besides, when you're trying to please God by your performance, you're never quite sure when you've done enough.

THE CONFUSION SURROUNDING FAITH

I wish I could say that this is just an academic issue between professional theologians. But I've seen too many believers who live in a "netherworld" of constant, nagging doubt regarding their salvation, and it's crippling to their spiritual growth. I don't think most Christians truly doubt God and His Word as much as they doubt themselves. But whatever the case, the outcome is still a life of uncertainty and stunted growth.

The problem for many Christians is that they don't fully understand what it means to trust Christ and then live by faith. The trouble usually starts when people add human effort either to salvation by faith or to the life of faith.

Getting Paid Versus Receiving a Gift

If your boss came to you on payday and said, "I have a special gift for you today," you would probably expect to receive something extra in addition to your paycheck. But if the boss simply handed you your check and said, "Here's your gift," you'd be disappointed because your salary is hardly a gift. You worked hard to earn that money, and your employer is obligated to give it to you if he wants to be fair and honest.

Let me add to the scenario. Suppose your boss left your office or cubicle and went around telling everyone else in the company what a gracious and generous person he was for giving you a paycheck and collecting all the credit that was due to you, the person who actually earned the money.

Now let's change the scene. Your boss comes in on an ordinary day and announces, "I want to give you a gift." Then he hands you a check for $100,000. After you get up off the floor, you ask him what you did to deserve this money. "Nothing really. The truth is that I just love being generous. In fact, every person in the company is getting $100,000 today."

If that happened in your company, would your boss have to go around trying to convince people how gracious he is and seeking their praise? No, you and all the other employees would gather in the halls and sing his praises yourselves. You would marvel at his generosity, and every time you saw him you would tell him how grateful you are for what he did. There would be no argument about who was worthy of the glory.

What I have just described is the difference between getting paid and getting saved. In the first case, you earned your salary and you get the credit for it. In the second case, you contributed nothing while someone else paid the price and gains all the glory. Salvation belongs to the latter category.

There is a great example of this difference in Romans 4, where Paul reached back to Abraham to illustrate the truth that salvation comes by faith:

> If Abraham was justified by works, he has something to boast about, but not before God. For what does the Scripture say? "Abraham believed God, and it was credited to him as righteousness." Now to the one who works, his wage is not credited as a favor, but as what is due. But to the one who does not work, but believes in Him who justifies the ungodly, his faith is credited as righteousness. (vv. 2–5)

God is not going to let anyone take credit for His salvation, because if we earned it by our own efforts, we would have something to brag about in heaven. But God will not share His glory with anyone. Jesus paid it all, and He's the One we will be praising in heaven.

Someone might object, "But didn't we at least contribute our faith? We had to exercise faith to believe in Christ, so we ought to at least get credit for that." Although our faith is the channel through which we respond to Christ, the idea that faith is a meritorious work on our part is another misunderstanding of the nature of faith. We'll talk more about that below.

As Bad Off As We Can Be

If salvation is a faith proposition totally apart from works, why should it surprise us that assurance is also a faith proposition totally apart from works?

The world, and too often the church, operates on a basic misconception about the nature of human works that says that the good things people do, especially if they're done in a religious cause, make the doer acceptable to God.

Let me be extremely clear about this. The Bible has a very graphic term for the "righteous deeds" that human beings do apart from faith to try to win God's favor. These things are like "a filthy garment" (Isaiah 64:6; "filthy rags," KJV)—a reference to the cloths that a woman used during her menstrual period. It is not an attractive picture.

According to Jesus, many people who thought they were pleasing to God are going to stand before Him at the judgment and say, "Lord, Lord, did we not prophesy in Your name, and in Your name cast out demons, and in Your name perform many miracles?" (Matthew 7:22). These are not bad people, but religious folk doing good things.

But Jesus' response to them is sobering. "I never knew you; depart from Me, you who practice lawlessness" (v. 23). This may not make sense to some people, but it does if you understand the doctrine of human depravity. The fact is that on the best day we ever had, our finest works are like a soiled garment in God's sight. God has ordained it so that we are saved by faith apart from works. Anything we try to add to that is a blight and a stain on salvation.

Faith Works for the Right Reasons

The wonderful thing about our God is that after He saves us without works, He gives us the privilege of working for Him and promises to reward us for everything we do in His name and for His glory. This is working for the right reasons.

I want to take another look at the right relationship between faith and works through the eyes and pen of the apostle James, whose treatment of this subject in James 2:14–26 has been a cause of misunderstanding and controversy for generations of Christians. When the great reformer Martin Luther read this portion of Scripture, he tore the book of James out of his Bible because he believed James contradicted Paul's clear statement in Romans 4 that Abraham was saved by faith.

James began this section with a question that might be considered controversial: "What use is it, my brethren, if someone says he has faith but he has no works? Can that faith save him?" (James 2:14). Then later he asked, "Was not Abraham our father justified by works when he offered up Isaac his son on the altar?" (v. 21).

Did Paul and James contradict each other, or was something else going on here? There are a number of clues in James 2 that tell us he and Paul were talking about two different things. In Romans 4, Paul was talking about how a person is made right with God, which is by faith without works.

But James was concerned with how a person who is already right with God is supposed to live out his or her new life in Christ. Each of James's faith illustrations involves people *demonstrating* their faith in God for others to see. James was contrasting a dead faith that makes no difference in a person's life with a living faith that results in service to God.

Romans 4 and James 2 complement each other. They show us two sides of the same coin. Paul's concern was how sinners become saints. James was saying that saints should act like saints. Paul wanted us to know how to get from earth to heaven. James showed us how to live heavenly on earth. Paul, the one who wrote so extensively about the importance of serving God and accumulating rewards in heaven, would have said amen to James's conclusion: "For just as the body without the spirit is dead, so also faith without works is dead" (James 2:26).

We could summarize this by saying that while we are saved by faith alone, the faith that saves is not alone. I hope this will help you grasp the difference so that you won't slip into a performance-based Christian life that robs you of the confidence the Lord wants you to have. Part of the solution to the problem is to dispel the confusion concerning the relationship between our faith in Christ and the works He has given us to do.

THE NATURE OF FAITH

In the excruciating hours, days, and even weeks after the deadly terrorist attacks in New York and Washington, we were brought face-to-face with the agony as thousands of New Yorkers took to the streets with photos and descriptions of missing loved ones. Their tearful expressions of hope in the face of overwhelmingly bad odds of survival were heart-wrenching.

One family held a birthday party the next weekend for their missing member. One young woman told the media that the family had so much faith he was still alive they decided to celebrate his birthday as if he were there. So the family gathered and sang "Happy Birthday" to the missing man, trying to smile and carry on bravely.

Other people who were interviewed in the aftermath of the tragedy expressed faith in the missing person's resourcefulness or ability to survive in a crisis. One distraught young husband in California whose wife was in one of the World Trade Center towers when it was attacked said that if anyone could survive in that situation, it was his wife. Sadly, as the days went on without more survivors being found, we heard fewer of these hopes being expressed.

If the sheer intensity of people's faith and hope could bring about a desired result, all of those families would have found their loved ones alive and well. And although we wish we could restore all the victims of this tragedy to their families, we must admit the reality that the object of a person's faith is more important than the size of that person's faith. This is a biblical principle that is crucial to the subject of assurance, and we will probably never see a more vivid real-life example of this truth in operation.

Faith Itself Doesn't Save

If "faith in faith alone" is not enough to guarantee certainty, how does faith work in relation to the assurance of salvation that so many believers seek? To answer that let's begin with a brief review of what faith is, and what it is not.

If Betty brings her friend Susan a beautiful gift and Susan reaches out her hand to receive it, people don't applaud Susan and say, "Look at what she just did! Isn't she marvelous?" That would be misplaced praise because there's no merit in opening your hand and taking a gift that is offered.

So it is with our faith. The Bible urges us to believe in Christ and receive His offer of salvation, and we are responsible to believe. But nowhere does the Bible assign any saving merit to our faith. When Jesus healed a man who was deaf and mute, the people who witnessed the miracle didn't congratulate the man. The Bible says they were astonished at Jesus and said, "He has done all things well" (Mark 7:37).

Faith Is the Conviction That God Is True

The Bible doesn't define faith precisely, but the famous description of faith in Hebrews 11:1 is a good starting point. "Now faith is the assurance of things hoped for, the conviction of things not seen." Faith is an inner conviction and persuasion that *what God says to us is true.* We see this in Romans 4, where Paul said of Abraham, "Abraham believed God, and it was credited to him as righteousness" (v. 3).

I want to emphasize the second part of my definition because without this, faith loses its shape and becomes vague and nebulous. When you're hurting or in need of comfort, the statement "Just have faith" with no object or reasonable ground for that faith won't help you much.

Again, the object of our faith is far more important than the intensity of our faith. People often say, "I wish I had more faith." But that's not our need, and I have Jesus' testimony on that. "The disciples said to the Lord, 'Increase our faith!' And the Lord said, 'If you had faith like a mustard seed, you would say to this mulberry tree, "Be uprooted and be planted in the sea"; and it would obey you'" (Luke 17:5–6). And just in case there's any doubt about that, Jesus also said, "Believe in God, believe also in Me" (John 14:1).

We don't need more faith per se, but either the right object to put our faith in or a deeper understanding of the object we have already put our faith in. That's why my prayer for this book is that it will comfort and confirm the saved, but discomfort and disturb the unsaved until they come to Christ for salvation.

We Exercise Faith Every Day

When you go to a doctor whose name you can't pronounce and receive a prescription you can't read, then take that prescription to be filled by a pharmacist you don't know and ingest a medication you never heard of before, you are exercising faith.

Now that's an everyday illustration, but it makes the point. You may have had people tell you they can't bring themselves to accept Christ because it just takes too much faith to believe in a God they can't see and touch and all of that. The next time that happens, ask them if they use electricity they can't see or listen to radio waves they can't touch. They might say they can see or hear the effects of electricity if they can't see it—and so it is with God.

Our Faith Needs the Right Object

In other words, everyone operates by faith on some level. The problem is a lot of people think saving faith is a special, "religious" faith that's entirely different from everyday faith. I don't find that distinction anywhere in Scripture. What separates saving faith from everyday faith is its object.

A number of years ago my doctor discovered a lump in my body during an examination. When he brought me this news I did not want to hear, I had three basic responses to choose from. The first was to trust my doctor completely and proceed with whatever treatment he prescribed. My second choice was to mistrust my doctor completely and accuse him either of incompetence or of an outright lie. My third option was to react with a mixture of faith and doubt, wanting to believe my doctor but not being fully convinced he knew what he was doing.

I'm happy to report that I trusted my doctor, I placed myself fully in his care, and the lump proved to be benign. But each of those potential responses revolved around my doctor's integrity. If Jesus tells me He has given me eternal life, that I will never perish, and that no one can take me out of His or His Father's hand (see John 10:28–29), do I really want to place myself in a position of questioning God's integrity? That's what happens when we put a question mark where God has placed an exclamation point.

At this point, I can hear a Bible student saying, "Wait a minute. The Bible commends Abraham for the strength of his faith." That's true. Paul wrote, "With respect to the promise of God, [Abraham] did not waver in unbelief but grew strong in faith, giving glory to God" (Romans 4:20).

Please don't misunderstand. I'm not at all saying that we shouldn't grow in our faith. My argument is that the kind of growth God wants us to enjoy can't really bloom in a life that is plagued by a constant cycle of doubt and spiritual defeat.

Having said that, though, I would still contend that the primary emphasis of Romans 4 is on the object of Abraham's deep-seated faith and confidence. Let's read on to verse 21, where we are told that Abraham was "fully assured that what God had promised, He was able also to perform."

In terms of the definition of faith I gave above, Abraham did not simply have an inner persuasion, period. He had an inner persuasion that what God had said to him was true. In fact, my definition of faith grows out of Romans 4:21. Did God say it? Can God pull off what He said? Then to doubt Him is to question whether He tells the truth or not.

THE OBJECT OF FAITH

On the night that the Jewish leader Nicodemus came to find out who Jesus was and what He was all about, Jesus upset Nick's religious categories by telling him, "You must be born again" (John 3:7). Nicodemus revealed his confusion and uncertainty about these things by asking, "How can these things be?" (v. 9).

Look at Jesus High and Lifted Up

In the process of explaining His Person and work, Jesus used an illustration that would have been very familiar to Nicodemus. I want to use it here in the hope that if you have put your trust in Christ alone, you will gain a deeper assurance of your salvation. And if you aren't saved, my prayer is that you will look to Jesus today and trust Him alone for salvation.

In John 3:14–15, Jesus said to Nicodemus, "As Moses lifted up the serpent in the wilderness, even so must the Son of Man be lifted up; so that whoever believes will in Him have eternal life." Jesus was referring to an incident in which the Israelites grumbled against God, who sent "fiery serpents" among them in judgment (Numbers 21:6; the full story is in vv. 4–9).

The Bible says that many people died, resulting in a plea to Moses to intercede with God to stop the plague. God told Moses to make a bronze serpent and set it up on a high standard or pole, with the promise that anyone who was bitten and looked up at the bronze serpent on the pole would live.

If you consult a medical book for the treatment for snakebite, you will not find "Look at a bronze serpent on a pole" as one of the remedies. It was a test of the people's obedience to God and a reminder that their salvation and well-being were found in God alone. Jesus used this story to illustrate the nature of His own death and the importance of faith in Him alone for salvation.

Just as the serpent was lifted up and suspended on the end of that pole, Jesus was lifted to hang suspended on the cross as a payment for sin. And just as every Israelite who had been bitten and looked at the serpent in faith was spared, so every person who looks to Christ and believes in Him is saved. In fact, the Israelites got so confused about the nature of that metallic snake that they later treated it as an idol, and it had to be destroyed (2 Kings 18:4). They were to obey God's command and look at the snake—but their faith was to be in God, not the snake.

Now let me give you the Evans version of this story and its

importance for salvation and assurance. Suppose you are a member of our church in Dallas, sitting in the auditorium with everyone else. Suddenly, everybody in the building is stricken with a poisonous substance shooting through our bloodstreams.

As everyone cries out in pain, I stand up and announce, "We're all dying, but God has provided a way of salvation for us. Outside these doors is a pole with a bronze snake at the top. If you don't want to die you must go outside and look up at the snake, just as God told me to tell you. If you look at the snake, you will live."

As the pastor, I'm going to plead for all I'm worth for people to go outside and take the cure. If someone calls, "Help me, pastor," I will be glad to offer my arm or hold the door, but that's all I can do because the answer to our fatal dilemma is outside on that pole.

But although you may believe me and go outside, it's possible that other people in the building would have different reactions. Some might say, "We refuse to believe that looking at a snake on a pole is going to heal anyone. Let's get a doctor in here with an anti-serpent serum."

Others might decide that the best thing they can do is stay in the church and pray, so they start praying and confessing their sins. Still others decide this is God's way of disciplining them for not being involved in ministry, so they hurriedly start filling out commitment cards volunteering to become part of the church's outreach. And others simply give up on the hope for a cure and organize a hospice so they can die together.

Since I've read the story and know how it ends, I'm leading the way to that pole! I'm going to put my faith in God's provision for my healing, and remind Him of His promise to cure everyone who trusts Him. I know everybody who joins me at the pole will be healed, while those who refuse to believe God or spend their time trying to get their lives in order die of their affliction. The question is whether or not they are willing to believe God.

By using the story of the fiery serpents to illustrate salvation to Nicodemus, Jesus was saying to him and to all of us, "Believe in Me and you will have eternal life." And in case you didn't notice, John 3:15 is followed by the wonderful promise of John 3:16. Jesus is the object of faith, and if your faith is in Him you are His for eternity.

Jesus Will Hold You Up

One day a boy was standing beside a frozen lake debating with himself whether to go ice skating. He really wanted to skate, but he wasn't sure that the ice would hold him. So he inched out very carefully and a little fearfully, almost afraid to trust his full weight on the ice. But just then he saw a man drive right out to the middle of the lake in his truck, get out, cut a hole in the ice, and begin fishing. The boy enjoyed a fine afternoon of ice skating on the lake.

Jesus has been holding people up long before you and I came along. You don't have to worry that the ground you're standing on is going to give way. You may say, "But Tony, you don't know what I've done." No, you don't know how great a Savior Jesus is. He saved Paul, who made killing Christians his profession. Your eternal salvation and your assurance aren't about you. They're about the strength of the support underneath you.

THE CONFIDENCE OF FAITH

If you're still full of doubts as you read this, let me give a word of hope and a suggested solution to that nagging sense of uncertainty. There were doubters in the Scripture, who had all kinds of doubts. In fact, several prominent people in the Bible had serious moments of doubt.

You're Not the Only Doubter

One biblical doubter was the father who brought his demon-possessed child to Jesus and said, "If You can do anything, take pity on us and help us!" (Mark 9:22). We'll call this the doubt of *desperation*.

John the Baptist is probably the leading example of a powerful figure of faith who fell into doubt. John had been arrested, and he began to wonder if Jesus really was the Messiah (see Luke 7:18–19). In other words, John became overwhelmed by negative circumstances. He was isolated, and all kinds of questions began running through his mind. Why was he in prison and facing death if Jesus was the Messiah? Had he misplaced his trust? We might call this the doubt of *defeatism.*

Then there was the most famous doubter of all, the disciple Thomas. Ten of his fellow apostles testified to Thomas, "We have seen the Lord!" (John 20:25a). But Thomas insisted, "Unless I see in His hands the imprint of the nails, and put my finger into the place of the nails, and put my hand into His side, I will not believe" (v. 25b). The man had ten reliable eyewitnesses and rejected them all. Thomas's problem was *deliberate* doubt.

So no matter what the cause of your doubt, you have company. Now let me show what each of these doubters did with their doubts, because each of them did the right thing.

Take Your Doubts to Jesus

When Jesus challenged the unbelief of the father with the sick child, the man cried out, "I do believe; help my unbelief" (Mark 9:24), and Jesus healed his son. John sent his disciples to ask Jesus, "Are You the Expected One, or do we look for someone else?" (Luke 7:20). Jesus performed miracles and preached the gospel, and then told John's disciples, "Go and report to John what you have seen and heard" (Luke 7:22). John never raised another doubt.

And we know what happened to Thomas. Jesus invited Thomas to touch His wounds and said to him, "Do not be unbelieving, but believing" (John 20:27). Thomas's response is the one we need to make when we realize who Jesus is and what He has done to save us: "My Lord and my God!" (v. 28).

If you have doubts you can't shake, bring them to Jesus. Pray, "Lord, I don't know whether or not I believe You can save and keep me forever, or whether I can do enough to keep myself saved. But I'm going to take my lack of assurance and look to Jesus—and like Jacob, I'm not going to let You go until You let me know that I'm Yours."

The story is told of a little girl who was looking at the beautiful reflection of the moonlight in a pond one night while taking a walk with her family. Her brother threw a large stone into the pond and ruined the reflection, and the girl began to cry. But her mother wisely said, "Honey, look up and you'll see that the moon is still there."

When Satan or circumstances or other people throw a stone into the pond of your life and your assurance is shattered, look up. Jesus is still there, and He is your security.

12

ASSURANCE
AND
SELF-EXAMINATION

You may not know this, but one reason God gives a preacher children is to keep him supplied with fresh illustrations.

When my younger son, Jonathan, was in high school, I went to watch him at football practice one day. The team was running plays with Jonathan at tight end, but he was not having one of his better practices. At one point the coach hollered out, "Jonathan, get in the game!"

That might seem like a curious statement. Jonathan *was* in the game. He was on the field and in uniform, not standing on the sidelines. He had been part of the huddle, so he knew the next play. He was lined up in the correct slot on the line of scrimmage. From all appearances, he was as ready to execute the play as any other member of the team. So what did the coach mean by yelling, "Get in the game!"?

Well, any sports fan knows that this expression means the player in question is messing up. Maybe he's not giving it his full effort, or he's not paying attention and needs to do a little mental self-examination and wake up. "Get in the game!" means that although the player may be filling his position, he's not *ful*filling the responsibilities of his position.

Now let me tell you what this expression does not mean, and why all of this is relevant to the assurance of salvation that God has for His people. Jonathan's coach was not questioning whether he was a member of the team, but focusing on how Jonathan was doing as a member of the team. And that is exactly what the Bible is doing in several key passages that encourage us as Christians to perform regular spiritual self-examination.

The question in each of these texts is whether this self-examination has to do with doubts about our salvation, or how we are functioning as saved people. Does the Bible encourage us to look within to see if we are still saved or in danger of losing our salvation?

A lot of people think so, especially those who deny that it's possible to know for sure we are saved. At first glance, the passages we will study do seem to teach that our salvation itself can be at stake in certain instances. If you've ever had a discussion on the issue of assurance and security, you may have run into these texts. Why does the Bible tell us to examine our own spiritual condition?

SELF-EXAMINATION AND SPIRITUAL FAILURE

Sometimes when you misbehaved as a child, your mother might have said something like this: "What is wrong with you, child? You didn't learn that in this house. You're acting like one of those wild kids down the street. I'm going to send you down there to live with them if you don't straighten up right now!"

Now your momma wasn't really planning to adopt you out. She just wanted you to know that you were not acting the way a child of hers was supposed to act. God has the same problem with some of His children, and there's nothing humorous about it. Consider the spiritually ill-mannered Corinthian believers who were making a sham of the Lord's Supper by being gluttonous and even getting drunk (see 1 Corinthians 11:21). Paul took on that mess in no uncertain terms:

> But a man must examine himself, and in so doing he is to eat of the bread and drink of the cup. For he who eats and drinks, eats and drinks judgment to himself if he does not judge the body rightly. For this reason many among you are weak and sick, and a number sleep. But if we judged ourselves rightly, we would not be judged. But when we are judged, we are disciplined by the Lord so that we will not be condemned along with the world. (vv. 28–32)

Saints Can Look Like Sinners

Sometimes it's hard to tell the saints from the "ain'ts" because some lost people live exemplary lives, while genuine believers can be capable of some really heinous behavior. That was the case in Corinth. Earlier in this letter Paul said that the church at Corinth was guilty of condoning incest, a sin so bad even the unbelievers around them blushed to mention it (see 1 Corinthians 5:1).

What about Paul's call for self-examination on the part of the Corinthians, and his warnings of judgment and condemnation? It sounds as if he was saying that if those folk who were sinning at the Lord's Supper didn't get their act together, they were in danger of losing their salvation. God had already killed some of them for their sin ("sleep," 1 Corinthians 11:30).

There's a lot to consider here, and to help us I want to give you two essential principles of Bible study that are necessary in understanding 1 Corinthians 11:28–32. The first principle is that the meaning of a word is established by its immediate context. If I asked a group of people what the word *bark* refers to, I might get several different answers. Some people would immediately relate the word to dogs, while others might suggest the bark of a tree. Until I use the word in a context, no one can be sure what I mean. But if I say, "I heard a loud bark outside my window last night," people know that I'm talking about a dog. The context guides the meaning of the word.

The second rule of Bible study we need to apply is the other side of the coin. It's also important that we plug an individual passage into the "big picture" of that book of the Bible, or even a writer's larger body of writing. Paul's works are a good example, so let's apply this second principle and work back to the first.

When we examine all of Paul's New Testament letters, it's clear that he was addressing believers. His message was for the church, not the world. First Corinthians itself opens with his greeting "to the church of God which is at Corinth, to those who have been sanctified in Christ Jesus, saints by calling" (1:2). Verse 4 may be even more significant for the purposes of our subject: "I thank my God always concerning you for the grace of God which was given you in Christ Jesus."

Although Paul reprimanded this church severely, we have to read his rebukes against the backdrop of these opening verses. He wasn't just tossing out flowers or being cordial when he called his readers sanctified saints who were the recipients of God's grace. This language would be out of place if he was fearful that they were about to become non-sanctified former saints from whom God had withdrawn His grace.

Even in the middle of his warnings in 1 Corinthians 11, Paul called the people "my brethren" (v. 33). My point is that since Paul is writing to Christians about self-examination, he is not talking about examination for the purpose of determining whether a person is saved or not.

Saints Can Be Disciplined Strongly

But what about the word *judged* in verses 31–32? It sounds like a reference to the eternal judgment reserved for unbelievers. But let's draw on the first Bible study principle explained above and evaluate this word in its immediate context. When we do that, several things become apparent.

For instance, we don't have to guess about the judgment Paul was talking about, because he provided that information. The judgment was physical discipline in the form of illness and even death (v. 30). The judgment mentioned in verse 32 must be read the same way. God was spanking His children for rebellious living, even destroying some of them physically the way the unbelieving world will also be destroyed someday.

By the way, there is very strong evidence for this interpretation in 1 Corinthians 5:5. In a similar situation, Paul said he had handed the incestuous person over to Satan for the destruction of his life if necessary. But Paul was careful to say that even if this extreme judgment had to be applied, the man would still be saved.

So the self-examination of 1 Corinthians 11 in relation to the Lord's Supper or Communion refers to a believer's discipline, not his or her eternal salvation. All of us are called to examine ourselves when we come to the Lord's Table, both for areas of sin that may invite God's discipline if not corrected, and to make sure that our lives are lined up with God's will and purpose for us.

A good father won't threaten to kick his children out of the family if they don't behave the way he wants. But that doesn't mean they won't ever get spanked, and sometimes the discipline may be severe. The Bible says, "Those whom the Lord loves He disciplines, and He scourges every son whom He receives" (Hebrews 12:6). We would be wise to examine ourselves to make it unnecessary for God the Father to spank us.

SELF-EXAMINATION AND SPIRITUAL PRODUCTIVITY

Given the spiritual track record of the Corinthian church, it's not surprising that Paul had to come back again and urge them to examine themselves. As he wrapped up his second letter to this church, the apostle wrote: "Test yourselves to see if you are in the faith; examine yourselves! Or do you not recognize this about yourselves, that Jesus Christ is in you—unless indeed you fail the test?" (2 Corinthians 13:5).

This passage is a little stickier to explain because it seems so obvious that Paul is saying, "Check yourselves out to see if you are Christians or not." In other words, "Check to make sure you are born again."

One strong objection to this view is the way Paul tied himself and his own apostleship in with the "test" he was urging the Corinthians to take. Whatever this test was, Paul expressed his hope that the believers in Corinth would realize that he certainly passed it. They knew of the godly service he had performed among them and the love he had shown for them. It's like saying, "You know—or at least you should know—that I pass the test, even if you've had a moment of doubt." The idea that Paul was inviting the Corinthians to see whether he too might have lost his salvation is ridiculous. We have no evidence that Paul ever doubted his salvation. He was ready on any day to "depart and be with Christ" (Philippians 1:23).

Another objection to the view that this passage is talking about assurance is its self-focus. Our assurance does not come from looking within ourselves, because our feelings and attitudes and actions change. True assurance only comes when we look to Christ, just as we looked to Him for salvation.

Pass the Test of God's Activity

If 2 Corinthians 13:5 is not about our eternal standing before God, what did Paul mean when he said, "Test yourselves to see if you are in the faith"? This is another case in which context is everything.

The larger context of 2 Corinthians establishes the readers' identity as believers. They were "the church of God" and "saints" who were the recipients of God's grace (1:1–2). If the apostle were to cast a serious doubt on their salvation, it would be the equivalent of saying to them, "I'm writing to you as if you are Christians, but I'm not really sure you are Christians at all, so you'd better check yourselves out to make sure you are Christians lest you prove not to be Christians." Taking this view leads to spiritual double-talk.

The book's context is also important because the theme of 2 Corinthians is Paul's vindication of his ministry and his love for the Corinthians. In answer to those who opposed and criticized him, and the Corinthians' own fickleness, Paul opened up his heart to demonstrate the sincerity and authenticity of his love and his apostleship.

This is key to understanding the test of faith Paul referred to in chapter 13. This was not a test of salvation, but a test of whether God was really at work in a believer's life. Some people in Corinth were questioning whether Paul really spoke with the authority of Christ. He was aware of the accusation, and he said he was coming back to Corinth to deal with those who were out of line (13:1–2).

Then Paul added that his visit would clear up the issue of his authority once and for all, "since you are seeking for proof of the Christ who speaks in me" (v. 3). It's like a father who hears his son acting up in the other room and says, "Son, you'd better start behaving yourself or I'm going to come in there and take care of the situation!"

Now when a father says that, what child who is clothed and in his right mind is going to holler back, "Oh, yeah? Prove it! I've got just as much authority in this house as you do. Who died and left you in charge?" That's just not going to happen if that boy is thinking straight. And if the father does have to go into the boy's room, whose authority and behavior do you think is going be up for examination?

What Paul did was turn the tables on his readers by saying, "You want to put me to the test to see if God is at work in me. But what you really should be asking is whether God is doing anything in you." Paul's concern wasn't whether the Corinthians were really saved. His fear was that they would "fail the test" by becoming spiritually unproductive and forfeit God's blessing and fruitfulness in their lives.

Don't Let Yourself Be Disqualified

How do we know this was the apostle's focus? Because he used the same Greek term translated "fail the test" in 2 Corinthians 13:5

to refer to the productivity of his ministry. "I discipline my body and make it my slave, so that, after I have preached to others, I myself will not be *disqualified*" (1 Corinthians 9:27, italics added). To be disqualified is to fail the test, lose the race, and forfeit the victor's reward.

Paul was not afraid that he was going to lose his salvation. He was the champion of the eternal security of the believer. But he *was* afraid that he would be unapproved and unrewarded by God because he had not been faithful to his calling. Paul wanted to finish the Christian race so that he would not appear before Christ empty-handed and receive no rewards in heaven.

We can be sure that Paul regularly and carefully examined himself with reference to his faithfulness and spiritual productivity. And although the Corinthians needed to stop questioning Paul and check out their own spiritual lives, he expressed his hope that even if they did insist on examining him, they would find that he passed the test.

Instead of telling the Corinthians to see whether they possessed eternal life, Paul called them to examine how well they were doing with the eternal life they already possessed.

SELF-EXAMINATION AND SPIRITUAL GROWTH

Paul wasn't the only apostle who wanted his spiritual children to perform regular checkups to make sure they were living in maximum faithfulness to Christ. Peter also charged the believers under his care to bring their lives into line with God's eternal purpose for them.

The passage I want us to consider doesn't use the term *self-examination,* but the meaning of what Peter wrote is the same:

> For he who lacks these qualities is blind or short-sighted, having forgotten his purification from his former sins. Therefore, brethren, be all the more diligent to make certain about His calling and choosing you; for as long as you practice these things, you will never stumble. (2 Peter 1:9–10)

It's obvious that we broke into the flow of thought here. You'll find "these qualities" itemized in verses 5–8, but I've set them aside for the moment to deal with the verses in question. At the end of this section, I want to come back to these qualities that make for spiritual growth to encourage you in your walk with Christ and increase your spiritual confidence.

God's Desire for Us to Grow in Grace

There are some potentially troubling words in 2 Peter 1:9–10. What did Peter mean by saying a believer could forget that he had been purified from his sins? And even more pointed for the issue of assurance, why would we have to make certain about our calling and choosing (or election) if these things are supposed to be certain in the first place? And does the word *stumble* refer to the potential loss of salvation?

Since the context of verses 9–10 also helps to explain their meaning, let's go back to the beginning of 2 Peter. There's a very telling phrase right in verse 1. Peter said his readers had "received a faith of the same kind as ours." It's hard to imagine that Peter would have said this if he was uncertain about his own relationship with Christ and afraid that someday he would do something to cause Christ to let him go.

Besides, Peter's language of certainty and celebration gets stronger and stronger all the way through verse 3. "[God's] divine power has granted to us everything pertaining to life and godliness, through the true knowledge of Him who called us by His own glory and excellence." Not only this, but we possess God's "precious and magnificent promises" and we have "become partakers of the divine nature" (v. 4).

These verses argue for the stability of our position in Christ. It's not until we come to verses 5–10 that Peter began to discuss the way we practice the faith we possess—our spiritual growth or lack thereof.

Verses 5–8 address spiritual growth. Therefore, in verse 9 Peter turned his attention to those who were failing to live up to their exalted standing in Christ. Notice, however, that he did *not* say a spiritually immature believer's former sins were no longer forgiven. The problem is that such a person is living as if he has forgotten whose child he is.

Verse 10 is Peter's call for self-examination. This is an interesting text because in one sense, we as believers don't make our calling and election certain. These are God's action to save us, and He is the One who guarantees our salvation.

So what did Peter mean? In the context of spiritual growth he was saying that by being diligent to grow in our faith, we produce for ourselves something like a deed that a homeowner has to prove that he owns his home. This is the background meaning of the Greek word translated *certain* in verse 10.

In other words, if you are growing in your faith and producing the qualities listed in verses 5–8, that's a proof of the reality of your salvation. Now don't misunderstand. This is very different from saying that your growth guarantees or secures your salvation. Salvation is not dependent upon your spiritual growth, but upon the finished work of Jesus Christ.

Interestingly, the word *certain* in 2 Peter 1:10 is translated "guaranteed" in Romans 4:16 and "assurance" in Hebrews 3:14, strongly suggesting that Peter used it here to convey certainty with regard to salvation. It's in this context that we must evaluate the word *stumble* at the end of verse 10. It cannot refer to a loss of salvation, but the failure to grow as we should.

Qualities That Strengthen Your Faith

Spiritual growth was definitely on Peter's heart when he wrote his second letter. His last word to the church was "Grow in the grace and knowledge of our Lord and Savior Jesus Christ" (2 Peter 3:18). And his first word of exhortation after greeting and encouraging his readers is the section on spiritual growth in chapter 1 that we set aside above (vv. 5–8).

We've done a lot of doctrinal study to this point, which is crucial to our growth and understanding. But I also hope that some brief reflection on this practical passage will deepen your walk of faith. Second Peter is a reminder that God wants us to get busy growing in the grace He has given us instead of fretting about whether we are still in God's grace.

With this in mind, we read in verse 5: "Now for this very reason also, applying all diligence, in your faith supply moral excellence." Applying diligence to supply the qualities that make for spiritual growth means that we must make a plan to grow and work that plan. We don't become strong Christians by watching videos of other Christians serving God. "Work out your salvation with fear and trembling" (Philippians 2:12).

The opening phrase of verse 5 gives us all the motivation we need. "For this very reason" points back to the magnificent position, power, and promises that are ours in Jesus Christ. What could be more encouraging than knowing that our efforts toward spiritual growth are not in vain because God is at work in us? Paul gave us the same encouragement and motivation in Philippians 2:13: "For it is God who is at work in you, both to will and to work for His good pleasure."

Since our standing in Christ is secure, we can move forward in the power of the Holy Spirit and supply the qualities in Peter's list to our faith. The first is moral excellence: "Like the Holy One who called you, be holy yourselves also in all your behavior" (1 Peter 1:15). If you want to excel in something, excel in holiness. Become a master in your "trade" of living for Christ, just as many of the trades refer to their most skilled practitioners as masters.

Supplying knowledge (2 Peter 1:5b) to our moral excellence increases our chances to grow. "Grow in . . . the knowledge of our Lord and Savior Jesus Christ" (2 Peter 3:18). Ignorance is not bliss when it comes to spiritual development. Your knowledge of God is directly related to your knowledge about God. The more time you spend getting to know Him, the better you will know Him. Grace and knowledge work hand in hand.

Self-control, perseverance, and godliness are the next three growth items on Peter's list (1:6). Self-control is another word for discipline, which is not just nice but necessary for spiritual growth. Do you know the areas where you are spiritually vulnerable, and are you working your plan to avoid those things? Are you keeping a daily appointment to meet with God in prayer and the Word? If you need someone like a prayer partner or accountability group, go for it. Do whatever it takes to develop self-control.

Perseverance is the quality that says, "Don't quit." You may feel like throwing in the towel at times, but if you're pursuing God, don't give up, because whatever you're going through is part of the plan.

Next is godliness, which for the Christian means becoming more like Jesus Christ. Peter had already said that God granted us "everything pertaining to life and godliness" (2 Peter 1:3). How's that for an encouraging word? We can grow in godliness because God empowers us to grow. This is the interplay of our work and God's work that Philippians 2:12–13 is all about.

The final two qualities Peter listed are brotherly kindness and love (2 Peter 1:7). These are closely related as the two the New Testament uses for love. "Be devoted to one another in brotherly love" (Romans 12:10) is about the best description of this first quality you'll find. This includes genuine affection and caring for other people as family, whereas love is the familiar word *agape*. This is the self-sacrificing love of God that leads a person to do what is best for somebody else regardless of the cost. The cross of Jesus Christ stands as the ultimate expression of *agape* love.

Where will these qualities take you as you grow in grace? Peter wrote, "For if these qualities are yours and are increasing, they render you neither useless nor unfruitful in the true knowledge of our Lord Jesus Christ" (2 Peter 1:8). Fruitfulness, usefulness, and the eternal rewards these will bring are the result of careful spiritual self-examination. Don't let yourself get sidetracked into fearful and paralyzing introspection over whether you're really saved—or even worse, whether Christ really meant what He said when He promised eternal life to all who trusted in Him.

THE SOURCE OF OUR ASSURANCE

There is a well-known Old Testament story that, with a little sanctified imagination, illustrates our thesis that assurance is not found in self-examination.

The story I have in mind is Passover, the night when the death angel of the Lord went through Egypt to slay all the firstborn, both humans and animals, in the final plague before Israel was released from bondage.

God commanded the Israelites through Moses to sacrifice a lamb and apply the blood to the lintel and doorposts of their houses. Then He warned that the death angel would slay the firstborn of any house that did not have the blood on its door. But when the angel saw the blood, he would pass over that house. There would be no judgment on those Israelites who obeyed.

Let's say I'm the firstborn son in one of those homes. My father gathers the family together and explains Moses' command concerning the Passover lamb and the terrible judgment that is going to fall on the Egyptians. Then at twilight on Passover evening my father kills a lamb and I watch as he takes a branch of hyssop, dips it in the blood, and applies it to the lintel and doorposts of our house. Then we eat the lamb that night and gather to wait for the death angel to strike, my father having firmly reminded us of Moses' warning not to go outside.

Now I don't know about you, but if I were the firstborn child in this family, I think I would find all these solemn preparations and my father's warnings a little bit scary. Imagine what this awesome scene of judgment and deliverance must have looked like to a child.

So as the firstborn in my family, I sit there thinking about the judgment against the firstborns. I become frightened as the thought of dying begins to take hold of me. I believe what my father said, but still I know I haven't been a perfect son, and suddenly the reality of my sins hits me.

As I become more afraid, I go to my father and say, "Daddy, are you sure we're going to be all right? I'm afraid I'm going to die tonight. I know I haven't been a very good son lately."

My father takes me over to the door and asks me, "Son, you saw me put the blood on our door tonight. What did God say?"

"He said when He saw the blood, His death angel would pass over our house."

"Right, Son. Passover has nothing to do with your behavior. This is not the time to worry about that. You're safe because God provided us with a lamb."

That word of reassurance calms me for a while. But a few hours later, as the night gets darker and quieter, a new rush of fear comes over me. I run to my father again, and he takes me to the same place and points to the door again. He reminds me of God's promise and tells me that we are going to be saved from judgment because our house is covered by the blood. This happens a few more times before the night is over, until finally I get the message and my heart is at peace.

If you doubt whether you're saved, don't sit around in self-contemplation until you're a bundle of fear. Turn to 1 Corinthians 5:7 and read these words: "Christ our Passover also has been sacrificed."

The blood of those lambs in the first Passover pointed forward to the coming sacrifice of *the* Passover Lamb, the Lord Jesus. If you have trusted Him as your Savior, His blood has been applied to your life and God's judgment will never touch you. You are safe in Christ forever.

13

ASSURANCE
AND
DISCIPLESHIP

First baseman Lou Gehrig epitomized the poise and profession-alism of the legendary New York Yankees teams of the '20s and '30s. It was said that Gehrig always came to dinner in the hotel wear-ing a jacket and tie, no matter how stifling the summer heat. And if a younger player dared to show up in the dining room without proper attire, Gehrig would pull the offender aside and say, "You're a Yankee now. Act like it."

That's about the most succinct description of discipleship I could give you. God's message to us as believers in Jesus Christ is, "You're My child now. Act like it." Therefore, our great challenge today is not to do everything we can to keep our salvation intact so God won't disown us, but to learn how to act like the sons and daughters of God that we already are.

In other words, discipleship is not your ticket to heaven. It is not the source of your assurance of salvation, but a process of growth whereby we get on with the business of becoming like Jesus Christ. Jesus Himself said, "A disciple is not above his teacher, nor a slave above his master. It is enough for the disciple that he become like his teacher, and the slave like his master" (Matthew 10:24–25).

This statement alone makes it clear that discipleship is not instantaneous. Instead, it involves a lifetime of learning. The word *disciple* means "student" or "learner," and so discipleship describes the process by which students absorb their teacher's instruction and skill so completely that they become just like that teacher. A more formal definition is that discipleship is a process of the local church that brings people from spiritual infancy to spiritual maturity. (I mention the church because it is God's school for making disciples.)

It is unfortunate that so many people are serving Christ in an attempt to validate their salvation. These are sincere believers, for the most part. They really want to follow Christ but have been led to believe that if they stumble along the way, or don't do enough good works, either their salvation will be revoked or they were never truly saved in the first place. Thus their service for Christ becomes a duty instead of a delight, a frantic search for security instead of a joyful journey inspired by gratitude for eternal life. Your salvation should inspire your discipleship, instead of your discipleship validating your salvation.

So let me say it again, just for the record. Assurance of salvation does not come from anything you do or fail to do. It comes from looking to and trusting the Savior, who not only gave you eternal life but guarantees the eternal life He gave you.

In order to find solid ground on which to establish assurance, we're having to clear away the debris of confusion that covers and obscures this topic. Part of this confusion is a faulty view of the relationship between salvation and discipleship. The two are intimately related, but they are not the same.

THE MEANING OF DISCIPLESHIP

In the ancient world, students often attached themselves to a teacher or master until they had acquired both a body of knowledge and the skills to use that knowledge effectively, no matter how long the process took. True disciples immersed themselves in their learning; it was a way of life, which is one difference between being a disciple and having a hobby.

Suppose a surgeon is preparing to operate on your heart when you ask, "Doctor, how many times have you performed this particular surgery?"

The surgeon replies, "Actually, I've never done this before. I'm just a general surgeon, not a heart specialist. But I've been studying the heart on the side, and I've always wanted to try this operation."

Most of us would be off the table and out the door if we heard that. That surgeon is merely a heart hobbyist, not a heart disciple. We want someone operating on us who studied the heart for years in medical school, spent more years under the tutelage of the top heart specialist in the country, and has performed at least one hundred successful operations.

As disciples of Jesus Christ we are His followers, but He has also appointed human teachers whose calling is to make disciples. Paul could say, "Be imitators of me, just as I also am of Christ" (1 Corinthians 11:1; see also 4:16 and Philippians 3:17). There is nothing wrong with following another person as long as that person is helping you become more like Jesus. All of us need teachers to help us align ourselves with Christ.

When we got saved, we were enrolled in Jesus' school of discipleship and introduced to its curriculum. This is a lifelong process of learning from which we will not graduate until we are promoted to heaven. And even there we will not stop learning, because we'll spend eternity discovering more and more about our great God (see Ephesians 2:7).

Our challenge as Christians, then, is to become such committed, excited, and teachable disciples of Jesus Christ that we begin to look and act like Him. The Bible calls it being "conformed" to the image of Christ (Romans 8:29). Assurance plays a key role in this process, because you can't be a focused, learning, and growing student when you're spending all of your time worrying about whether you're still enrolled in the course. Assurance of salvation makes effective discipleship possible.

HOW DISCIPLESHIP DIFFERS FROM SALVATION

Now that we have defined our terms, we need to decipher the relationship between discipleship, which is a lifelong process of growth, and salvation, which is complete the moment we trust Christ. Our thesis is that confusing these two leads to a lack of assurance and sends us searching for it in the wrong places.

You may be surprised by one passage which shows that discipleship and salvation are distinct. The Bible says that Jesus had disciples who were not even saved. According to John 6:60, a group of Jesus' disciples became offended at His teaching about His flesh and blood. They objected to what Jesus said, to which He replied, "There are some of you who do not believe" (v. 64). And it gets worse, because John went on to say, "As a result of this many of His disciples withdrew and were not walking with Him anymore" (v. 66).

It's obvious from this text that the term *disciple* was applied broadly to anyone who wanted to learn more about what it meant to follow Jesus Christ. Jesus had a large following at one point, but He thinned out that crowd when He began showing them the true cost of being His disciple.

Why would Jesus allow unsaved people to follow Him as disciples? For the same reason we don't stand at the church door on Sunday morning checking spiritual ID's so no lost people will be admitted to the service. Unsaved people have a far better chance of getting saved if they are under the hearing of the Word than if they turn away and leave.

Jesus didn't worry about weeding out the crowd that followed Him until the time was right. And since those who followed and listened to Him were functioning as students, the Bible refers to them as disciples. But unsaved people are never called saints or told they are on their way to heaven. There is no such thing as an unsaved Christian.

Discipleship Is a Costly Commitment

The Bible closes with this invitation to partake of God's salvation: "The Spirit and the bride say, 'Come.' And let the one who hears say, 'Come.' And let the one who is thirsty come; let the one who wishes take the water of life *without cost*" (Revelation 22:17, italics added). Salvation is free.

Discipleship, on the other hand, is costly. Jesus said on one occasion, "If anyone wishes to come after Me, he must deny himself, and take up his cross and follow Me. For whoever wishes to save his life will lose it, but whoever loses his life for My sake and the gospel's will save it" (Mark 8:34–35). It will cost you your life to become Jesus' disciple.

Jesus was referring to the fact that to follow Him requires an exchange of our life for His. Discipleship is the process designed to get rid of the old you and accentuate the new you, which is the life of Christ within you.

Now you may say, "But Tony, didn't we become new creations in Christ the moment we trusted Him? Doesn't the Bible say the old things have passed away and everything is new?"

Yes, the Bible does say, "If anyone is in Christ, he is a new creature" (2 Corinthians 5:17). This is true instantly in terms of our *position* before God. You will never be more saved than you were the day you came to Christ. But in terms of our *practice,* we have to learn to put off the deeds and attitudes of our old sinful selves.

Remember that when you came to Christ, you received His life in seed form. But don't misunderstand. I'm not saying that your salvation was incomplete. Just the opposite, in fact. It's because you are made complete in Christ that you even have the wherewithal to grow as a maturing disciple. Discipleship addresses the importance of nurturing and developing the seed of the gospel while starving out the flesh.

Paul called the Galatians "my children, with whom I am again in labor until Christ is formed in you" (Galatians 4:19). He wasn't saying that these people were on their way to getting saved and were about to make it. He was speaking of their progress as disciples, which was shaky at the time. The difference between a defeated and a victorious Christian is not a defect in their salvation, but a difference in the quality of their discipleship. It's costly to be a disciple.

Discipleship Makes Radical Demands

Here's another difference between salvation and discipleship. The former demands only faith (although faith is to issue in works [James 2:14]), while the latter makes radical, ongoing, and long-term demands.

When the Philippian jailer cried out, "What must I do to be saved?" Paul and Silas answered, "Believe in the Lord Jesus, and you will be saved" (Acts 16:30–31). They did not make any other demands, because faith is all that's necessary to be saved. That jailer didn't do anything to earn his salvation, but he got forgiveness and a home in heaven that night.

People who say they are trying to make heaven their home are confused. They don't understand the gospel. You do not try to make heaven your home. If you could make heaven your home by yourself, Jesus wouldn't have had to leave His home in heaven to come down and die on the cross so He could take you back to heaven with Him.

Salvation is guaranteed, but not discipleship, because discipleship makes radical demands that some people are not ready to meet. There are Christians who are truly saved but do not continue on the road of discipleship. People in this condition certainly need to check their hearts and their standing before God, but this is not to deny that it is possible for a believer to fail to follow the Lord in discipleship.

You see, we love hearing about salvation because it's free, but not this talk about losing our lives and paying a price and giving up all to follow Christ. But discipleship is undeniably radical. Jesus said, "If anyone comes to Me, and does not hate his own father and mother and wife and children and brothers and sisters, yes, and even his own life, he cannot be My disciple" (Luke 14:26).

You don't have to hate your mother or your father to get saved. You don't have to hate yourself to come to Christ and find eternal life. But to become a disciple requires such radical self-abandonment to Christ that compared to your love for Him, your love for even the people closest to you looks like hate.

After Lois and I had been dating for a while, she hit me with this statement: "Tony, you will never be first in my life because my commitment to Jesus Christ will override my relationship with you." I understood what she meant, and it made me want to marry her more than ever because I wanted someone who was radically committed to Christ.

Let me tell you something. If you have never made the decision to follow Jesus Christ whatever the cost, don't be surprised if you do not see the power of God operating in your life. If you're still sitting on the fence, don't be surprised if heaven doesn't come down and glory doesn't fill your soul. Don't be surprised if you don't see much answered prayer.

The reason for this is explained in an interesting passage at the end of John 2. We read in verses 23–25:

> Now when He was in Jerusalem at the Passover, during the feast, many believed in His name, observing His signs which He was doing. But Jesus, on His part, was not entrusting Himself to them, for He knew all men, and because He did not need anyone to testify concerning man, for He Himself knew what was in man.

This is amazing. These people believed in Jesus, but the Bible says that Jesus did not entrust or commit Himself to them. Is it possible for there to be Christians to whom Jesus is not committed?

It is, because the issue is not salvation but discipleship. The question is not whether a person is in the family of God, but whether he or she can be trusted to handle the things of God faithfully and maturely.

Many parents understand this difference because they have some children they're more committed to than their other children. We're not talking about the parents' love for their children, but the matter of trust. Parents can safely commit time, money, and other things to some children because they are going to do something good with what they've been given.

But with other children the more money they are given, the more they waste it. The same is true for their time, educational opportunities, or any number of other benefits. It has nothing to do with the children's position in the family, but with their practice as family members. God won't commit Himself to some of us in terms of our discipleship because He knows we are going to wind up abusing His good gifts.

It's radical to tell people they have to hate their own lives. That means if you say one thing and God says another, you choose God. This is not polite Christianity, but it's the only way to live. Where else but in living for Christ will you find a cause to give yourself to that will last for eternity? Salvation will get you up to heaven, but discipleship will get heaven down to you because Christ will commit Himself to you in all of His power and glory.

Discipleship Is Observable

Another important contrast between salvation and discipleship is what we might call their observability. That is, salvation is a transaction of the heart. No one can see it take place. Salvation takes place in the privacy of a person's heart and soul.

But discipleship is always meant to be public and therefore observable. John 19:38 refers to Joseph of Arimathea as a disciple of Jesus who had followed the Lord secretly because he was afraid of his fellow Jews. But guess what happened to Joseph? There came a day when he had to declare himself publicly, and you can read about it in the same verse. He went to Pilate and asked for Jesus' body to bury, and he laid Jesus in his own tomb. It would have been impossible to do something like that in Jerusalem without making his true allegiance known.

Jesus may have some "secret-agent saints," but He does not want disciples who function as covert operatives when there are no restrictions on the practice of their faith. "Therefore everyone who confesses Me before men, I will also confess him before My Father who is in heaven. But whoever denies Me before men, I will also deny him before My Father who is in heaven" (Matthew 10:32–33).

We may fall on our knees and say, "Father, I need a miracle. I've got a disease the doctors can't cure. In Jesus' name. Amen." Or, "Lord, I need a better job so I can get out of debt. I pray this is Jesus' name. Amen."

Praying in Jesus' name means that He has to sign off on the requests we make. So when we ask for something, God the Father wants to know if His Son can agree to our request.

But for some of us, Jesus would have to say, "Father, I can't trust this person with a better job because He has been on his present job for ten years and My name never comes up in his conversations. He is afraid that someone will see him praying in the lunchroom. Father, how can I give this person more when he is going to leave Me out?" If we deny Christ in our public lives by our actions, He will deny us before His Father. God may have other reasons for not answering prayer as we might wish it to be answered, and even the most committed saints have unanswered prayers and deep sorrows. But you can be sure that being a part-time disciple is going to lead to little blessings.

Discipleship Is Conditional

If there is any truth about salvation that you take away with you after reading this book, I hope you grab hold of this: Salvation is unconditional and, therefore, the assurance of that salvation is unconditional because it is all of God and none of you.

But discipleship is conditional. "Jesus was saying to those Jews who had believed Him, 'If you continue in My word, then you are truly disciples of Mine; and you will know the truth, and the truth will make you free'" (John 8:31–32). To continue means to abide or remain in the truth.

Many people want truth without the abiding that it takes to get the truth inside of them. If someone says, "I know the truth, but I'm not free," then we have an abiding problem.

John 8:32 is one of the most quoted verses in the New Testament, but don't forget the Bible study principle we learned earlier: the importance of context. The problem comes when people want to skip verse 31 and claim verse 32. We want to be free of our problems, our addictions, our vices, or our circumstances. But in order to be free we have to know the truth. And in order to know the truth we must continue or abide or remain in Christ and so prove to be true disciples.

Whenever I read this I think of drinking tea. Too many Christians live their lives the way people make tea, constantly dipping the bag in and out of the water. These folk dip in to church on Sunday morning and then pull back. Then they dip on Wednesday night for another "dunk" in the Christian cup.

One day I asked a man I was eating with why he dipped his tea bag in the cup and pulled it out. "Because, Pastor, if I leave it in there too long the tea will get too strong."

Watch out if you remain in Christ, because you may find yourself getting strong! If you're wondering where your victory and joy and peace went, check to see if you've been dipping or abiding in Christ.

Discipleship Deals with Intimacy

There is one more difference between salvation and discipleship I want us to see. Salvation deals with our legal relationship to Christ, and is forever sealed and settled. Discipleship has to do with the level of intimacy we have with the Savior who guarantees our eternal life.

The disciple Philip made an interesting request of Jesus in John 14:8, "Lord, show us the Father, and it is enough for us."

Notice Jesus' response: "Have I been so long with you, and yet you have not come to know Me, Philip?" (v. 9). That's very important because Philip was one of the first to believe in Jesus and follow Him (see John 1:43–44). In other words, Philip had been with Jesus for a long time, and yet he still was a long way from getting the picture.

Maybe you became a Christian when you were ten years old. Now you're forty-five, and you're still asking to see God. Maybe the intimacy you're missing is waiting for you in a deeper commitment to Christ in discipleship.

HOW DISCIPLESHIP RELATES TO ASSURANCE

If the goal of discipleship is not to produce assurance, how are the two related? Let's deal with this question in a little more detail.

Discipleship Is Rooted in Assurance

It's pretty hard to get serious about growing if you're not sure you were ever born in the first place. Now that sounds like doubletalk, but it's the logical conclusion of any teaching that denies that we can be absolutely sure we are saved. Salvation gives us new life, and assurance gives us the security and confidence to develop that new life as we follow Christ in discipleship.

There is a tremendous interplay of salvation, assurance, and discipleship in Titus 2:11–13. "For the grace of God has appeared, bringing salvation to all men, instructing us to deny ungodliness and worldly desires and to live sensibly, righteously and godly in the present age, looking for the blessed hope and the appearing of the glory of our great God and Savior, Jesus Christ."

Notice that the grace of God appeared to us and brought us salvation (v. 11). And that same grace will be manifested to us at the end of this age when Jesus appears and takes us to be with Him in glory (v. 13). Do you read any doubt on Paul's part here that those who are saved by God's grace will one day be present with Him in glory? There is no doubt at all. In fact, this entire passage is one sentence, suggesting even by its grammar the uninterrupted movement from grace here on earth to grace in eternity.

What about verse 12? This speaks to our discipleship "in the present age" and the way we should conduct ourselves on our journey from earth to heaven. It's like a sandwich, with the "meat" of discipleship in between the two pieces of bread called grace. The bread holds the meat in place, and the meat fills out the sandwich. Assurance is an integral part of the formula.

The relationship between assurance and discipleship is also evident in Jesus' invitation: "Come to Me, all who are weary and heavy-laden, and I will give you rest. Take My yoke upon you and learn from Me, for I am gentle and humble in heart, and you will find rest for your souls" (Matthew 11:28–29).

Verse 28 is an invitation to salvation. Jesus offers us rest if we will do nothing more than come to Him, which is another way of saying believe in Him. This rest is purely a gift.

But verse 29 is a call to discipleship. It's only as you take Jesus' yoke and learn from Him that you find the rest a disciple enjoys. A yoke is a classic illustration of what it means to be a disciple or a learner. In biblical days farmers would yoke an older, experienced ox with a young, inexperienced ox so the younger could learn how to pull the plow. The older ox would do most of the work until the younger one grew accustomed to the yoke and became productive.

Since a yoke suggests hard work, and a lot of it, we wouldn't normally associate it with rest. But Jesus said the person who yokes up with Him will find rest. What gives you and me the assurance to take Jesus at His word and accept His yoke that leads to rest? Because we have already experienced His rest in salvation, the cessation of all our efforts to make ourselves acceptable to Him. Assurance is a crucial antecedent to discipleship.

Assurance Motivates Our Discipleship

Assurance is the motivation and the power of discipleship. God wants us to be grateful for our eternal salvation. He wants us to be thankful that because of Christ's death on the cross, heaven is our home. If we will look at what God has given us and stop fretting about whether He is going to take back His gift of salvation, we'll be ready to follow Him in committed discipleship here on earth. If we can trust Christ with our eternity, can we not trust Him with our few days on earth?

There was once a girl who was ashamed of her mother because her mother had a terribly disfiguring scar that ran across her face. The girl would never bring her friends home or invite her mother to school functions because she was embarrassed by her mother's appearance.

The mother knew why her daughter was so ashamed of her and afraid for anyone to meet her. So one day she said to her daughter, "Honey, sit down. I'm going to tell you how I got this terrible scar. One day when you were a baby, I went out to the well to draw water. But when I turned around, the house was on fire. I dropped the bucket and rushed back into the house to grab my precious little baby out of her crib.

"The fire was engulfing your room, but I got there in the nick of time. But on my way out of the house, a burning beam collapsed and hit me across the face. I had you cradled in my arms and managed to protect you, but I took the full force of the beam on my face. So darling, the next time you feel ashamed to introduce me to your friends, just remember that the only reason I have this scar is because I was saving your life."

Jesus has some scars too, in His hands and feet and side. The next time you don't feel like being His disciple and introducing Him to your friends, remember how He got His scars. And when you remember, tell Him you'll follow Him for the rest of your days out of gratitude for the fact that He has saved you for eternity.

14

ASSURANCE AND SPIRITUAL FAILURE

In the aftermath of the September 11, 2001, terrorist attacks on New York and Washington, one of the statements we heard expressed again and again was utter shock that an attack of this magnitude could happen in America. This nation was far too secure and well-protected, we thought, to be struck in its heart and brought to its knees by an unseen enemy.

Even weeks later, as the details of how the attacks happened became known, millions of Americans were still asking, "How could this have happened?" One reporter spoke for many when he said, "We thought this could never happen in America. Now we know better." On September 11, 2001, it became tragically obvious that we had been living under a false sense of security that didn't allow for terrorism on this scale.

False security is always dangerous. The last thing I want to do in this section of the book, or in the section that follows, is to give anyone who doesn't really know the Lord a false sense of assurance. That's why we keep coming back to the central truth that our assurance rests in *nothing* but the finished work of Jesus Christ and the witness of the Holy Spirit that we are truly children of God (see Romans 8:16).

I also do not want to see Christians develop a false sense of security that often manifests itself in one of two ways: either the belief that we are above falling into temptation and failure because we are secure in Christ, or the equally mistaken notion that our eternal security means we can live in unrepentant sin or spiritual lethargy because we will make it to heaven anyway.

I don't think it will come as a surprise to you that even saved and secured people can and do stumble in their walk of faith. After all, assurance is tied to God and His perfect ability to save and keep us, not to our perfect ability to remain faithful to Him. Spiritual failure happens to all believers at various points and to varying degrees in their spiritual journey, because we are still living in sin-contaminated bodies and immersed in a sin-wrecked world.

But that doesn't give us an excuse for failure and spiritual lethargy and coldness. Nor does it mean that spiritual failure is a small thing. It's a real issue in the Christian life, and it will erode your sense of assurance faster than anything I can think of.

The question many believers ask after slipping is, "How could God still love a person like me?" The short answer is that He does, because you can't do anything to take yourself out of His hands. But He also loves His children enough not to let them continue on the wrong road, because God disciplines every child He receives.

Let's talk about how spiritual failure can happen, what its consequences are, and what we can do about it. We'll also see how all of this relates to the doctrine of assurance, because spiritual failure and eternal security seem to be incompatible.

THE POSSIBILITY OF SPIRITUAL FAILURE

There is no denying the fact that saved people who are sealed by the Holy Spirit until the day of redemption and secure forever in Christ can still fall into sin and failure. The Bible contains many examples of people who fell, some for short periods and others for a good part of their lives. These examples range from spiritual insensitivity and coldness to moral failure and even outright denial of the truth.

The Bible's "Hall of Failure"

David is an example of moral failure in his adultery with Bathsheba and murder of Uriah (2 Samuel 11–12). David covered his sin for about a year until confronted by the prophet Nathan. Then David immediately confessed and repented, and he told the Lord, "Against You, You only, I have sinned and done what is evil in Your sight" (Psalm 51:4). That's an important truth, because all spiritual failure ultimately is against the Lord.

David's predecessor, King Saul, became spiritually insensitive and calloused. He disobeyed God and didn't think anything was wrong until Samuel confronted him (1 Samuel 15:1–31). Saul's life and reign went downhill from there, and God rejected him as king.

King Solomon is another example of spiritual failure. He started his reign under God's unusual blessing and anointing, but then married many foreign women who led his heart away from God for an extended period of time (1 Kings 11:1–4). But I expect to see David, Saul, and Solomon in heaven.

The early church also contained examples of spiritual failure. The incestuous man in Corinth fell into deep moral failure (see 1 Corinthians 5:1–5), but as we noted in a previous chapter, even in this case the man's eternal salvation was not at stake. Paul pronounced his discipline with the expressed desire that the man's soul would be saved (v. 5).

Paul's pastoral involvement with the churches he had founded brought him into contact and conflict with people who failed in their faith. Every pastor sees people who come into the church and are on fire for the Lord the first year or so, become lukewarm the second year, and can't be found by the third year. They fade and fall away, and they may even end up denying the truth of God either by their words or by the way they live. Some of them may never have been truly saved in the first place, but that can't be said for every person who loses the fire.

Two such people were in the church at Ephesus where Paul left Timothy as pastor (see 1 Timothy 1:3). Paul urged Timothy: "Fight the good fight, keeping faith and a good conscience, which some have rejected and suffered shipwreck in regard to their faith. Among these are Hymenaeus and Alexander, whom I have handed over to Satan, so that they will be taught not to blaspheme" (vv. 18–20).

Whatever these men were guilty of, this was serious discipline for serious spiritual failure. We might think there was no way these men could be true Christians, but the parallel situation in 1 Corinthians 5 suggests that Hymenaeus and Alexander were believers who fell into serious spiritual error. You can't suffer shipwreck in regard to a faith you don't have. The only way to be part of a shipwreck is to be on the ship.

Hymenaeus is mentioned again in 2 Timothy 2:17, where we find out what he was doing. He and a man named Philetus were teaching that the resurrection of saints had already taken place, and by doing so they had "upset the faith of some" (v. 18). Now if you are waiting for Jesus to come back and the resurrection to take place, but you are told you have missed it, your faith is going to be shaken up.

But notice what Paul said next. "Nevertheless, the firm foundation of God stands, having this seal, 'The Lord knows those who are His,' and 'Everyone who names the name of the Lord is to abstain from wickedness'" (v. 19).

Despite those who get off track and even fall into error, the Lord knows who His people are. In other words, if you're His you're His, period. And that includes people who go astray either morally or doctrinally, although God will discipline them severely unless they repent.

The declaration at the end of 2 Timothy 2:19 is especially important for our purposes. Can we come to the Lord and live any way we please because we are His? No, if you name the name of the Lord, your goal should be to separate yourself as far from sin as possible. We all stumble at times, but a deliberate departure from what we know to be true invites God's discipline.

Hymenaeus and his pals had to learn not to blaspheme and lead people away from the truth. If a Christian won't listen to the Word of God and the Spirit of God, God will turn that person over to the devil for severe discipline.

We Need to Be on Guard

You say, "Tony, I would never fall away from the faith like that and end up in false doctrine." That's great, but we slip up in much more ordinary, everyday ways. Paul addressed these in 1 Timothy, saying to men, "If anyone does not provide for his own, and especially for those of his household, he has denied the faith and is worse than an unbeliever" (5:8).

Then he addressed the situation of younger widows: "I want younger widows to get married, bear children, keep house, and give the enemy no occasion for reproach; for some have already turned aside to follow Satan" (5:14–15).

And in chapter 6, Paul had this word for those in the church who had fallen in love with money: "Those who want to get rich fall into temptation and a snare and many foolish and harmful desires which plunge men into ruin and destruction. For the love of money is a root of all sorts of evil, and some by longing for it have wandered away from the faith and pierced themselves with many griefs" (vv. 9–10).

Spiritual failure doesn't have to be a huge leap into doctrinal error that denies the truth of Scripture. We can deny the faith by the way we live, failing to fulfill our biblical responsibilities or allowing the world to pull us away from faithfulness to Christ. I think of Demas, one of Paul's ministry companions who deserted the apostle because he "loved this present world" (2 Timothy 4:10).

Demas was ministering with Paul and helping take care of the aged apostle. But the world just looked too good to Demas, and he turned from serving Christ with Paul. It is possible for a Christian to be detoured from the faith.

You may be thinking that these people certainly don't sound like true Christians. But let me remind you of the carnal Corinthians, who were so messed up they turned the Lord's Supper into a drunken party. God killed some of them for their sin ("sleep," 1 Corinthians 11:30), but it's interesting that this word for their death is used only of believers in the New Testament.

Lost people don't sleep when they die, because they don't have any hope beyond the grave, only judgment awaiting them. So they are not seen as being at rest awaiting the resurrection. Some of the Corinthian believers were dead, but their eternal salvation was not the issue. It's possible for saved and secure people to fail spiritually in large and small ways.

THE ROAD TO SPIRITUAL FAILURE

Admitting the possibility of spiritual failure is the first step to being on guard against it. None of us is perfect, but that doesn't mean we have to live in spiritual mediocrity, stumbling along from one setback to another. There are plenty of warning signs along the road that leads to spiritual failure. Let's note some of them so you'll know what to watch for.

We have a lot of help because an entire book of the Bible was written to warn believers who are about to head down the wrong road. Hebrews was addressed to Jewish believers who were encountering persecution and were considering throwing in the towel and going back to Judaism. And by the way, Hebrews also contains the passage that is used maybe more than any other as "proof" that it is possible to lose your salvation. We'll deal with that text in our study later.

The writer of Hebrews addressed his readers as "holy brethren" (3:1), and his basic message to them was, "Do not throw away your confidence, which has a great reward" (10:35). Since the Hebrews were on the verge of losing their spiritual confidence (not their salvation) and turning back, this letter contains some clear warning signs we can read and heed as we seek to avoid going into a ditch in our Christian lives.

First Warning Sign: Spiritual Neglect

We don't have to curse the Lord or teach false doctrine to get into trouble. We can simply neglect our faith. "For if the word spoken through angels proved unalterable, and every transgression and disobedience received a just penalty, how will we escape if we neglect so great a salvation?" (Hebrews 2:2–3).

Spiritual neglect is so lethal because the Christian life is so "daily." We may experience bursts of spiritual growth, but by and large it is the product of daily faithfulness and discipline.

For instance, we get fired up about reading our Bibles or praying. But after a while, the Bible winds up on the shelf again and prayer goes lacking. Or we find a church we love and jump in, only to lose our fire and start neglecting to make the effort to fellowship with other believers.

Spiritual neglect is so subtle that we can fall into it without feeling particularly sinful. People in this situation may console themselves by the fact that they aren't really doing wrong. It's not like they're lying or cheating or being unfaithful to their spouses. They still pray and read their Bibles and attend church sometimes.

But no Christian ever "neglected" himself or herself into spiritual growth. Students don't get promoted just because they don't do something bad enough to get expelled from school. They get promoted because they don't neglect to study.

If you're neglecting things like time with God in the Word and prayer, and time with His people in fellowship and service, this should be a warning sign to you that you are on the road to spiritual neglect. The truth that we are secure forever in Christ was never meant to lull us into spiritual indifference.

Why do we neglect such a great salvation as Jesus gives? Because it loses its value. It's not so great anymore. Jesus Christ becomes ordinary. The exciting truths of the faith become stale. They're old hat to us now.

The same thing happens in a marriage. A marriage gets stale when the love relationship is neglected. The partners don't have to be unfaithful, just ignore each other and take each other for granted. Do that long enough and a marriage can die from neglect. The couple is still married. They still have the ring, but the zing is gone. The things they used to do that made their relationship exciting don't get done anymore. What is true in marriage is true in any relationship: Neglect causes damage. Neglect is a big warning sign on the road to spiritual failure.

Second Warning Sign: Spiritual Insensitivity

If allowed to persist, spiritual neglect leads to spiritual insensitivity. Hebrews 3 contains this warning: "Take care, brethren, that there not be in any one of you an evil, unbelieving heart that falls away from the living God. But encourage one another day after day, as long as it is still called 'Today,' so that none of you will be hardened by the deceitfulness of sin" (vv. 12–13).

Insensitivity sets in when Christ stops being real to you and you stop looking to Him for your life. When you stop looking to Christ, unbelief sets in. And when unbelief sets in you become susceptible to the deceitfulness of sin.

Insensitivity means you've lost your ability to feel. How do you know when you're being spiritually insensitive? Sin isn't as painful as it used to be. Before, when you sinned you were crushed. You had failed your Savior. You had the right heart attitude about your sin.

But when spiritual insensitivity sets in, sin isn't that painful anymore. After all, everybody else is doing it. What hurts the heart of God doesn't hurt you the way it used to. This is a dangerous condition, which is why the author of Hebrews gives the Holy Spirit's warning, "Do not harden your hearts as when they provoked Me, as in the day of trial in wilderness" (3:8).

Our prayer must be, "Lord, keep my heart tender and sensitive so that I feel the way You feel about everything." We need this because it's easy for a spiritually insensitive world to encase us in its hardness toward God.

Third Warning Sign: Spiritual Stagnation

If you've ever seen a clouded, stagnant pond you know what happens when the flow of fresh water is cut off. Nothing gets in or out. Even if you poured a bucket of fresh water into a stagnant pond, the new water would soon become green too.

When we allow our hearts to become insensitive toward the things of God, the next sign on the road to spiritual failure reads: "Warning: Stagnation Ahead." This was the case with the Hebrews.

In chapter 5 the author began teaching some deep truths about the priesthood of the Old Testament character Melchizedek, who was a type of Christ. But then it's as if the author realized whom he was addressing in his letter, because he stopped and said:

> Concerning him [Melchizedek] we have much to say, and it is hard to explain, since you have become dull of hearing. For though by this time you ought to be teachers, you have need again for someone to teach you the elementary principles of the oracles of God, and you have come to need milk and not solid food. For everyone who partakes only of milk is not accustomed to the word of righteousness, for he is an infant. But solid food is for the mature, who because of practice have their senses trained to discern good and evil. (vv. 11–14)

The phrase "dull of hearing" means mule-headed, or stubborn as a mule. These believers had been saved long enough to be spiritually mature. But they had stagnated in their development because they had quit practicing the faith.

Now that doesn't mean they had quit being Christians. What was at stake here was not these Jewish believers' eternal salvation, but the fruitfulness and effectiveness of their lives on earth. Eternally secure Christians can become so dull and stagnant that they are basically useless to the kingdom of God. And when that happens, we shouldn't be surprised that there is no sense of assurance and peace of heart concerning salvation.

The Hebrews had quit learning and growing in Christ and practicing the things that bring believers to maturity. Their hearts and minds were like a stagnant pond, and the writer of Hebrews realized that giving them deep new truth was like pouring a bucket of fresh water into a stagnant pond.

The principle here is that if you don't use it, you lose it. That's true of almost anything: your physical health, your ability to speak a language, your knowledge in a particular field. It also works that way in the spiritual life.

Suppose your child keeps failing his senior year, and all he can say is, "Well, at least I'm not a junior anymore." Would that satisfy you? Of course not, because by this time he should be out of high school. It's not a compliment to be voted "Most Popular Senior" three years in a row!

The key phrase in Hebrews 5 is "by this time." If you've been saved for five or more years, by this time you ought to know how to lead someone else to Christ. Why are so many Christians still stuck in elementary school spiritually speaking (the idea behind "elementary principles" in v. 12)? Because they aren't practicing their faith.

You see, we grow by practicing and using the truth, not just by knowing the truth. You can buy the workout equipment and watch the accompanying video on which the expert shows you how to use the equipment and get in shape. But you'll continue to stagnate on your couch until you practice what you are learning.

The cure for spiritual stagnation is to get moving. "Therefore leaving the elementary teaching about the Christ, let us press on to maturity" (Hebrews 6:1). Some people don't like the exhortation to "press on" because it sounds too much like work. Well, let me tell you something. To move forward in your Christian life requires some pressing. You have to exercise some serious spiritual discipline in order to grow. Don't expect God to levitate you out of bed in the morning and onto your knees. Don't expect Him to open your Bible and float it in front of you. You must press on to maturity.

Now in case this sounds as if you have to do it all, let's move on to Hebrews 6:3, which says, "And this we will do, if God permits." If you don't want to become stagnant, if you're not satisfied to be stuck in the same spiritual rut, you need to get up and start pressing on. But you do so in the strength God provides. Your pressing on is only effective because God is also at work in you. "Work out your salvation with fear and trembling; for it is God who is at work in you, both to will and to work for His good pleasure" (Philippians 2:12–13). You can only work out what God has worked into you.

Salvation and assurance are all of God because it is Christ who saves you and gives you the assurance that you are saved. But spiritual growth involves your response to God's enabling. You must press on, but God must permit. So you say, "Lord, I'm going to press on, but I'm depending on Your strength to enable my pressing on to take me somewhere." Spiritual growth demands faith and works.

For example, was David able to kill Goliath because he trusted in God, or because he used his slingshot? The answer is both. David had to fire the stone, but God had to "permit" it to hit Goliath in the right spot. David acted in complete dependence on God, but he still had to act. The cure for spiritual stagnation is to get the flow of fresh water going again.

Fourth Warning Sign: Spiritual Defection

If we miss the warning sign of stagnation, we're really heading into some serious territory on the road to spiritual failure. The Hebrews were on the verge of spiritual defection, so they received this admonition:

Let us hold fast the confession of our hope without wavering, for He who promised is faithful; and let us consider how to stimulate one another to love and good deeds, not forsaking our own assembling together, as is the habit of some, but encouraging one another; and all the more as you see the day drawing near. (Hebrews 10:23–25)

It's much harder to get on the wrong road and wind up falling away if you're in fellowship with the rest of the body of Christ. Holding on to your confidence is closely tied to your involvement in a local assembly, because God never intended the Christian life to be a solo act. Remember, we are taught to pray "Our Father who art in heaven," not "My Father."

You and I are not God's only children. We belong to something bigger, which is what God is doing with His entire family through the church. If we storm out of the house like a teenager because we want to do our own thing and we're tired of the rules and the other family members, then the next time God has a family meeting we're not part of it. When He starts making plans for His children, we are not part of those plans.

Forsaking the assembly of the local church is tantamount to spiritual defection. The Bible knows nothing of a Christian who is severed from the church and going it alone. Let me tell you what the assembly of believers can do for you. If you're slipping toward spiritual failure and lethargy, the body of Christ can reel you back in.

The author of Psalm 73 knew the power of worship to correct wrong thinking. He was about to slip and stumble (v. 2) because he began looking at the wicked people around him and got all upset. They seemed to be free of trouble and having all the fun. They were getting all the promotions and making all the money, and he started feeling sorry for himself. He decided that being faithful to God wasn't worth it.

But then the psalmist came into "the sanctuary of God" (v. 17) and everything changed. He saw the true end of wicked people, who would soon be judged by God. His perspective changed completely and he was kept from spiritual defection. If you're a vital part of the church, you are more likely to detect potential spiritual failure so you won't defect from the faith. The early believers in the book of Acts met together daily in worship and the teaching of the Word, and the fellowship of the church helped them keep their priorities fixed on praising God and reaching others (Acts 2:42–47).

THE CONSEQUENCES OF SPIRITUAL FAILURE

God takes spiritual defection very seriously, as He does spiritual failure on any level. There is always forgiveness available when we repent and come back to God, because we are still God's children even when we fail. If your trust is in Christ alone as your Savior and the guarantor of your eternal destiny, you are saved for eternity. But consequences await God's children who turn away from Him.

God May Have to Discipline Us

One of these consequences is divine discipline. In Hebrews 6:4–6a we read, "For in the case of those who have once been enlightened and have tasted of the heavenly gift and have been made partakers of the Holy Spirit, and have tasted the good word of God and the powers of the age to come, and then have fallen away, it is impossible to renew them again to repentance."

This is the passage that causes such confusion and is a favorite of those who deny the truth of eternal security. Some people try to get around the problem by saying that the people in question were not real believers because they only "tasted" of salvation.

But that view doesn't stand up, because the author of Hebrews used the same Greek term to say that Jesus tasted death for every person (2:9). Did He just nibble at death, or did He die? If Jesus didn't really die on the cross, we have a major problem. But He drank the cup of death down to its dregs. The word *taste* means to appropriate, not to dabble with. The people of Hebrews 6 were believers.

So if that's true, don't these verses clearly teach that believers can lose their salvation? If this is true, then the text is also clear that it is "impossible" for them to get it back again—a view that no one who denies the possibility of assurance wants to hold.

So if the text is talking about true Christians and it is *not* talking about them losing their salvation, what is the author's point? He is saying that Christians can become so hardened in spiritual failure and departure from the truth that it becomes impossible to renew them again to repentance.

Now this is certainly not impossible for God, because the Bible says nothing is impossible for God. But believers who turn away from God can become so hard other people can't win them back, and their lives may end in spiritual ruin as far as their earthly service is concerned—even though they are saved.

What does this process look like, and where does it end? The Bible says of these people, "They again crucify to themselves the Son of God and put Him to open shame" (Hebrews 6:6b). That is, a believer's life can become such an embarrassment to Jesus Christ that it's like putting Him on the cross again and holding Him up to public ridicule of the kind He endured when He was crucified.

Then we read, "For ground that drinks the rain which often falls on it and brings forth vegetation useful to those for whose sake it is also tilled, receives a blessing from God; but if it yields thorns and thistles, it is worthless and close to being cursed, and it ends up being burned" (Hebrews 6:7–8). The ground here is our hearts, and the rain is the grace of God that rains down on us when we are saved and that continues to shower our lives.

God sends His grace of His own accord, but we have a decision to make as to what that grace will produce in our lives. We can either be obedient and growing and fruitful, or we can produce nothing but thorns and thistles.

Thorns and thistles are not useful. When a farmer back in Jesus' day had a field full of thorns and thistles, he would burn the field to get rid of them. That's a picture of divine discipline on a believer who has turned from the faith.

God disciplines His children, both in the sense of pruning our lives to make them more fruitful and in the more negative sense of ridding us of things that pull us away from Him. The Hebrews had forgotten that, so the writer had to admonish them:

> You have forgotten the exhortation which is addressed to you as sons, "My son, do not regard lightly the discipline of the Lord, nor faint when you are reproved by Him; for those whom the Lord loves He disciplines, and He scourges every son whom He receives." It is for discipline that you endure; God deals with you as with sons; for what son is there whom his father does not discipline? (Hebrews 12:5–8)

God spanks every child who lives in His house. Our goal should be to learn from the first spanking so the Father doesn't have to resort to more severe discipline. Pull out those thorns and thistles as soon as they appear, so God won't have to scorch them out. Better still, pay attention to what you're sowing.

God May Have to Take Us Out

By now you shouldn't be surprised to know that God sometimes has to resort to putting a sinning believer to death to keep that person from embarrassing the kingdom. Death is a very severe consequence of persistent spiritual disobedience and unrepentant sin. The book of Hebrews also addresses this issue:

> If we go on sinning willfully after receiving the knowledge of the truth, there no longer remains a sacrifice for sins, but a terrifying expectation of judgment and the fury of a fire which will consume the adversaries. Anyone who has set aside the Law of Moses dies without mercy on the testimony of two or three witnesses. How much severer punishment do you think he will deserve who has trampled under foot the Son of God, and has regarded as unclean the blood of the covenant by which he was sanctified, and has insulted the Spirit of grace? (10:26–29)

Now I said this was extremely serious. An offender against the Mosaic Law was stoned to death. That's how seriously God takes His character and His Word. The punishment for the offending Christian isn't specified, except that it is "much severer" than stoning.

We don't see this kind of judgment carried out very often, because God is gracious and it brings Him no pleasure to have to judge His erring children.

But He won't put up with His children abusing the gift of salvation indefinitely. If we trample the blood of Christ underfoot either by our words or our lifestyle, God will see to it that we are stopped.

That's why James said, "My brethren, if any among you strays from the truth and one turns him back, let him know that he who turns a sinner from the error of his way will save his soul from death and will cover a multitude of sins" (James 5:19–20). The sinner here is a sinning saint, and the soul refers to our life. Death is severe but a possible means of judgment—but again, what's at stake here is a Christian's physical life and testimony on earth, not his or her eternal salvation.

God May Have to Disinherit Us

A third consequence of spiritual failure is disinheritance in the coming kingdom of heaven. Jesus said in Matthew 8:12 that the sons of the kingdom were cast in outer darkness at the start of the kingdom banquet. That is, they were not admitted to the banquet to enjoy this thousand-year party called the kingdom. They're still saved people, but they are the ones whose works are burned up at the judgment seat of Christ and so they have nothing to present to Him from their time on earth. Their judgment is to be put outside, not of heaven, but of the kingdom banquet.

Jesus said this judgment would cause "weeping and gnashing of teeth." This isn't the suffering of hell, but the anguish of those who miss the greatest party of all time and eternity. That's why Paul cautioned us to be careful what we build our lives with (see 1 Corinthians 3:10–15).

THE CURE FOR FALLING AWAY

Many people who agonize over whether they have lost their salvation need to be reminded that their deep concern is one of the best signs that they are truly saved. Lost people don't usually lose any sleep wondering if they are saved or not.

The same principle applies to spiritual failure. If you are concerned about your walk with God and you agonize over your sin, that's the best sign of all that you have not become hard of heart and uncaring.

So how does a Christian recover from spiritual failure? I don't have any secret message or magic formulas for you, just an admonition and encouragement to begin where you are. I like to compare this to halftime in football or basketball.

The great thing about halftime is that you get to step back and reassess your game, make adjustments, and come out fresh in the second half. Some amazing turnarounds have happened in the second half of games after a team has taken the time to adjust. If you know the Lord, you're still in the game. Let's all come out and play the second half for His glory.

15

ASSURANCE AND ETERNAL LIFE

John McGraw was the legendary manager of the New York Giants baseball team from 1902 to 1932, a time when major league baseball was a rough-and-tumble game and some ballplayers were considered by decent folk to be little more than hoodlums.

McGraw fit this image perfectly. He was called the Little Napoleon because of his autocratic style. His players feared him. McGraw hated umpires, but an umpire in that same era named Bill Klem was as legendary as McGraw, and just as tough. One day during an argument a furious McGraw roared, "Klem, I'll have your job for this!"

Klem roared back, "McGraw, if you can have my job, I don't want it!"

Bill Klem understood an important principle about security. He realized that if his job was so insecure an angry manager could get him fired, then he might as well go on to something else because the job really wasn't his at all.

This same principle applies to the Christian life. If the life that Jesus gave you is so insecure the devil can get you "fired" any time he feels like it, or if you or anyone else on earth can do something to take yourself out of Christ's hand, then the life you were given at salvation was not eternal at all and you had better be looking somewhere else for your security.

But when Jesus said of His children, "I give eternal life to them, and they will never perish" (John 10:28), that's exactly what He meant. As desperate and as hopeless as we would be without Christ, that's how secure we are in Him. Jesus made the promise of eternal life to a desperate woman one day, and we need to hear again what He said.

OUR ENTRANCE INTO ETERNAL LIFE

The story of the woman at the well is one of the most familiar in the New Testament. This Samaritan woman who came to Jacob's well to draw water had her life changed forever because Jesus was there that day. Since Jesus wanted to get a discussion started about water, He said to her, "Give Me a drink" (John 4:7). That got her attention because she was shocked that Jesus would want to put His Jewish lips to her "unclean" Samaritan cup and take a drink.

The woman expressed her surprise that a Jew would have anything to do with a half-breed Samaritan, but Jesus had something much more shocking and surprising in mind. In response to her comment, He said, "If you knew the gift of God, and who it is who says to you, 'Give Me a drink,' you would have asked Him, and He would have given you living water" (v. 10).

The woman didn't realize yet that Jesus was offering her eternal life, so she questioned His ability to give her a drink when He had nothing to draw water with. I want to focus on Jesus' answer to her confusion. "Everyone who drinks of this water will thirst again; but whoever drinks of the water that I will give him shall never thirst; but the water that I will give him will become in him a well of water springing up to eternal life" (vv. 13–14).

All It Takes Is One Drink

You've probably read this story, or heard it preached, more than once. But don't let its familiarity cause you to miss what Jesus was saying. Notice the certainty contained in His promise of eternal life. Those who take a drink of His living water—that is, those who receive the gift of eternal life—never have to worry about being thirsty again.

Think about that for a minute. One drink is all that is required to partake of eternal life. That's a clear picture of salvation. It's a decisive moment of faith, just as taking a drink is a decisive act. And notice that this drink never has to be repeated. Salvation is a once-for-all transaction. Jesus could not have made it any clearer. To make sure she wouldn't misunderstand Him, Jesus contrasted the water of eternal life He offered with physical water, which only satisfies our thirst for a while and then leaves us thirsty again.

Now this raises two questions that need to asked. First, if the Bible teaches that salvation is a once-for-all, never-to-be-repeated, decisive moment of faith, what does this say about the kind of teaching that denies believers the assurance of their salvation and keeps them constantly coming back to the altar to be saved again and again?

To put it plainly, this "theology of uncertainty" devalues God's gift of salvation because it is based on the assumption that He takes His gift back every time we do something to tick Him off. Others who deny real certainty say that we must keep on proving that we really took the drink of eternal life by our perseverance in good works.

Both of these perspectives leave us with a serious question: If one drink really isn't enough, how do we know when we have drunk often enough to be really saved? What if we die between drinks? The issue gets absurd when we take these ideas to their logical conclusion. People who keep getting saved over and over again are trying to create their own well, but it doesn't work that way.

Jesus promised the woman at the well that if she drank of His living water, she would not need to keep drinking. Her response in John 4:15 indicates that she was still thinking of physical water, but whatever it was Jesus was offering her, she definitely wanted it: "Sir, give me this water, so I will not be thirsty nor come all the way here to draw."

A second question that arises out of this story is this: How can taking one drink of Jesus' living water satisfy our thirst forever? Jesus answered that in verse 14: "The water that I will give him will become in him a well of water springing up to eternal life." It's one thing to take a drink from a well and then move on. It's another thing entirely to have a well within you that continually satisfies your thirst. If you are a believer but you feel thirsty today, it isn't because the well of salvation has dried up on you.

Assurance Comes with the Gift

This water of life that Jesus gave us at salvation is a special gift. Jesus didn't say it would well up within us as long as we toe the line and don't do anything to displease Him. Neither did He say that once the flow of eternal life was interrupted, we would have to come and drink and start the process all over again. He said the well He places within us will flow eternally. Assurance of salvation is built into the gift of eternal life.

So the entrance of eternal life does not depend on our ability either to create our own well or to keep the well of living water flowing. That is God's responsibility. Eternal life also does not depend on our worthiness to receive it. We didn't dwell on the spiritual condition of the woman whom Jesus met in John 4, but you may recall that she was rather notorious.

In John 4:16–18 we find out that she had gone through five husbands and was living with a man to whom she was not married. Now that mess needed to be taken care of, but Jesus didn't start there (although He *did* get there) because He knew that if she got saved, these other things would take care of themselves. Salvation was her greatest need, and she needed to come to Jesus right where she was. And when she came to Him just as she was, she received the gift of eternal life.

If someone stood in your church's pulpit next Sunday and began teaching that sinners had to clean their lives up before Jesus would accept them, I'm sure that people would cry foul. We know that salvation is not dependent upon what we can do to make ourselves presentable to God. So why do we insist that our assurance of salvation depends on what we can do to *keep* ourselves presentable to God?

On the contrary, it is the fact of assurance that is the ground of our sanctification (Romans 12:1–2; Ephesians 4:32; 5:8; 1 Peter 1:3–7, 13–25). It is living in light of the eternal life we have been given that gives us victory over sin (Romans 6:11–15).

THE ESSENCE OF ETERNAL LIFE

We've been saying throughout this section that if we will keep our eyes on Christ, finding the assurance we seek won't be a problem because the Savior who saves us is the Savior who assures and secures us.

That's one reason I believe that Jesus defined the essence of eternal life as a relationship with Him. If the "man on the street" was asked to define eternal life, he would probably say that it means to live forever. But length of existence is an insufficient definition of eternal life. Lost people are going to exist forever in hell, so there has to be more to eternal life than just its "foreverness." You and I were created as eternal beings.

Knowing Jesus Is Eternal Life

Jesus gave us the "more" of eternal life in His prayer to the Father in the Upper Room just before His crucifixion. "This is eternal life, that they may know You, the only true God, and Jesus Christ whom You have sent" (John 17:3). Eternal life is the knowledge of God, the kind of intimate relational knowledge between a parent and child that people in hell will not be able to experience because they will be separated from God for eternity.

No wonder the Bible tells us to "[fix] our eyes on Jesus" (Hebrews 12:2). We don't focus on Christ just to gain assurance. It is actually a by-product of our commitment to look to Christ as our life and develop the eternal life that God has placed within us. One of the challenges involved in studying about assurance is that the New Testament doesn't address the subject very often, and for a good reason. To the writers of Scripture, the possibility of losing their salvation was a nonissue, which is in itself a good argument for the permanence of salvation. As far as the apostles were concerned, God said it and that settled it.

In fact, when a person says he has a problem with assurance and can't get any peace about whether he is saved forever or not, there is often a deeper spiritual problem present. Let me illustrate what I mean.

Imagine an Olympic runner who bursts from the starting blocks in a race, only to pull up short halfway around the track because he is suddenly gripped with doubt that he really qualified for the race in the first place. He thinks about it for a few seconds, then shrugs his shoulders and starts running again, only to stop in doubt again, convinced that the judges have already disqualified him because he wasn't really a legitimate competitor and didn't belong in the race.

To my knowledge, that has never happened. An Olympic runner spends all of his time and energy developing himself to run the best race he can possibly run. My point is that believers who are busy developing a vital, vibrant, and growing relationship with Jesus Christ won't have time to obsess over whether they still belong to Christ. A believer who is constantly obsessed with a lack of assurance often doesn't have much happening in his or her spiritual life.

We Need to Grow in Knowing Jesus

A baby who remains a baby will never know the joys that come with growth and the development of satisfying interpersonal relationships. I can take you to the nursery in our church and show you a roomful of individuals who are basically oblivious to the presence of other individuals just like them, at least in terms of the ability to form meaningful relationships.

Babies love the crib, live in the crib, and don't want anybody bothering the crib. But no parent who cares will let a baby stay in the crib forever. God didn't save you and me so we could hang out in the spiritual nursery our whole lives. That's why Peter said, "Grow in the grace and knowledge of our Lord and Savior Jesus Christ" (2 Peter 3:18). Eternal life is a relationship with Christ.

Jesus said, "I am the way, and the truth, and the life" (John 14:6). John said of Jesus, "The life was manifested, and we have seen and testify and proclaim to you the eternal life, which was with the Father and was manifested to us" (1 John 1:2). In this same letter John also said of Jesus, "This is the true God and eternal life" (5:20).

You won't have an assurance problem if you are growing and developing in your relationship with Jesus Christ, "who is our life" (Colossians 3:4). And by the way, this verse also ties our life with Christ to the certainty of our spending eternity with Him, because Paul wrote, "When Christ, who is our life, is revealed, then you also will be revealed with Him in glory."

Someone may say, "I'm a believer but I don't feel close to Christ. I'm not experiencing the intimacy of that relationship." We all know this can happen, just as we know how a married couple can begin to grow apart and function as two distinct individuals. They may still go through the motions of marriage, but the relationship has deteriorated.

The problem is not that the couple's marriage isn't legitimate or still intact, but there is no development of that union. The same thing can happen to you in the Christian life. When it does, the solution is to look to Christ and restore that intimacy, not question Christ's love for you and the soundness of your salvation.

THE EXPERIENCE OF ETERNAL LIFE

Have you ever looked at something and yet not really seen it in terms of realizing it was there? It happens all the time, especially as we get older. Something similar can happen with the eternal life we have been given by Christ. It's there, but we have to realize it and do something with it to fully experience all that God has for us.

The Bible says, "Do not be deceived, God is not mocked; for whatever a man sows, this he will also reap. For the one who sows to his own flesh will from the flesh reap corruption, but the one who sows to the Spirit will from the Spirit reap eternal life" (Galatians 6:7–8). The reaping of eternal life here is not salvation, because this was written to Christians ("brethren," v. 1).

We Must Sow to Eternal Life

Paul's point was that in order for us to experience—not achieve—eternal life, we must sow to eternal life. In other words, we must starve the flesh and cultivate the Spirit.

Paul chose the most common metaphor of his day to illustrate what he meant. A farmer has to prepare the ground before he can sow the seed. It takes work to sow good seed and reap a harvest. If we want to experience and enjoy the benefits of eternal life we must "sow to the Spirit." Paul told Timothy, "Take hold of the eternal life to which you were called" (1 Timothy 6:12). Timothy already possessed the gift of life in Christ. But that gift needed to be cultivated.

How many parents have said to their children, "You need to start taking responsibility for your life"? Those parents aren't denying that the child belongs to them. But they know that their children need to mature in order to become fully functional and productive. And another benefit of maturity is that children can actually grow closer to their parents because they can now relate to Mom and Dad on a much more fulfilling level as friends, much like we grow in our relationship to Christ, who wants to call us His friends (John 15:15). So the issue is not the child's membership in the family, but the development and growth that the child needs to begin exhibiting. Too many Christians exist but never get around to living even though they're on their way to heaven. If you want to make something of your eternal life, you have to invest in it.

Paul likens that investment to sowing and reaping in Galatians 6. It's important to remember that even as Christians, we have a choice as to whether we are going to sow to our sinful flesh or to the Holy Spirit who lives within us. The Bible says, "If you are living according to the flesh, you must die; but if by the Spirit you are putting to death the deeds of the body, you will live" (Romans 8:13).

If you sow to the flesh, the unrighteous part of you that doesn't want to please God, you will die. That means we will be spiritually impoverished. The eternal life within us will begin to shrivel and become unproductive, like a crop that is sown but then neglected.

That's because the flesh is like an in-law you can't get rid of. The flesh is never satisfied. Even when you give the flesh what it wants, it always wants more. That's why God has consigned these sin-contaminated bodies of ours to the grave and will give us new bodies in the resurrection. But in the meantime, the Bible says that to get rid of sin we must feed the Spirit, or sow to the Spirit, and starve the flesh. By the way, this is the opposite of the ancient heresy of Gnosticism, which said the material body itself was bad and therefore it didn't matter what you did with it, which gave Gnostic followers permission to indulge in sin and debauchery.

Jesus Calls Us to Abide

Jesus also used an agricultural metaphor to describe the way He wants us to experience eternal life, "Abide in Me, and I in you. As the branch cannot bear fruit of itself unless it abides in the vine, so neither can you unless you abide in Me" (John 15:4). To abide in Christ means to maintain intimate connection and fellowship with Him. That's essential because Jesus is the vine, another way of saying that He is our life.

Several years ago I had a problem with my lawn sprinkler system. It wouldn't come on to water my lawn even though it was set on a timer. The repairman who came out worked for about an hour and found the problem. A wire in the electrical timer had become disconnected, so there was no transfer of electrical power to turn the system on and water the lawn.

The problem wasn't that I had a poor sprinkler system. And it wasn't as if the city of Dallas wasn't supplying all the water I needed through its lines. The problem was the wire's failure to "abide" or remain connected to its power supply. Once that connection was restored, my brown grass started to turn green again.

Now you know where I'm going with this. If your spiritual life is starting to turn brown, the problem is not in your "system." God's salvation is flawless and complete. Neither is your problem the water supply. Jesus said your salvation would be a well of water eternally springing up within you. The problem is that you have ceased to abide in your source of life and your power supply. The wire that connects your life with God's power has been disconnected, so there is no flow of water and your life is turning brown.

It comes back to our relationship with Christ. Since He is our life, abiding in Him is the only way to experience the continual flow of that life. Our relationship with Him is what must power our spiritual development.

I like to illustrate the principle of abiding by comparing it to my enjoyment of hot weather. You'd think I was a native Texan because I love the heat. I'm not big on air conditioning. I like to go walking in the heat. I drive with the air conditioning off in the summer, which is saying a lot in Dallas.

Now when you "abide" or remain in the heat the way I like to do, you don't have to do anything special to experience the incredible power of the sun. Even a short walk from one of our church's buildings to another in the Dallas heat can cause you to begin perspiring. The sun affects you simply because you are underneath its influence. It rubs off on you because it is such a powerful presence you can't help but feel its power.

Let me tell you about abiding in Jesus. He is so powerful that all you have to do to experience His power is abide in His presence. He will urge and convict you to be holy and cause you to want to live right even during those times when you don't want to be holy or live right. He is the Son, and His power is all-pervasive.

Jesus will affect and empower you no matter where you are, because He is your life and your power source. All you have to do is put yourself in His abiding presence.

Jesus will change you, develop you, encourage you, strengthen you, and empower you. He'll give you victory because "greater is He who is in you than he who is in the world" (1 John 4:4). And you won't have to wonder whether God still loves you enough to keep you in His care now and for eternity.

16

ASSURANCE AND REWARDS

Teachers are always eager for signs that their students are maturing and ready to get on with the business of learning. One sign that students are progressing is when they quit asking questions such as "Is this going to be on the exam?" or "What time does this class end?" or "Are you going to grade on the curve?" and start asking things like "What does this mean?" and "How can I use this knowledge?" and "How should I adjust my life in relation to what I'm learning?"

There is a spiritual parallel to this phenomenon. One sign that we are maturing and progressing in our Christian lives is the kind of questions we ask and the thoughts that occupy our minds. For instance, some believers are still hung up on what I call "ABC" questions of the faith such as "How can I know that I'm really saved?" or "Could I ever sin so badly that God will reject me?" or "Are my doubts a sign that I've lost my salvation?"

Don't misunderstand. These issues are important, and it's not necessarily wrong to have times of doubt. But these periods of uncertainty should become shorter and less frequent as we grow in the grace and knowledge of our Savior. Part of my purpose has been to deal with these foundational questions that have to do with our security in Christ. But I also want to help us move beyond "the elementary principles of the oracles of God" (Hebrews 5:12) because God has so much more for us.

OUR MOTIVATION TO SERVE CHRIST

Part of this rich store of truth and blessing is the rewards that God offers us for faithful service. But I'm convinced that we can't really step out confidently and give ourselves fully to serving Christ if we're afraid that the ground of our salvation may give way beneath us at any time and we fall out of God's grace. Assurance is an essential part of the foundation we need to serve God effectively.

Therefore, I want to discuss assurance as it relates to our service and rewards. My thesis is that the fact of our eternal salvation, and our knowledge of that fact, should spur us to please God by offering Him a life of grateful service. And the amazing thing is that when we do this, God turns around and rewards us based on our faithfulness.

Serving Out of Appreciation

I fear that too often we fail to appreciate our great salvation. We lose our sense of awe and wonder that Jesus would die for us. A good reminder is the story of the woman who came to Jesus at a dinner party and wept in repentance at His feet, washing His feet with her tears and wiping them with her hair.

You can read the story in Luke 7:36–48. I want to focus on Jesus' response to the self-righteous Pharisee who was His host for the dinner and who was appalled that Jesus would allow this sinful woman to approach Him. Jesus said to the Pharisee, "Her sins, which are many, have been forgiven, for she loved much; but he who is for-given little, loves little" (v. 47). The message to all of us is that we are in the same predicament as this woman, needing much forgive-ness. And those who are forgiven much should love much.

The Bible says, "The gifts and the calling of God are irrevoca-ble" (Romans 11:29). That's a very important truth for our assurance because it means that God doesn't change His mind and take back the gifts He has given us, including the gift of salvation. That issue is settled, which frees us to serve God not to try to stay in His grace, but simply because we can't get over His grace.

Our Opportunity to Reign with Christ

In his second letter to Timothy, Paul included a great statement that may have served as a confession of faith for the early church: "It is a trustworthy statement: For if we died with Him, we will also live with Him; if we endure, we will also reign with Him; if we deny Him, He also will deny us; if we are faithless, He remains faithful, for He cannot deny Himself" (2 Timothy 2:11–13).

Here is plenty of truth both to encourage us in the security of our salvation and to motivate us with the rewards of faithfully serv-ing Christ. The first of these four lines or couplets is a clear refer-ence to salvation, for when we trust Christ we identify with Him in His death and resurrection, dying to our sins so that we "might walk in newness of life" (Romans 6:4).

Let's set aside the second statement for a minute and deal with the last two, which have to do with God's faithfulness in the face of our unfaithfulness. Our denial of God and His denial of us do not relate to salvation, but to the life we live for Him on earth. We learned earlier that if we deny the Lord by our words or our deeds, Christ will deny us in terms of unanswered prayers and unmet needs.

The last statement is a great affirmation of our eternal security, even though the context is human faithlessness. Our lack of faith-fulness does not affect God, because even if we fail, He doesn't stop being our Father. Even if we stop living for Him, He doesn't renege on His promise to save us—not because we are worthy of His faithfulness, but because the only way God could change His mind about our salvation would be to deny His own character. And that will never happen because God can never cease being God and because when God saved us He gave us His nature and adopted us into His family.

In other words, God always leaves the lights on the way loving parents leave the light on at night until the last of their children is safe at home.

With this kind of security undergirding and supporting us, we have every reason to do what the second of Paul's four couplets urges us to do: "If we endure, we will also reign with Him." Notice that this is a conditional phrase on the human side, just like the other statements. God's salvation is unconditional and assured, but His rewards for service are conditioned upon our response.

Endurance here means more than just hanging on until the end. It means enduring the way a skilled and well-conditioned runner runs a race: not barely making it to the finish line, but running a strong race and blasting through the tape with a final burst of speed. Those are the kinds of runners who "reign" in a race, who win the crown and the prize.

Similarly, our endurance in running the Christian race results in our winning the crown and reigning with Christ. This is not talking about salvation, for if so it would teach that if we can just hang in there we'll make it to heaven someday. That would make salvation dependent on us in the end, a denial of the Bible's clear teaching that salvation is all of God and nothing of us.

Instead, Paul was looking ahead to the reward that comes with faithful service for Christ. Paul was motivated by the promise of rewards from Christ, as we'll see later. He was expecting not just to squeeze through the door of heaven, but to reign with Christ in a place of honor, authority, and responsibility. The Bible contains many hints of what that position will entail, but for our purposes now it is enough to note that those who endure with Christ in service on earth reign with Him in glory in eternity.

The Fear and the Love of Christ

We find two very enlightening statements about Paul's motivation for his ministry in verses 11 and 14 of 2 Corinthians 5, which follow a thought that he wanted to emphasize.

In verse 11 the apostle said, "Therefore, knowing the fear of the Lord, we persuade men" (we'll see below what "therefore" refers to). Then in verse 14 he said, "The love of Christ controls us." These two attributes of God stand like two great boundary lines or bookends between which Paul conducted his ministry. In them he found all the motivation he needed to serve the Lord.

The King James Version translates the word *fear* in verse 11 as "terror," which is closer to the idea that Paul was trying to convey. He wasn't terrified of the Lord, but he knew some things about God that we forget too easily. For example, "Our God is a consuming fire" (Hebrews 12:29). "It is appointed for men to die once and after this comes judgment" (Hebrews 9:27). "It is a terrifying thing to fall into the hands of the living God" (Hebrews 10:31).

In other words, Paul was highly motivated to rescue the perishing from the burning fires of God's judgment. And even if we interpret the "fear of the Lord" to be reverence for Him, the motivation is still there because we serve God out of reverence for His person and His great love for us.

Second Corinthians 5:11 begins with the transitional word "Therefore," which points back to the previous thought. There is another reason that Paul was motivated by the fear of the Lord: the knowledge that he would have to stand before Christ and give an account of his life. "For we must all appear before the judgment seat of Christ, so that each one may be recompensed for his deeds in the body, according to what he has done, whether good or bad" (v. 10).

The judgment seat of Christ is not a judgment of our eternal destiny, but an evaluation of Christians to determine our rewards, or lack thereof, for the way we have served Christ. We might think Paul wouldn't have been quite as concerned about this judgment, since everyone who appears before Christ is already saved.

But that's not the case. Paul did not want to appear before Christ with nothing to show for his Christian life, because his primary ambition was to please Christ (see v. 9) and because he knew he would suffer loss if his works were rejected.

The perfect complement to the fear or terror of the Lord is His love, and as the people of God we need to say with Paul, "The love of Christ controls us" (2 Corinthians 5:14). Christ's love took Him to the cross, where "He died for all" (v. 15a). Such amazing love is more than enough motivation for us to give our lives in service to Christ. The remainder of verse 15 sums it up so well. Jesus Christ died for us, "so that [we] who live might no longer live for [our]selves, but for Him who died and rose again on [our] behalf."

THE GLORY OF GOD'S REWARDS

Whenever the subject turns to rewards, someone objects that it seems self-serving to talk about what we get for serving Christ. My answer to that objection is that neither Jesus nor the apostles seemed the least bit reluctant to discuss the subject or encourage believers to consider the benefits as well as the sacrifices of following Him. As long as our conversation contains this same balance between rewards and the sacrifices it takes to reap them, then there's nothing wrong with focusing on our spiritual rewards.

A classic example is the exchange between Jesus and His disciples in Matthew 19:23–30. Their discussion grew out of the well-known incident in which a rich young man came to Jesus and asked what he needed to do to inherit eternal life (vv. 16–22). Jesus looked into the man's heart and knew that his real problem was his wealth, so He told him, "If you wish to be complete, go and sell your possessions and give to the poor, and you will have treasure in heaven; and come, follow Me" (v. 21).

But the Bible says the young man turned away and left because he didn't want to part with his wealth. (An important side note on rewards: This man couldn't see that following Jesus would bring a reward far greater than the collective value of his possessions. What a contrast to Moses, who left the wealth of Egypt behind to identify with the people of God, although they were slaves, "for he was looking to the reward" God had for him [Hebrews 11:26].)

The disciples watched this man approach Jesus and leave, and they heard Jesus say how hard it is for a rich person to enter heaven. They also expressed astonishment that someone like the rich young man who appeared to them to have it all together would have such a hard time making it to heaven (Matthew 19:23–26).

Now while all of this was going on, Peter had been doing some calculating. It seemed to him that since the rich man got to keep all of his wealth while the disciples had to give up everything to follow Christ, something was out of kilter. So he asked Jesus the question the other disciples probably were thinking too, but were afraid to voice: "Behold, we have left everything and followed You; what then will there be for us?" (Matthew 19:27).

We know this was a valid question because Jesus did not rebuke Peter at all for asking it. Peter, Andrew, James, and John had put it all on the line, giving up their fishing business to become Jesus' disciples. Matthew was probably doing pretty well as a tax collector, and no one knows what the other disciples had to give up to follow Christ. So Peter wanted to know what they could look for in terms of return on the investment of their lives in the kingdom of God.

Getting Back More Than We Give Up

According to Matthew 19:28–29,

Jesus said to them, "Truly I say to you, that you who have followed Me, in the regeneration when the Son of Man will sit on His glorious throne, you also shall sit upon twelve thrones, judging the twelve tribes of Israel. And everyone who has left houses or brothers or sisters or father or mother or children or farms for My name's sake, will receive many times as much, and will inherit eternal life."

Obviously, part of the reward Jesus promised to the disciples was unique to the Twelve. You and I are not going to sit on thrones judging the twelve tribes of Israel. But this promise illustrated the basic principle of rewards Jesus announced in Matthew 19. When you give yourself and everything you have to serve Christ, you always get back far more than you give up. None of the apostles gave up a throne for Christ, but that's what they received in return.

Then in verse 29 Jesus broadened His promise to include you and me. Some people are puzzled by Jesus' reference to various categories of people and property and the promise that we will receive "many times as much." This is not some new kind of investment plan in which you give up one farm and receive many more in return.

Jesus was speaking in the context of His kingdom and His people, and it's true that when we become part of the family of God we gain many times more brothers and sisters than we ever had before. And in a very real sense, as we serve Jesus Christ we have all the material resources we will ever need because God moves His people to share abundantly with His servants.

If you are willing to get serious about being the slave of Christ, you won't have to worry that you'll end up being embarrassed. Some people are slaves to their careers because they want to reach a certain level and have a certain title by their name. Others are slaves to their education because they want to earn a certain degree and have certain initials after their name. Still others are slaves to a sport or even a hobby because they want to win a trophy or an award.

These achievements aren't wrong in themselves. But they will fade someday and their return will diminish. If you're going to throw yourself into something and give it your all, go for the gold of God's rewards. Whatever you may lose along the way you'll get back, and more than you lost.

The Inheritance of Eternal Life

Did you notice what Jesus said at the end of verse 29? One of the rewards for serving Him is that we will "inherit eternal life." We know that eternal life in terms of our salvation is a gift. But there's a difference between eternal life as a gift and as an inheritance. Every believer will make it to heaven, but believers will not all have the same level of reward and honor in heaven. All Christians will enjoy eternal life, but they will experience that life at different levels.

Jesus taught this principle again and again in His parables, giving the servant who was the most faithful on earth the greater reward (see Matthew 25:14–30). God is an equal opportunity rewarder, but the rewards vary based on the response of the individual.

The bottom line is that Peter didn't have to worry that he was taking a risk and losing something valuable. Not only was his eternal salvation secure, but he was laying up eternal rewards in heaven as Jesus commanded us to do (see Matthew 6:19–21).

Some Christians haven't given it all up to serve Christ because they're worried about what they are going to lose. But that's not how most of us conduct our earthly business. You don't often hear someone say, "I don't want to put my money in the bank because then I won't have it in my pocket anymore."

We take our money to the bank because it's safer there than it is in our pockets, and because we have our eye on a return. Nobody pays interest on the money in your pocket. You have to let it go to get it back with interest. Jesus offers a better deal than that because His returns are guaranteed, and the interest rate is astronomical, not 5 or 10 or even 20 percent, but "many times" our original investment. Serving God turns earthly expectations around because heaven's economy is nothing like earth's.

God's Grace and Our Rewards

The grace that God displayed in salvation is always the foundation for our service. The God who saved us by grace alone through faith also crafted us as His workmanship to do good works (see Ephesians 2:8–10). The Bible exhorts us, "Therefore, since we receive a kingdom which cannot be shaken, let us show gratitude, by which we may offer to God an acceptable service with reverence and awe" (Hebrews 12:28).

In other words, in light of all that God has done for us, we need to express our gratitude in our service. Have you ever been offended when you've done something for someone and never heard a word of thanks? We teach our children to say thank you for what they are given because we don't want them to be ungrateful, grasping people and because givers want to know that their gifts are appreciated. The greatest Giver in the universe wants us to show our gratitude by our reverent service—and then He turns around and rewards us for that service with blessings even beyond the unspeakable gift of eternal life.

The Criteria for Our Rewards

I've saved one of the most crucial and detailed passages on rewards for now so we could give it the attention it deserves. God graciously allows us to serve Him and promises us rewards for faithful service, but that doesn't mean we can bring Him shoddy, half-hearted, haphazard, or self-centered service and expect a full reward. God's Word provides standards or criteria by which our service will be evaluated at the judgment seat of Christ. These are described in 1 Corinthians 3:10–15.

Paul compared our Christian lives to builders erecting a building. Paul himself was laying the foundation of this building through his own apostleship as "a wise master builder" following God's blueprint (v. 10). The foundation is none other than Jesus Christ Himself (v. 11).

With the foundation in place, Paul turned to the work we do in building on that foundation: "Now if any man builds on the foundation with gold, silver, precious stones, wood, hay, straw, each man's work will become evident; for the day will show it because it is to be revealed with fire, and the fire itself will test the quality of each man's work" (vv. 12–13).

The difference between these building materials is all-important.

The first three materials are costly, permanent, and of the highest quality. The next three materials are cheap, temporary, flammable, and easily obtained on a scrap pile or by the side of the road. It's obvious that the materials you use to construct the "building" of your Christian life and service will reflect the value you place on the grace God has bestowed on you.

None of us is perfect, but all of us know when we are giving God our best and when we are offering Him the scraps and leftovers of our time, talent, and treasures. The quality of our work will be revealed at "the day," the judgment seat of Christ mentioned in 2 Corinthians 5:10. Christ will use the perfect instrument to determine the difference between diamonds and straw—the fire of His holy gaze. The Bible says Jesus' eyes are like "a flame of fire" (Revelation 1:14).

When Jesus turns His attention to our works, they will be tested by fire. "If any man's work which he has built on it remains, he will receive a reward. If any man's work is burned up, he will suffer loss; but he himself will be saved, yet so as through fire" (1 Corinthians 3:14–15). That's both a tremendous promise and a very sobering reminder that God demands our best.

Paul closed this section with a word of assurance, but we need to remember that the doctrine of assurance is not meant to be an excuse for us to sit back and coast our way to heaven. The person whose works are consumed by fire at Christ's judgment seat while he is saved through the fire will feel the sting of that loss. Job said, "I have escaped only by the skin of my teeth" (Job 19:20). That's the idea here. I don't want to barely make it to heaven smelling like smoke. I want to inherit the rewards God has for me, and I want the same for you.

Four Ways to Test Your Service

Here are four ways by which you can measure the quality of your Christian service.

The first is *dependability*. "It is required of stewards that one be found trustworthy" (1 Corinthians 4:2). We may not all be equal in gifts, abilities, and opportunities, but all of us can be faithful to God's call on our lives. Abraham left Ur and went to Canaan because he saw and believed God's promises before any of them were fulfilled. Noah spent 120 years faithfully building the ark and preaching righteousness simply because God commanded him to do so. Everybody fails at times, but is dependability the pattern of your life?

A second standard or measure is your *declarations*. Jesus said in Matthew 12:36 that every careless word we speak is recorded. According to Luke 12:3, "Whatever you have said in the dark will be heard in the light." Use your words to bless God and build up others.

Then you can examine your *deeds*. We've talked a lot about this, so let me remind you of what the risen Christ said: "Behold, I am coming quickly, and My reward is with Me, to render to every man according to what he has done" (Revelation 22:12).

Fourth, God will test your *desires*. When Jesus comes He will "disclose the motives of men's hearts" (1 Corinthians 4:5). Make sure that in the secret place of your heart, your desires reflect the desires of God's heart.

Service for Christ that meets these standards and endures His test of fire will result in rewards that are so eternally safe Jesus said that nothing on earth can ruin or steal them (see Matthew 6:20). Your salvation is just as secure, so you are free to serve Christ with everything you have, because you are eternally grateful to Him.

THE
CASE
FOR
ETERNAL
SECURITY

17

THE IMPORTANCE OF ETERNAL SECURITY

One day a friend of mine drove to the ATM machine at his bank and withdrew one hundred dollars from his savings account. He made the transaction and took the money, then pushed the button to get his card and receipt. The card popped out, but apparently the printer wasn't working because no receipt came out. He waited a few seconds, then drove away without his receipt.

My friend said a funny feeling hit him as he left the bank. He had a good idea of his savings account balance before he withdrew the hundred dollars, but he also knew that he had to leave enough in the account to cover several automatic payments that were deducted each month. Without a receipt to look at and reassure himself of the balance, he said he had a quick twinge of doubt and did some hurried mental arithmetic to make sure he was OK. As it turned out his balance was not only adequate to cover everything, it was more than adequate.

I tell you this story to illustrate the relationship between the doctrines of assurance and eternal security, which is the subject of this section. Eternal security is like the money in my friend's bank account. It means that our salvation is safely on deposit in the bank of heaven, secure forever. But we tend to forget that fact and succumb to times of doubt. So assurance is like the receipt that God gives us as a reminder that our salvation account really is secure and more than able to cover all of our needs.

In case you're thinking that the need for a "receipt" of salvation indicates weak faith, let me show you that issuing a receipt for salvation was God's idea. According to Romans 4:25, "He [Jesus Christ] was delivered over because of our transgressions, and was raised because of our justification." The resurrection was God's proof that His Son's payment on the cross for our sins was accepted. The reason we can know that we are saved and secure today is that we have God's "receipt," the resurrection of Christ, to prove that our sins are forgiven.

So don't let anyone make you feel bad about your need for a sense of spiritual security. Eternal security is important to our spiritual lives for a number of reasons beyond that of helping us deal with doubt and get on with living for Christ.

As we study the truth of eternal security in its various aspects and applications, there will be some inevitable repetition from the assurance section since these two doctrines dovetail so closely. But I think you'll see these passages in a slightly different light.

ETERNAL SECURITY AND EVANGELISM

Many people would not necessarily put these two subjects together because they seem to be at opposite ends of the spiritual spectrum. But eternal security bears on the message of evangelism that we deliver because it is built into the nature of the gospel.

I know there aren't any verses in which we find the apostles saying to someone, "Let me show you how you can know for certain that you are saved and eternally secure." But if it is not possible to know that we have eternal life, and if salvation is contingent upon anything within us, then the offer of the gospel is compromised whether the subject ever comes up or not.

Recall, for example, the confidence with which Paul and Silas answered the Philippian jailer's question, "What must I do to be saved?" (Acts 16:30). They were able to say without hesitation, "Believe in the Lord Jesus, and you will be saved" (v. 31). The integrity of that promise demands that there be no conditions attached or caveats that would cause the apostles to have to back up and qualify their offer.

Peter addressed his second letter "to those who have received a faith of the same kind as ours" (2 Peter 1:1). We pointed out earlier that if Peter had a halting, doubting faith in which he could get no lasting peace about his relationship with God, he would hardly wish that on others.

Do you think Peter's salvation was secure? Do you know that Jesus Himself prayed for Peter to stand true during the greatest failure of his life? Just before His crucifixion and Peter's denial, Jesus said, "Simon, Simon, behold, Satan has demanded permission to sift you like wheat; but I have prayed for you, that your faith may not fail" (Luke 22:31–32).

Now Jesus wasn't talking about the risk of Peter's losing his eternal salvation, but his yielding to the temptation to deny the Lord and be totally crushed by his sin so that he would be rendered useless. The danger to Peter was real, but Jesus could say what He said because God had already secured Peter's restoration. We know that because the only time God the Father ever turned down His Son's prayer was when Jesus prayed for the cup of suffering at the cross to be taken from Him.

The point is that Peter was more secure than he even understood at that moment. You say, "Well, that's fine for Peter because Jesus prayed for him." Jesus is praying for you too! He is your Great High Priest in heaven today, of whom the Bible says, "He is able also to save forever those who draw near to God through Him, since He always lives to make intercession for them" (Hebrews 7:25).

If "save forever" doesn't mean forever, then we don't have a gospel that is truly "good news" to a lost world.

ETERNAL SECURITY AND THE FEAR OF JUDGMENT

One of the great promises in the Bible, and one of the anchor verses for the argument of this book, is John 5:24, "Truly, truly, I say to you, he who hears My word, and believes Him who sent Me, has eternal life, and does not come into judgment, but has passed out of death into life."

I don't know of any fear that is greater than the fear of judgment. Those who deny the truth of eternal security have to admit the possibility that a believer who fell from grace and lost his salvation, and died in that condition, would face God's judgment. It's no wonder that in some churches people are at the altar every week, begging God to save them again.

In fact, this issue gets very serious when we realize that many false religions and cults use the fear of judgment to control their people. One cult is famous for putting white-haired people out on the streets to work the neighborhood. If you've ever wondered why these people are working so hard at their age, one reason is that this particular cult teaches its adherents that they can never really be sure they are in the "in group," so they keep pounding the pavement to earn their place in heaven.

You can get people to do a lot of things out of fear, especially if they fear that their eternal destiny depends on what they do. I'm not suggesting that legitimate Christian groups and denominations intentionally instill fear, but the result of instilling fear, even without intentionally doing so, is that people live their Christian lives walking on eggshells to make sure they don't mess up and cause God to loosen His grip on them. If eternal security is not true, then we cannot fully obey the biblical command, "Be anxious for nothing" (Philippians 4:6).

ETERNAL SECURITY AND THE CROSS

When we understand the finality of the transaction that took place when Jesus died on the cross, the truth of eternal security comes into clearer focus. Understanding the Cross also lifts the issue above all the wrangling about whether people can sin their way out of God's grace, or whether they will abuse their security and live any way they want.

Paul wrote concerning the Cross,

> When you were dead in your transgressions and the uncircumcision of your flesh, He made you alive together with Him, having forgiven us all our transgressions, having canceled out the certificate of debt consisting of decrees against us, which was hostile to us; and He has taken it out of the way, having nailed it to the cross. (Colossians 2:13–14)

Notice that God speaks in the past tense of our sin debt being completely paid for by Jesus Christ on the cross, so much so that the "certificate" containing our sins has been "paid in full." This is what Jesus was referring to when He cried out from the cross, "It is finished!" (John 19:30).

Paul teaches that all of our transgressions—past, present, and future—have been forgiven. But those who deny eternal security cannot really affirm this because their position necessitates the view that only those sins that we committed *before* we became Christians were really forgiven at the cross.

How can I say that? Because if we can commit a sin tomorrow, next week, or next year that can cause us to be severed from God's grace and pass from life back into death, then that future sin is not truly paid for at the cross. The problem with that view is that all of our sins were still future when Jesus went to the cross. Yet the Bible makes no distinction between past, present, and future sins, speaking of all our sins as though they are already under the blood.

ETERNAL SECURITY AND GOD'S LOVE

The following chapter will discuss this aspect of eternal security in detail, so let me just whet your appetite. We could quote pages of Bible verses that speak of God's eternal love for us, but let me show you something exciting from Romans 4. Speaking of Abraham's faith, Paul wrote:

> Therefore it [Abraham's faith] was also credited to him as righteousness. Now not for his sake only was it written that it was credited to him, but for our sake also, to whom it will be credited, as those who believe in Him who raised Jesus our Lord from the dead, He who was delivered over because of our transgressions, and was raised because of our justification. (vv. 22–25)

This is good. These verses say that God loves you so much Jesus Christ not only died to save you, but He rose to keep you justified. The resurrection is not only the receipt for your salvation, it is the power by which you are kept secure until the day of redemption. We read earlier that Jesus ever lives to make intercession for us.

That means every time Satan comes before God to accuse us and insist that He toss us out of His family, Jesus steps in as our Advocate and says, "Father, these people belong to Me. I died to pay for those sins, and they are Mine." If we were in church right now, I'd be saying someone ought to be praising God on this one.

ETERNAL SECURITY AND HERMENEUTICS

Your view of eternal security also affects your hermeneutics. Now you may not know that you have a hermeneutics to be affected, but you do. This is just a big word for the art and science of interpreting Scripture. Everyone interprets the Bible by some standard, whether good or faulty. Our view on the doctrine, or even the possibility, of eternal security affects the way we read and interpret God's Word.

What It Means to Abide in Christ

Let's take one classic text as an example. In John 15:1–5, Jesus taught us the importance of abiding in Him if we expect to produce spiritual fruit. Then He issued this warning: "If anyone does not abide in Me, he is thrown away as a branch and dries up; and they gather them, and cast them into the fire and they are burned" (v. 6). Is this referring to eternal judgment and the possibility of someone who was once a believer being cast into the fires of hell? Or is this a serious and sober warning to us to make sure we stay in close, vital connection with the Vine, Jesus Christ (see v. 1)?

Most people make two major assumptions when they read this passage. The first is that a failure to abide means a loss of salvation. The second assumption is that fire as a symbol of judgment refers to hell, which would make sense in John 15:6 if the person who failed to abide was stripped of his or her salvation.

But do these assumptions make for good hermeneutics or Bible interpretation here? Consider the question of being tossed in the fire and burned. Fire in the Scripture does often refer to hell, but not always. In fact, in 1 Corinthians 3:13, 15, Paul said there would be fire at the judgment seat of Christ to test the quality of believers' works. The issue there is not the person's salvation, but fruitfulness. Given the context of John 15, understanding fire as symbolic of God's purging and discipline of an unfruitful, spiritually dried-up believer gives us a better meaning of Jesus' warning in verse 6.

What, then, is the context of John 15? The concept of abiding in the New Testament has to do with intimate relationship and fellowship. It is not a test for salvation, but for intimacy. God takes His relationship with us very seriously, so when we stop abiding or pursuing intimacy with Him, He will do whatever it takes to get our attention, and it could get hot. When I misbehaved, my father used to tell me, "Boy, I'm going to burn your backside." It did feel like fire, but the point is my father meant he was going to discipline me.

John 15 is important for us as Christians, and it becomes even more crucial when we understand it in its true light. Instead of worrying that we are going to be cut *from* Christ, we had better be concerned about how fruitful we are *for* Him. If we fail to produce the fruit that should flow from our intimate connection to our Vine, God is going to take drastic measures to prune us and make us fruitful, or if we refuse to abide, our lives will become dried up and useless like dead branches.

Abiding, Fruit, and Salvation

I want to make two important observations about the question of abiding and spiritual fruit, and their relationship to salvation. First, if producing spiritual fruit is proof that we are saved, then we can't know for sure we are saved until we have had time to bear fruit. Jesus does say that people will be known by the fruit their lives produce (Matthew 7:20), but my focus here is on the immediacy of the offer of the gospel, as in Acts 16:31. The Philippian jailer probably went on to become a fruitful Christian, but to be saved all he had to do was believe in Jesus. Also, Jesus promised the thief on the cross that he would be with Jesus in Paradise before that day was over (Luke 23:43).

Second, the Bible teaches that it is possible even for unbelievers to produce what looks like good spiritual fruit. A lot of people are going to present their works to Jesus at the judgment, and the list is impressive (Matthew 7:21–22). But Jesus will say, "Depart from Me" (v. 23). Some sinners live outwardly better lives than some Christians. Now don't misunderstand. There are plenty of people who ought to be worried about whether they are saved because their lives are bearing no spiritual fruit or good works, which James says will accompany true salvation (James 2:14). I urge you to look at your life today to see if this fruit is evident. For the non-Christian or someone who merely professes to be a Christian, lack of real fruit may be a warning sign. But for the Christian, fruit is not a salvation issue, but a fellowship issue.

ETERNAL SECURITY AND SPIRITUAL GROWTH

Here's another point we've made before that I want to underscore: A lack of clarity on eternal security leads to stunted spiritual growth. "It was for freedom that Christ set us free; therefore keep standing firm and do not be subject again to a yoke of slavery" (Galatians 5:1).

Failing to look to Christ and trust Him for your security is tantamount to putting yourself back under the Law in terms of putting yourself on a performance basis with God. Just as a baby must be on a certain basic dietary standard in order to grow and develop, we as Christians must be on the grace standard if we expect to grow. Peter did not say, "Grow in your ability to keep God's law and please Him by your performance." Peter said, "Grow in grace" (see 2 Peter 3:18).

Now don't misunderstand. Believing that you are eternally secure does not guarantee you will grow in grace. You still must abide in the Vine and draw strength and nourishment from Christ. But once you get your spiritual feet under you and realize that in Christ you are standing on solid ground that won't give way beneath you, the Christian life takes on an incredible new sense of freedom and a new dynamic. One way you know you're living on a performance basis is that you feel yoked to your performance list, or someone else's, all the time.

ETERNAL SECURITY AND GOD'S CHARACTER

I asked the people at our church one Sunday, "Who wants to be the first person to stand up and call God a liar this morning?" No one took me up on my offer. Who would want to accuse our great God of lying to us or breaking His Word? But if God says He has given us eternal life and nothing can separate us from Him (see Romans 8:38–39), and yet we try to say that He will take back His eternal life under certain circumstances, then we are in effect calling God a liar. Why? Because we are denying the clear teaching of His Word.

I also believe that to deny that we are secure in Christ has the effect of making Jesus' work on the cross a failure. Why? Because it means that He died to give you and me something, eternal life, that He is ultimately unable to deliver or guarantee.

More than that, if our salvation can be lost the first time we sin or slip along the way, then the Holy Spirit would be found to be impotent. Why? Because it is through His power and on the strength of His seal on us that we are supposed to be kept and guarded and secured until the day of redemption (see Ephesians 1:13).

You can see why I call a denial of the biblical doctrine of eternal security an attack on God's character. The work of every member of the Triune Godhead in salvation is undermined if God doesn't really mean it when He says we are His forever.

ETERNAL SECURITY AND GOD'S PROMISES

I want to close this chapter with a review of some tremendous promises from Jesus' lips that you know well. He said, "All that the Father gives Me will come to Me, and the one who comes to Me I will certainly not cast out. For I have come down from heaven, not to do My own will, but the will of Him who sent Me. This is the will of Him who sent Me, that of all that He has given Me I lose nothing, but raise it up on the last day" (John 6:37–39).

Again, Jesus said, "My sheep hear My voice, and I know them, and they follow Me; and I give eternal life to them, and they will never perish; and no one will snatch them out of My hand" (John 10:27–28).

Jesus said to Martha, "I am the resurrection and the life; he who believes in Me will live even if he dies, and everyone who lives and believes in Me will never die. Do you believe this?" (John 11:25–26).

That's the real question, isn't it? Jesus turns the searchlight from Himself to our hearts. He demonstrated that He was the resurrection and the life by raising Martha's brother Lazarus from the dead that day. No problem or question there. The only question is whether we really believe what God says in His Word.

If Jesus had not done His Father's will, He wouldn't be the perfect Son of God. And if He's not the perfect Son of God, He's not qualified to be our Savior. And if He's not qualified to be our Savior, we don't have a Savior. And if we don't have a Savior, we might as well quit church and go home. And if Jesus could lose some of those who have come to Him, then He would not have been the perfect Savior we love and follow.

Speaking of promises from God's Word, here's one that motivates me every day: "Therefore, my beloved brethren, be steadfast, immovable, always abounding in the work of the Lord, knowing that your toil is not in vain in the Lord" (1 Corinthians 15:58). I am so excited that God looked at this sinner and not only forgave me but secured me forever. I am so excited that I am unshakable in Him that I want to be unshakable in my service for Him. Is eternal security important? In every way!

18

THE PASSION OF ETERNAL SECURITY

One of the hardest courses I took during my student days at Dallas Theological Seminary was a class on the theology of Karl Barth. Barth was a very influential Swiss theologian from the middle of the twentieth century whose impact is still being felt today. Barth's sentences as they were translated from German into English were extremely long and hard to follow, and his thought processes so deep, that we got headaches just trying to work through the course and grasp what he was saying.

Ever since taking that course, I've enjoyed the story of the time when Karl Barth visited America. A young journalist was assigned to interview Dr. Barth for a Christian magazine, and in the course of the interview he asked Barth, "What is the greatest thought that has ever come across your mind?"

I can see this young man sharpening his pencil (this was more than fifty years ago) and getting ready to write furiously as the great theologian cut loose with some grand and complicated thought.

Dr. Barth paused for a moment and replied, "The greatest thought that has ever come across my mind is this: 'Jesus loves me, this I know, for the Bible tells me so.'"

Karl Barth was not being facetious. He understood in a profound way the importance of a very simple truth that is a cornerstone of the Christian faith. We've sung about Christ's love since we were little children, but sometimes we forget the basics. If we fully understood the enormous scope of that love, we wouldn't have any problem with the doctrine of eternal security.

God's promise to secure all those He saves is rooted in His love. To deny that truth is to admit that we really don't understand very much about the love of God. We're going to see that He passionately cares for His own. Security is a work of love on God's part.

THE MEANING OF GOD'S LOVE

One reason that so many people struggle with the concept of eternal security is that they struggle with the concept of God's love. It's important to remember that our definitions of love and God's definition aren't always the same. If you grew up in a loveless environment, in an environment in which the love you received was conditional on your behavior, then you may be using a human definition of love to define an infinite divine attribute.

Starting with human definitions of love leads to statements such as, "I don't see how God could love me perfectly and eternally in spite of what I do. I don't even like myself all that much at times." It's true that human love is often inconsistent, misplaced, and bestowed for the wrong reasons—the very opposite of God's love. Let's take a quick refresher course in the nature of God's love and see how it relates to the doctrine of security.

God's Love Is Visible

By this I mean that God did something to show us how much He loves us. Someone said, "I asked Jesus how much He loved me. He said, 'This much,' and stretched out His hands and died." Jesus said, "Greater love has no one than this, that one lay down his life for his friends" (John 15:13). Paul gave a classic statement of the atonement when he wrote, "God demonstrates His own love toward us, in that while we were yet sinners, Christ died for us" (Romans 5:8).

Some of us talk a good game when it comes to love, but God so loved that He gave. Guys are good at rapping with girls about how great their love is, but too often the girl discovers that there is no reality behind the rap, no real willingness to love sacrificially and completely.

God's Love Is Sacrificial

Sacrifice is another word for love as far as defining God's eternal, saving love. The *agape* love that God lavished upon us in Christ is characterized by a commitment to act in the best interest of the person loved, regardless of the cost or self-sacrifice demanded of the one doing the loving.

One way we can measure love is the price tag that a person is willing to pay to love someone else. I don't mean the financial price tag, because it's possible to shower a person with expensive gifts and yet not have that person's best interests at heart. That happens far too often because one of the inadequate definitions of love that many people accept is that love means goodies and trinkets, and lots of them. God's love is extremely costly because it cost Him heaven's best, but love cannot be quantified in dollars and cents. But love can be measured in what the lover is willing to sacrifice.

God's Love Is Unconditional

God's kind of love also comes without conditions. This doesn't mean that He never has any demands to make on us, but rather that we don't have to be a certain kind of person to merit His love. The only condition for receiving God's love is being a sinner, and we all qualify.

This is very important for eternal security. God loved us despite the fact that we were "helpless," "ungodly," and "sinners" (Romans 5:6, 8). In other words, we weren't very pretty at all when God saved us. In fact, we were downright ugly in our sin.

So here's the question: If God was not too repulsed by our sin to reach down into the pit and save us, why should it be so hard to believe that He is not too repulsed by our sin now to keep us by His grace? Don't misunderstand. This is not permission to live unfruitful, lackadaisical Christian lives.

Just the opposite, in fact. Knowing the great price God paid to save us, and our unworthiness to be saved, should make us want to serve the Lord with everything we have. Paul said, "I count all things to be loss in view of the surpassing value of knowing Christ Jesus my Lord" (Philippians 3:8). If you aren't counting all things as loss for Christ, you're missing the point of your security in Him. It's not a truth to hide behind, but a foundation to stand on.

God's Love Is Judicial

Besides being visible, sacrificial, and unconditional, God's love is also judicial. Here's a corrective to the mistaken view that teaching the security of the believer leads to license and lazy Christian living. Being judicial means to act as a judge, to weigh both sides of a case and come to a firm decision. The human race has already been put on trial in the court of heaven and the verdict has been announced: "There is none righteous, not even one"; "For all have sinned and fall short of the glory of God" (Romans 3:10, 23).

The fact that God's love is judicial is good news for us, because He didn't just let us go in our sin to be condemned to eternal hell. He brought us up on charges and alerted us to our need. Then He did something very judicial and very loving. He exacted payment for those sins, as a righteous judge must do, but He carried out that judgment on His own Son so we could be forgiven and go free.

Now think about this. When you were saved, God set aside His guilty verdict against you and declared you righteous in Jesus Christ (the act of justification, see chapter 2). For you to slip out of God's hands and be lost again would require a reversal of God's declaration, then a reinstatement of it when you got saved again, then another reversal when you fell again, and so on. The scenario gets to be ridiculous.

God's Love Is Eternal

Let me tell you one more thing about God's love that bears on eternal security. God's love is eternal because God Himself is love. "Love is from God . . . for God is love" (1 John 4:7–8). The statement "God is love" has been twisted and abused to mean all kinds of things, but don't let the distortions obscure what the Bible is saying. God loves because He *is* love. Love is an integral part of God's being. His love for us is eternal because God is eternal. His love toward us will never cease, because God cannot contradict who He is.

THE GREATNESS OF GOD'S LOVE

In the book of Ephesians, the apostle Paul explained the greatness of the love God has bestowed on us in Christ. Two of the most important words in the Bible are "But God . . ." (Ephesians 2:4). We were dead and hopeless in our sins, but God did something about it. Why? That's the rest of verse 4. God acted because He is "rich in mercy" and "because of His great love with which He loved us."

The Dimensions of This Love

In Ephesians 3:17–19, Paul invited us to explore all the dimensions of God's love. Breaking in at mid-sentence, we read, "That you . . . may be able to comprehend with all the saints what is the breadth and length and height and depth, and to know the love of Christ which surpasses knowledge, that you may be filled up to all the fullness of God."

The context of these verses is worth noticing. All three members of the Godhead are involved in delivering our salvation and securing us in the love of Christ: God the Father (v. 14), God the Spirit (v. 16), and God the Son (v. 17). We are joined together with each member of the Holy Trinity in a relationship of love that is so deep it is beyond anything we can understand.

A popular gospel song of a few decades ago asked the question, How big is God? We could ask that in relation to God's love. It's as big as God Himself because God is love. We could also ask, How deep and high and wide and long is the love of God? Paul said that no matter in which direction you look, you'll never discover the outer limits of the love of God in Christ Jesus, because it is beyond our finite understanding.

The Election of God's Love

There's another aspect of God's love that bears on the issue of eternal security, which is the electing nature of this love. We'll discuss this in the next chapter, but here's a preview. Some believers are put off by the teaching of election because it seems to deny human beings any freedom in the choice.

But the fact is that God's election of us in Christ "before the foundation of the world" (Ephesians 1:4) is a tremendous argument for our security because once again, the motivation for action resides in God's loving character and not our actions, either good or bad. A love that is based in God's changeless, eternal being is not one that He is going to keep withdrawing and giving back.

The clearest example of God's sovereign choice in love is Jacob and Esau.

Though the twins were not yet born and had not done anything good or bad, so that God's purpose according to His choice would stand, not because of works but because of Him who calls, it was said to her [their mother, Rebekah], "The older will serve the younger." Just as it is written, "Jacob I loved, but Esau I hated." (Romans 9:11–13)

There is a lot going on here in terms of God's covenant and His dealing with the family of Abraham, but the bottom line is that God set His love on Jacob as an act of His sovereign choice. Paul made it abundantly clear that God did not look at Jacob and see that he was good, while noting that Esau was a godless man. Remember, even though Jacob had a heart for God he wasn't all that great through a large part of his life.

God made a determination within Himself to love Jacob—and by the way, it was not just that God liked Jacob better than Esau for whatever reason. That wasn't a matter of playing favorites or some kind of petty preference. Loving Jacob included God's decision to fulfill His promises through Jacob's line. The point is that Jacob was precious to God, period. You are precious to God, period.

The Tenacity of God's Love

Paul talked about the length of God's love. The good news is that God will go to any length to bring you to Himself. His love is tenacious, with a reach you can't outrun.

The Old Testament prophet Hosea is a powerful example of the tenacity with which God loves His people. Hosea's story and prophecy are about God's determined, everlasting love. God told Hosea to marry a prostitute named Gomer and settle down with her (see Hosea 1:1–2). Hosea married Gomer and loved her, but after their children were born, Gomer forsook Hosea and her family and went back to her old ways.

But in spite of Gomer's unfaithfulness and the pain and humiliation it must have caused Hosea, God told him, "Go again, love a woman who is loved by her husband, yet an adulteress, even as the Lord loves the sons of Israel, though they turn to other gods" (Hosea 3:1). So the prophet bought his wife back from whatever bondage and degradation she had fallen into, took her to their home again, and restored her to his love.

God told Hosea to do all of that to serve as a picture of His pursuing, tenacious love for Israel. God had entered into a covenant with the nation of Israel like a marriage covenant between a husband and wife. Israel was God's wife, and no matter how far the people strayed from Him, no matter how far they sank into sin and degradation, God was telling them that He would not let them go. He was going to be faithful to His marriage covenant even when His wife was faithless.

Even when the people of Israel went chasing after other gods, God's love was like a hand on their shoulder drawing them back. And just as Hosea finally redeemed and restored Gomer despite everything, God wanted Israel to know that the day would come when He would finally and fully redeem them, and they would be a holy people to Him.

We find it easy to love that which is successful, attractive, and pleasing to us. It's fairly easy for us to love those who return our love. But God's love is the kind that pursues the unlovely. God came after us when we were going away from Him. He tracked us down and would not let us go.

THE FINALITY OF GOD'S LOVE

God's love is the love to end all loves. When God sets His love upon a person, He does not change His mind and He doesn't quit until His purposes have been fulfilled—whether we're talking about His chosen people Israel or individuals in the church like you and me. That's the sense in which I refer to the finality of His love.

Here's an example of what I mean. John 3:16 says that God gave "His only begotten Son" so that we might have eternal life. We've talked a lot about the price that God paid to save us, so let me put it in a little different context.

The Finality of Christ's "Forsakenness"

"Only begotten" means unique, one-of-a-kind. There has never been anyone like Jesus Christ, nor will there ever be again. He is the only Son of God and the second person of the Trinity. The Bible teaches that the three members of the Godhead are distinct in personality but one in their divine essence, self-existing in perfect harmony from all eternity. This means we can't even begin to comprehend the disruption that took place in the Godhead when Jesus cried out to His Father from the cross, "My God, My God, why have You forsaken Me?" (Matthew 27:46).

For that moment when God the Son was bearing the sin of the world and God the Father had to turn away from His one-and-only Son, their fellowship and communion was disrupted. That had never happened before even for one second in all the ceaseless ages of eternity past, and it will never happen again. God only forsook His Son once, when the Son was paying for our sins. There was a terrible finality to Jesus' abandonment by His Father on the cross.

The Finality of Christ's Payment

Jesus testified to the finality of the transaction on the cross when He uttered His final words before releasing His spirit and dying: "It is finished!" (John 19:30).

You may know the background of that phrase. It meant, "Paid in full!" Jesus was announcing to the angels in heaven, to the people of earth, and to Satan and the demons of hell that no more debt was owed for sin. I don't know how anything could be clearer than that. Even the tearing in half of the temple's huge veil from top to bottom (see Matthew 27:51) was a visible testimony to the fact that no more sacrifices for sin would ever be needed again.

To quote baseball great Yogi Berra, "It ain't over till it's over." Well, when Jesus demonstrated His love for you and me on the cross, it was over! God was signaling to every person and every power on earth and under the earth that the transaction was complete. Why would we want to reopen a case that God has declared closed by questioning the validity of our salvation?

The wonder of God's love is what keeps drawing us back to Romans 8:31–39, which moves from no condemnation to no separation. According to 2 Corinthians 5:17–18, we are new creations in Christ Jesus, the old things have gone and everything is new, and we have been reconciled to God. Why would we mess with that provision by worrying about whether we have been separated from God again, are back under His condemnation, have our old life back, and are no longer reconciled to God but are His enemies again?

Every time the Bible addresses the subject of our salvation, it speaks with wonderful and unmistakable finality. That's why the Greek word selected by the Holy Spirit to describe the saving message of Christ means "good news." There is no better expression of that good news than the message of John 3:16. I want to conclude our discussion of the magnificent, saving, and securing love of God with an encouraging summary of this great verse:

"For God so loved." That's the greatest degree.
"The world." That's the greatest company.
"That He gave." That's the greatest act.
"His only begotten Son." That's the greatest gift.
"That whoever." That's the greatest opportunity.
"Believes." That's the greatest simplicity.
"In Him." That's the greatest attraction.
"Shall not perish." That's the greatest promise.
"But." That's the greatest difference.
"Have." That's the greatest certainty.
"Eternal life." That's the greatest possession.

There are a lot of periods in John 3:16 when you read it this way. And as someone has said, don't ever put a question mark where God has put a period. If God says nothing on earth or in hell can ever separate you from His love, you can believe it!

19

THE
PROCESS
OF
ETERNAL SECURITY

A number of years ago the Federal Express delivery company had a very effective television commercial that featured an older CEO-type executive sitting at his desk putting a letter together. A voice-over came on, asking in a very incredulous tone: "This is the most important letter of your life, and you're going to trust it to the post office?!"

The executive suddenly got a scared look on his face as the voice pointed out that the post office handles millions of pieces of mail each day, suggesting it was highly possible that this man's all-important letter might never reach its destination. The more the voice talked, the more nervous the man became, thinking about his precious letter disappearing into the postal system and being lost forever. He started shaking violently as he held the envelope to his lips and tried to lick the flap shut. You could hear the paper crinkling loudly as the man's hands shook.

But when the voice suggested that he send the letter by Federal Express, the man's face suddenly brightened. He smiled, relaxed, and heaved a sigh of relief at the reassuring thought of Fed Ex's secure tracking and delivery system.

That old commercial is a pretty good analogy of two possible ways to live the Christian life when it comes to your view of eternal security. You can either shake in your shoes wondering when and if you are going to disappear from God's care and be lost, or relax and rest in the reassuring knowledge that He is "tracking" you for eternity.

This may be a little bit of an overstatement of the case, but that's what the issue boils down to for us as individual believers. What I'd like to demonstrate in this chapter is another facet of the reassuring fact that your salvation and mine are parts of a divine program that is so incredible it reaches from eternity to eternity and encompasses both the human and angelic realms. And since God's salvation program has never been in danger of failing at any time, we are as secure as we could possibly be.

THE PROGRAM OF ELECTION

God's program of salvation involves His electing purposes, as the Bible states in Ephesians 1:4: "[God the Father] chose us in [Christ] before the foundation of the world, that we would be holy and blameless before Him." I want to look at the program of election under several headings and see how it relates to the security we should be enjoying as believers.

The Participation of Election

By participation I don't mean that we help God along in His plan, although we are responsible to respond in faith to the gospel. The Bible sets these two truths in perfect balance, as Paul wrote to the Thessalonians: "We should always give thanks to God for you, brethren beloved by the Lord, because God has chosen you from the beginning for salvation through sanctification by the Spirit and faith in the truth" (2 Thessalonians 2:13). God's work is to choose and to save; our response is to put our faith in the truth.

I'm using the term *participation* simply to mean that our salvation is tied to our participation or identity with Jesus Christ. The Christian life is Christ from beginning to end. It is all in Christ, from Christ, for Christ, with Christ, through Christ, and to Christ. The opening chapter of Ephesians shouts this truth in almost every line (note verses 1–7, 9–10, 12–13, 15, 17, 20, 23). Everything that God is accomplishing in salvation is intimately tied to His own relationship with His Son and to our relationship with Christ.

The Conception of Election

In 2 Timothy 1, the apostle Paul urged Timothy to stand with him unashamedly in the work of the gospel and even to suffer by the power of God, "who has saved us and called us with a holy calling, not according to our works, but according to His own purpose and grace which was granted us in Christ Jesus from all eternity" (v. 9).

Here Paul located the origin of our salvation in eternity past, as he did in Ephesians 1:4. We can't pinpoint the exact beginning of God's electing plan because eternity doesn't have a beginning or an end. Paul even said that God's plan to display His grace in Christ was "from all eternity," which takes the process back farther than our limited minds can comprehend.

What I want you to see is that salvation didn't suddenly appear when we showed up. In fact, the plan of salvation had been drawn up in the council chambers of God for an eternity before the earth was created or Adam was made.

Understanding that our election reaches back into eternity is important for several reasons. For example, it reveals the great lengths to which God went to save you. The three persons of the Trinity having conferred and agreed on the plan of salvation, it is unimaginable that They would say, "This is the best plan for the redemption of mankind, but We cannot secure its results." The fact is that God's elect were already chosen, redeemed, sealed, and secured in His mind "from all eternity."

Another reason the eternal nature of election is important is that, as I want to demonstrate, election did not begin with the human race. We cannot fully comprehend and appreciate the purpose of our election until we understand what happened in heaven with the first beings God created.

The First Elected Beings

According to Ephesians 1:5–6, the purpose of election is that we might bring praise and glory to God as Exhibit A of His grace. We'll develop this theme later, but first we need to go back into eternity because we humans are not the first beings God created to praise and glorify Him. In eternity past God created the myriads of angels in heaven to execute His will and to lead heaven in His praise and worship.

But when Lucifer, the chief of angels, declared, "I will make myself like the Most High" (Isaiah 14:14) and rebelled against God, one-third of the angels joined him in his rebellion (see Revelation 12:4). But God defeated Lucifer and his angels, and he was cast to earth as Satan with the fallen angels becoming his demons. We know this from 2 Peter 2:4 and Jude 6, which say that God condemned the rebellious angels to judgment and hell. There was no second chance or redemption offered to the angels who sinned.

What happened at this point is crucial to understand in relation to election. When Satan rebelled, God judged him and his angels (see Matthew 25:41; 2 Peter 2:4; Jude 6; Revelation 20:10). Remember, the devil is not the king or the ruler of hell. He will be the most tormented being in that awful place.

Now we come to the election of angels, because the Bible refers to those angels who remained true to God as "chosen" (1 Timothy 5:21). This is the same Greek root as the word *elect,* and could just as easily be translated that way (as in the NIV). While judging the angels who rebelled, God also confirmed the two-thirds of the holy angels who remained true to Him in their holiness. In other words, the angels were "locked in" to their decision to follow God or follow Satan. Since Satan's rebellion did not surprise our sovereign God who knows all things perfectly, it shouldn't surprise us that God preempted Satan's actions by securing the devil's defeat and preserving two-thirds of His angels in holiness.

Theologians often use the term *inscrutable* to describe God's plan, meaning that it is beyond our understanding. What we know for sure is that God elected some angels to eternal holiness while permitting others to "abandon their proper abode" (Jude 6) and fall into sin. The basis of that election was intimately related to the angels' decision to accept or reject Satan's overtures to join him in rebelling against God. It was not an arbitrary overruling of their capacity to choose.

So the principle of divine election was established with the angels. This is crucial because what happened to the angels happened to mankind, with one very important difference.

The Election of Mankind

Satan's attempt to usurp God's throne was smashed before it ever got started. But the rebellion in heaven also gave God a unique opportunity, if you will. This was the opportunity to receive greater glory by demonstrating that He could do more with lesser beings, when those beings were dependent on Him, than He could do with superior beings (the angels) when those beings rebelled against Him. This new creation would also allow God to express a part of His nature that had never been fully revealed before: namely, His grace.

So God decided to create the human race, a group of beings temporarily made a little lower in rank than the angels (see Hebrews 2:7) as creatures to do what the fallen angels failed to do, which is bring Him praise. Human beings sinned and fell from their original position and purpose too, but in grace God redeemed a body of people who will be with Him in heaven for all eternity and render Him the praise and glory due His name.

Now let me clarify something before we go any further. When we talk about God doing this and then deciding to do that, we're not suggesting that God waited for one thing to happen before deciding to do something else. God does not think and act in sequence as we do. We're trapped in time, but God is outside of time and is not subject to its limits. Everything is the eternal now for God. We only use sequential language because that's the only way we can discuss His actions.

Contrary to what some theologians are teaching today, God does not need to wait until an event unfolds to see how it is going to end. Neither is He ever surprised or caught off guard by human actions. God has no Plan B. With that clarification in place, we're ready to talk about human election.

THE PURPOSE OF ELECTION

We referred earlier to Ephesians 1:6 as stating the purpose of God's election. Let me begin with verse 5: "He predestined us to adoption as sons through Jesus Christ to Himself, according to the kind intention of His will, *to the praise of the glory of His grace,* which He freely bestowed on us in the Beloved" (italics added).

God's purposes in election will stand (see Romans 9:11), so you don't need to fear that one iota of His program will fail. Every person God saves will be in heaven singing the praises of His grace. God will accomplish this for His own glory.

We Are God's Gift to Jesus

In accomplishing His elective purposes, God the Father decided to present a redeemed humanity as a love gift to His Son. Now to understand this, you have to realize how much God the Father and God the Son love each other within the Trinity, and how much they are committed to each other's glory. We see this again and again in John 17, which is the great prayer that Jesus prayed the night before He was crucified.

For example, the first words Jesus said were, "Father, the hour has come; glorify Your Son, that the Son may glorify You" (v. 1). The prayer makes several other references to the Father's glory and the Son's glory, and to Their love (see vv. 23–24, 26). This context is crucial because it is in this setting of mutual love between the Father and the Son that Jesus spoke of redeemed people as His gift from the Father. Notice in particular what these verses say about our security.

In verse 2 of John 17, Jesus said that God had given Him authority, "that to all whom You have given Him, He may give eternal life." Every person in God's gift to His Son receives salvation. No one is overlooked. And it gets even better, because Jesus not only saves the elect, He keeps them.

Every Believer Will Make Heaven

"Keep them in Your name," Jesus prayed (John 17:11). Then He asked the Father to keep His people from "the evil one" (v. 15). And in case you think He was only talking about the disciples who were with Him in the Upper Room, Jesus prayed "for those also who believe in Me through their word" (v. 20). That's you and me. And then Jesus asked of His Father, "I desire that they also, whom You have given Me, be with Me where I am" (v. 24).

Now if language means anything, Jesus was asking His Father to protect the gift He had given His Son, and to make sure that every believer whom the Father elected and the Son redeemed would be with Christ in heaven. It sounds to me as if we are as secure as we could possibly be.

Suppose the Father doesn't want to protect the gift that He has given the Son? That will never happen, because it was impossible for Jesus to pray a prayer that His Father would not answer—the only exception recorded in Scripture being in the garden when Jesus prayed that the cup of suffering be taken from Him. There is no hint at all in John 17 that any of Jesus' requests would be denied. After Jesus prayed, He was ready to go to Gethsemane and agonize with the Father about the suffering that was ahead for Him (see John 18:1).

Don't miss the significance of what happened between God the Father and the Son that night in the Upper Room. You are a gift from God to Jesus Christ, who asked His Father not to let the Evil One remove you from Him on your way to heaven. Jesus also asked that you would be with Him in heaven. And since the Father always hears and answers His Son, you are already in heaven in the mind and purpose of God.

In other words, you and I are tied into something much bigger than ourselves. God is going to make sure that His Son has a redeemed body of people who will sing the praises of His grace in heaven. If you are truly saved, you are going to be part of that heavenly redeemed chorus.

THE PREDESTINATION OF ELECTION

Once you understand that God's plan of salvation encompasses eternity past and eternity future, and not just these few years of earth's history, then doctrines such as election and its companion truths that have caused so many people so much confusion should not be hard to accept. Our range of vision and understanding is very limited, but God sees everything in one complete package.

God Preplanned Our Salvation and Security

The doctrine of predestination is one of those teachings that we ought to be able to accept and believe even if we don't fully understand it. The Bible says clearly, "[God] predestined us to adoption as sons through Jesus Christ to Himself" (Ephesians 1:5). That should communicate security to you because your salvation is the result of careful planning on the part of the eternal God.

To predestine means to preplan, or to plan beforehand. Before He brought the world into being, God conceived a plan to save those whom He would choose and to keep them saved. Now this suggests an issue that is for most people the biggest stumbling block in believing the truth of election. If God chose some people for salvation, that means He did not choose others. The Bible is clear that many people will wind up in hell, although the Bible also says that God loved the world so much He sent His Son to die for the world.

The short answer to the dilemma is that election and predestination do not rule out human responsibility. We've dealt with this issue in earlier chapters, so allow me just to review it briefly here.

Paul said in 2 Corinthians 5:19 that "God was in Christ reconciling the world to Himself." So God has rendered the whole world "savable" through the death of Jesus Christ. In fact, according to Romans 5:18, Christ's sacrifice on the cross has dealt with the sin of Adam for all people: "So then as through one transgression there resulted condemnation to all men, even so through one act of righteousness there resulted justification of life to all men."

The Bible says that the same "all" who were condemned are the "all" who are justified. Now this either means that everyone was automatically saved when Jesus died on the cross, which we know is not true, or Paul had something else in mind.

The answer is found in the apostle's reference to the one act of sin and the one act of righteousness. The former speaks of Adam, whose sin in the Garden of Eden spread the contamination of sin to the entire human race. The result is that every person who has ever been born is born in sin and stands under the judgment and condemnation of God.

But what Adam messed up, Jesus Christ "the last Adam" (1 Corinthians 15:45) fixed up. Christ's act of righteous obedience on the cross reversed the condemning effects of Adam's sin, so that the Bible can say the whole world has been justified and reconciled to God in Christ.

What this means is that people are no longer condemned for Adam's sin. Nobody goes to hell because Adam sinned, because Jesus Christ paid for that sin. This is why babies and people who are mentally incapacitated from infancy and cannot be held accountable go to heaven. They have no sin of their own to answer for. Anyone who goes to hell goes there because of his or her own sin, not Adam's.

God Gave Us a Way Back

How does this reconciliation of all people intertwine with God's predestination of the elect to salvation? Let me go back to the angels for a minute to help us. When the angels who fell sinned against God, we learned that they were sealed in their doom. But God did something with humans that He didn't do with angels: He gave us a way back. It's called grace.

In other words, even though the human race exercised its option to sin and fell under God's condemnation, God has given mankind a way to "opt back" into His favor. But each person must still accept or reject God's offer of grace that forgives the sins they have committed. Those who accept God's grace do so because they are His elect, but those who refuse His plan of salvation are held accountable for their rejection. In the councils of eternity, God predetermined to provide salvation for all and secure it for those who are in Christ.

There is still an element of mystery to election and predestination. But the Bible teaches them plainly, and also says that we are responsible to respond to God's call. The beauty of grace is that God gives us a way back to Him from our sin and rebellion. That's what it means to be elected.

It's necessary to deal with these issues, and they are sometimes difficult to understand. But the real bottom line for us as Christians is that we are secure in Christ forever. Jesus said that no part of the gift His Father has given Him will be lost. "This is the will of Him who sent Me, that of all that He has given Me I lose nothing, but raise it up on the last day" (John 6:39). The author of Hebrews said that God has demonstrated "to the heirs of the promise" His unchangeable purpose by His oath (6:17). Therefore, the hope we have in Christ is "an anchor of the soul, a hope both sure and steadfast" (v. 19).

The imagery here is that of sailors who leave the mother ship in a smaller vessel in order to carry the anchor forward to a place where it can be firmly lodged. By His entrance into heaven's sanctuary as our Great High Priest (Hebrews 9:11–12), Jesus has anchored our salvation there. Just as the security and stability of a large ship is tied to the holding power of the anchor, reardless of how unstable are the weather conditions, so our security is tied to the Anchor of our souls (see Hebrews 6:19), regardless of the winds of sin or circumstances.

THE PATERNITY OF ELECTION

Some people want to make the doctrine of election out to be some kind of cold, impersonal action on the part of a somewhat distant, rather impersonal God. But that's not the way the Bible presents election. Notice Ephesians 1:5 one more time: "He predestined us *to adoption as sons* through Jesus Christ to Himself" (italics added). You were not only born into the family of God when you got saved, you were adopted into His family, which means He wanted you in His family so much that He pursued you and took out papers on you for the purpose of adopting you to be His child.

The Permanence of Your Adoption

People who believe they can lose their salvation are living in a foster home. There's all the difference in the world between being a foster child and an adopted child. Foster homes are not permanent. Foster parents don't have all the legal responsibility of adoptive parents, and foster children have no part in the family's inheritance. It's hard for children in a foster home situation to develop security because they never know how long they're going to live in that home.

God did not bring us into His house and His family to stay a while until we move on or He loses custody of us. He adopted us; we belong to Him forever. One of the reasons people give for wanting to adopt a child is that they have so much love to give they want a child to shower their love upon.

Guess what God is saying in election? He's saying there is so much love in the Godhead that what the triune God wants to do is adopt some people and bring them into the family so they can share that love and enjoy all the rights and privileges that come with being part of God's family. Through election our adoption was already complete in eternity past, which is why Ephesians 1:3 says we have been blessed with every spiritual blessing "in the heavenly places" even though we're not there yet. It's a done deal as far as God is concerned. Election is a paternal act; a loving Father has chosen us.

The Father's Home

Whenever I think of this truth, my mind goes to Jesus' story of the prodigal son (Luke 15:11–32), which is really the story of a loving father. The prodigal son is like a lot of Christians who have been adopted and raised by a loving heavenly Father, but then go left on Him and use His money to get there.

You know the story. The prodigal took his part of the family inheritance and then used it to totally degrade himself and completely abuse his family's name, his family's resources, and his father's love. But when that Jewish boy got so low that he wound up living with and eating with pigs, he decided to get up and go home—not as his father's son any longer, but simply as one of the hired servants.

So the boy set off for home to confess his sin and beg his father to let him live in the servants' quarters. But his father had other ideas, because, you see, this son was still a member of the family and he had not lost his sonship.

I love the way Jesus said the prodigal's father saw him coming when he was still far off. That means Daddy had kept the lights on and was looking for his son to come back home. The boy's father ran to meet him and greeted him not as a returning sinner or a lowly servant, but as his privileged son. The father even bestowed on the boy all the symbols of his sonship with all of its rights and privilege.

Was confession and repentance necessary on the son's part? Absolutely. Did he have to decide he was tired of the pigpen and turn back to the father? Of course. But when he came back, his loving daddy was looking for him and forgave him.

Aren't you glad that God didn't give up on you when you gave up on Him? Aren't you glad that when you turned away from Him, He didn't turn away from you? That's because you never stop being His child. What that ought to do is make you want to stay home when you come home. It ought to make you want to love your Father because He kept on loving you. It ought to make you want to praise Him for His great salvation that remains secure forever.

20

THE PAYMENT OF ETERNAL SECURITY

When I was growing up in Baltimore, Earl was my man because Earl was the philosopher of the neighborhood where I grew up. Everybody who has ever lived in the "hood" knows that you always had a philosopher on the streets. He was the guy who couldn't make it out of the 'hood, so he learned everything about the 'hood and how to survive. The philosopher on the street corner was the person who educated you about "hood-ology."

Earl served that purpose on our street, and he was always saying things that made sense to me as a kid. So I would go home and repeat them, but my father wasn't impressed. I'd start a sentence by saying, "But Dad, Earl said . . .", but that's as far as I would get.

"Well, Earl is as ignorant as you are. Let me tell you something, boy. When Earl starts feeding you, clothing you, taking care of you, and taking you to the hospital when you're sick, then you can quote Earl. But until he starts doing that, I don't want to hear about Earl, because what he says means nothing around here. I'm the father in this house."

What my father was saying was, "Son, I'm the one who's paying the price to take care of you and put a roof over your head and make sure you have a secure home and a future away from the 'hood. And since I'm the one doing all of that, what anyone else says about you is irrelevant—and that includes Earl and even you."

God says about those who belong to Him, "I am the One who paid the price to redeem you and secure you and give you an eternal future in heaven. And since I am the One who did all of this, what anyone else says about the security of your salvation is irrelevant, even if that someone is you." When God says we are forgiven and declared righteous in Christ, we are forgiven and righteous in His sight. When Jesus says not one part of His gift from the Father will be lost (see John 6:39), then we are secure and it doesn't matter what anybody else says because Jesus paid it all.

We have examined the issue of eternal security from a number of perspectives, and in this chapter I want to review again the tremendous price that Jesus Christ paid to save you and keep you. Paul's prayer for the Thessalonians speaks powerfully about God's intention to keep all of those who belong to Christ and deliver them to heaven: "Now may the God of peace Himself sanctify you entirely; and may your spirit and soul and body be preserved complete, without blame at the coming of our Lord Jesus Christ" (1 Thessalonians 5:23).

Please notice that Paul pointed ahead to the culmination of our salvation at the return of Jesus Christ. I have good news for you. If you are found blameless, which means if you are saved, when Jesus returns you have made it, because when He comes back He's taking all of His children home to be with Him. Paul's prayer is another way of saying you *will* make it because it is God's will and good pleasure to preserve you. All who know Christ are eternally secure because of the saving death and the saving life of Jesus Christ.

THE SAVING DEATH OF CHRIST

Let me ask you a question. Since the Bible says that Jesus is "the author and perfecter [or completer] of faith" (Hebrews 12:2), can you think of anything that can crop up between the beginning and the end of salvation that can interrupt the work Jesus has begun and will complete? I can't either.

Jesus began your salvation in eternity past when in the council of the Godhead it was decided that the Son would take on human flesh and die as the payment for the sins of the world. Jesus then died to accomplish the transaction of redemption and rose from the grave to prove that the deal was done. And He ascended and is alive in heaven today as our High Priest, continuing to perfect and complete our salvation until the day He returns for us.

Your Debt Has Been Canceled

The heart of what Jesus Christ did for us in His saving death is captured in two great passages of Scripture, one from Paul and the other from the lips of Jesus Himself on the cross, that tell us the debt of our sin has been fully paid. The apostle wrote:

> When you were dead in your transgressions and the uncircumcision of your flesh, He made you alive together with Him, having forgiven us all our transgressions, having canceled out the certificate of debt consisting of decrees against us, which was hostile to us; and He has taken it out of the way, having nailed it to the cross. (Colossians 2:13–14)

Paul was referring to the bill of indebtedness that was prepared against a prisoner in Roman days and posted outside his cell, often having been signed by the prisoner himself as an admission of his debt. The bill stayed there until the debt was fully paid and the prisoner was set free, at which time the bill was taken down and, according to some ancient sources, was first blotted out and then canceled.

Paul said that God was holding a bill of indebtedness against us because of our sin and failure to live up to His standards. But when Jesus was nailed to the cross, our bill was nailed there along with Him just as surely as Jesus' own bill of accusation was nailed above His head by the Romans (see Matthew 27:37). And when Jesus died, the offenses on our sin bill were blotted out and canceled.

Imagine receiving your biggest bill in the mail with the record so completely obliterated that you couldn't even see how much you owed, and a note at the bottom indicating that the bill had been paid in full. It's one thing to pay a bill out of your own pocket, but it's something entirely different to see your bill paid at no cost to you. That's the grace of God.

Jesus Paid It All

The word that was written across a debt to cancel it after all its demands were met was the Greek word *tetelestai,* which means "paid in full." You may not recognize this word, but you are probably familiar with Jesus' usage of it on the cross. It was the last word He spoke before dismissing His spirit and dying: "It is finished!" (John 19:30). In other words, the sin debt of the world had been settled.

Tetelestai is an accounting term. By using it at that dramatic moment on the cross, Jesus was announcing to every authority and power in heaven and on earth and under the earth that every demand of God against sinners like you and me had been met. From that day forward, the sin bill of every child of God would read zero on the line labeled "Amount due." The death of Christ was so complete that it totally and completely satisfied God's righteous demands. In the wording of a great term we learned in an earlier chapter, God has been propitiated or satisfied with regard to us.

What About the Future?

My experience as a pastor has been that many of the people who struggle with the security of their salvation have a harder time believing that their future is covered by Christ than they do believing that He forgave their past. These are people who fear that they will commit some sin in the future that will cause God to cut them off from His grace. The only way that could happen is if Christ's death is somehow insufficient to pay for all sins, but let's hold that thought for a minute.

In one way, the problem these believers have is the problem that the Old Testament Israelites faced. The people of Israel could never rest from offering their sacrifices because Jesus Christ, the once-for-all sacrifice for sin, had not yet been offered. The blood of the animals they brought to the priests to be sacrificed had to flow continually. The reason for this is explained in the opening verses of Hebrews 10:

> For the Law . . . can never, by the same sacrifices which they offer continually year by year, make perfect those who draw near. Otherwise, would they not have ceased to be offered, because the worshipers, having once been cleansed, would no longer have had consciousness of sins? But in those sacrifices there is a reminder of sins year by year. For it is impossible for the blood of bulls and goats to take away sins. (vv. 1–4)

Israel's sacrificial system was designed to reinforce the fact that animal sacrifice was a temporary measure to cover sins until God's promised Redeemer would come. The system was also meant to point forward to that Redeemer, whom John the Baptist identified as Jesus, "the Lamb of God who takes away the sin of the world!" (John 1:29).

One reason that the letter to the Hebrews was written was to demonstrate the superiority of Christ over the Law, and the superiority of His sacrifice over the animal sacrifices of the Law. The writer fleshed out this contrast in a number of ways, including this reference to the Israelite priests' service as opposed to Christ's sacrifice: "Every priest stands daily ministering and offering time after time the same sacrifices, which can never take away sins; but He [Christ], having offered one sacrifice for sins for all time, sat down at the right hand of God" (10:11–12).

Did you notice the contrast between the standing priests of Israel and the sitting Christ? One piece of furniture you would never find in the tabernacle or the temple was a chair for the priests. That's because their work was never done. The priests never got a chance to sit down because the people had to come every day with sacrifices for their sins. There was no rest for the priests. When they got tired, a new group of priests came on duty, because the blood had to keep on flowing to cover sins.

That's why the people of Israel had what I call salvation on the layaway plan. Their obedience to God in offering the prescribed sacrifices was credited to them against the day when the Messiah and Savior would come and take away sin forever.

This contrast between the old way of atoning for sin and Jesus' payment for sin on the cross speaks directly to the fear that we might commit a sin someday that Jesus can't cover. The point is that *all* sin was taken into account when Jesus said "It is finished!" In fact, if Christ's death is not sufficient for our future sins, then it is not really finished at all.

Think about it. All of our sins were still future when Christ died, at least from our perspective, so why should we be so insecure about our future, so unsure in regard to our salvation? Remember that all this talk about past, present, and future is irrelevant to God. Every sin that you and I will ever commit was placed on Christ that day on Calvary, and because of Him we will never face our sins again. Instead of lying awake at night worrying about what we might possibly do to forfeit our salvation, we should be asking for strength to remain true to Him and grow in grace.

I love the way Hebrews 9:12 states it: "Not through the blood of goats and calves, but through His own blood, He entered the holy place once for all, having obtained eternal redemption." After He rose from the dead and ascended back to heaven, Jesus entered the heavenly tabernacle with His own blood and made the perfect, final sacrifice for sin. Then He sat down forever to prove that it is finished.

As far as heaven is concerned, the sin issue is settled and will never come up again. We can move on to the meatier stuff of the faith. That's why the writer of Hebrews told his readers that the time was far past for them to leave behind the ABCs of the faith and "press on to maturity" (6:1).

If you want a promise for the future you can hold on to and rest in today, consider 1 Thessalonians 1:10, which instructs us to wait for Jesus, "who rescues us from the wrath to come." We are delivered from the wrath to come. Notice that this rescue is present tense, not future. Your full and final deliverance in the presence of God is already accomplished in His mind.

We haven't arrived at the coming day of wrath yet, but we don't have to worry about it. Why? Because of Jesus: "For by one offering He has perfected for all time those who are sanctified" (Hebrews 10:14).

THE SAVING LIFE OF CHRIST

Most Christians are familiar with the saving death of Christ because it is one of the pivotal truths of our faith. Peter told the Jewish enemies of Christ, "There is no other name under heaven that has been given among men by which we must be saved" (Acts 4:12).

But the salvation Jesus Christ has provided is even more wonderful than a lot of people realize, because it encompasses His life as well as His death. Concerning this, Paul made a very interesting comparative statement: "For if while we were enemies we were reconciled to God through the death of His Son, *much more,* having been reconciled, we shall be saved by His life" (Romans 5:10, italics added). You are not only saved by Christ's death, you are also saved by His life.

We Need Righteousness

What does the life of Christ have to do with our security? To answer that, we need to note another important doctrinal statement that Paul made in 2 Corinthians 5:21. Speaking of what God did for us in Christ, Paul wrote: "He [God] made Him [Christ] who knew no sin to be sin on our behalf, so that we might become the righteousness of God in Him."

This great verse actually encompasses both the saving death and the saving life of Christ. God made Christ to be sin on our behalf when Christ bore the sin of the world on the cross. The cross took care of our sin problem forever, because our sins were charged to Christ's account and His death was credited to our account, His blood washing our sin debt away.

But we have another problem or need as sinful creatures. We not only need to have something *subtracted* from our lives, our sins which separated us from a holy God, but we need to have something *added* to our lives. We need an infusion of perfect righteousness in order to be able to stand before a perfectly righteous and holy God and find acceptance. The life of Christ has to do with providing us with the perfect righteousness we must have to come into God's presence.

Righteousness in the New Testament refers to a rightness of life or a right standing before God. Sin is wrong, and getting rid of sin is good. But getting rid of sin does not automatically ensure that we will start doing what is right. We not only need a positive infusion of righteousness to be right before God, but according to Paul we need the very "righteousness of God," which means being as righteous and holy as God Himself.

If you're reading this and wondering where you are going to get such a right standing before God, you're asking the right question. Now let me ask you a question: Is Jesus Christ righteous enough to stand before God as perfectly acceptable and blameless? Of course, because Jesus *is* God. So the answer to the question of where we can obtain perfect righteousness is the same as the answer to the question of where we can obtain enough credit to forgive our sins. The answer is Jesus Christ.

Jesus' Righteousness Covers Us

You see, Jesus lived a sinless life on earth for thirty-three years to provide you and me with the righteousness we need to be acceptable to God. This is why Jesus wasn't born as a full-grown adult who appeared suddenly on earth one day, died on the cross, and then went back to heaven. He had a specific mission to fulfill through His life. Jesus announced that mission during the Sermon on the Mount: "Do not think that I came to abolish the Law or the Prophets; I did not come to abolish but to fulfill. For truly I say to you, until heaven and earth pass away, not the smallest letter or stroke shall pass from the Law until all is accomplished" (Matthew 5:17–18).

What Jesus did during His earthly life was to completely and perfectly obey the righteous Law of God without any sin or failure at all, which qualified Him to be our sin-bearer. Jesus had to satisfy all of God's demands for perfect obedience and perfect righteousness in order for His death to be an acceptable payment for our sins.

When Jesus came at the beginning of His ministry to be baptized by John the Baptist, John was reluctant at first to baptize Jesus because he recognized that he was in the presence of the Son of God (Matthew 3:13–14). But Jesus made a very interesting statement in response to John's refusal to baptize Him: "Permit it at this time; for in this way it is fitting for us to fulfill all righteousness" (v. 15). Jesus didn't have any sin to repent of and be baptized for, but it was important that He identify with John's message of repentance. Jesus called it "fulfill[ing] all righteousness," and this was what His earthly life was all about. It took the thirty-three or so years that Jesus lived to fulfill this mission.

This is why at various points in His ministry, Jesus refused to let other people push Him into the spotlight or make Him declare publicly who He was and what He was doing. Jesus would respond to these efforts by saying that His time had not yet come. What He meant was that His work of fulfilling God's righteous requirements was not yet complete.

People sometimes wonder why Jesus lived the number of years He lived and why He died at the particular time He died. Both His ministry and His life were short by our standards, but He lived just as long as He needed to live to satisfy the demands of God's Law. Jesus also had to face every kind of temptation we would face so that we would have a High Priest in heaven who can "sympathize with our weaknesses" (Hebrews 4:15). That's one reason His temptation by Satan was so important.

So what God does when we are saved is not only credit Christ's atoning death to our account, but also credit Jesus' perfect righteousness to our account. The former takes away our sin, and the latter clothes us with Christ's righteousness so that when God looks at us now, He sees not our sin but the perfection of His Son.

Paul called this putting on Christ (see Romans 13:14), and he described salvation as "put[ting] on the new self, which in the likeness of God has been created in righteousness and holiness of the truth" (Ephesians 4:24). This righteousness is absolutely necessary for us to enter heaven, because God is not going to allow the smallest hint of unrighteousness to spoil His heaven.

The truth of Christ's righteousness being applied to us is crucial support for the doctrine of security. If we are not only in Christ as believers but also clothed with His righteousness, for God to turn us away would mean canceling the credit that Christ earned for us by His life and death. It would be as if the Father suddenly turned down the credit of His Son. You are secure not only because Christ took away your sin, but because He gave you His perfect righteousness.

Jesus' Intercession Keeps Us

Everything we have talked about to this point applies to Christ's life on earth prior to His death. But He is also alive from the dead today and ministering on our behalf in heaven to keep us saved. The writer of Hebrews said:

The former priests [under the old system], on the one hand, existed in greater numbers because they were prevented by death from continuing, but Jesus, on the other hand, because He continues forever, holds His priesthood permanently. Therefore He is able also to *save forever* those who draw near to God through Him, since He always lives to make intercession for them. (7:23–25, italics added)

This is one of the many references in Hebrews and other parts of the New Testament to the high priestly ministry of Jesus Christ in heaven today. You may be wondering why you still need Jesus to intercede for you in heaven today if He has already forgiven your sins and you are on your way to heaven.

There are several reasons that Jesus' priestly intercession is necessary for us today. One reason relates to the passage we noted above referring to Jesus as our understanding and sympathetic High Priest (Hebrews 4). If Jesus had gone back to heaven and simply detached Himself from everything on earth until His return, you and I would not have a merciful and faithful High Priest we could call on in times of need. Don't ever think you are pulling off this thing called the Christian life on your own. Jesus keeps us by His present life and ministry of intercession before the Father on our behalf.

There's another way in which Christ's life in heaven today saves us. This has to do with His role as our Advocate or defense attorney before the Father. "My little children, I am writing these things to you so that you may not sin. And if anyone sins, we have an Advocate with the Father, Jesus Christ the righteous" (1 John 2:1). We have discussed this before, so let me just review it here, because it's an exciting verification of our security.

The reason we need Jesus to defend us is that Satan is our accuser (see Revelation 12:10). The devil's self-appointed job is to bring our many sins and failures before God in the court of heaven to see if he can get our salvation reversed, so to speak, and get our acquittal in Christ overturned.

It's not as if Satan doesn't have any evidence to work with, because we sin and fail God every day. But every time Satan shows up as our accuser and prosecutor, Jesus shows up as our Defender, opens the Book of Life, and reminds the Father that our sins have been paid for and that we are clothed in His perfect righteousness.

In fact, Satan's case doesn't stand a chance anyway because heaven's courtroom is stacked in our favor. The Judge is our Father, and the Defender is the Judge's well-beloved Son and our elder Brother. My family owns the court!

Staying with the courtroom analogy for a minute, the only way you and I could have our salvation overturned is if our Defender either failed to prove His case, or if His sacrificial death and right-eous life were no longer allowed to be admitted as evidence that we belong to Him. That means God the Father would have to throw out His Son's work, which is an absurdity not even worth mention-ing. You are saved and secure forever because Jesus Christ lived a perfect life that perfectly satisfied God's righteous demands, then died on the cross to pay for your sins and lives today to argue your case in heaven and keep you saved.

The story is told of a man in Europe who owned a Rolls Royce. The rear axle broke one day and the man called the Rolls Royce com-pany in England. He was instructed to ship the car to England, where it was repaired before being returned to him. When the man did not receive a bill for some time, he called to inquire about the situa-tion. But he received a great surprise when the Rolls Royce repre-sentative told him, "We have no record of a Rolls Royce with this problem."

If a car manufacturer will go to this length to protect its good name and reputation, how much more will God do to protect His name by securing those whom He has saved?

THE
PROTECTION
OF
ETERNAL SECURITY

One business that has been popular for a long time, especially in large urban areas like Dallas, is home security. A number of companies will come to your home and install any one of a variety of systems to protect your home from intruders.

One telltale sign of a home security system in our part of the country is the dark screens that cover a home's windows and are wired to the alarm system. The doors are also usually wired to detect any tampering or opening, and the system is usually monitored twenty-four hours a day by a person at the security company. The family chooses a password to give to the security company in case the company has to call the house to see if there's a problem. The company will even put a little sign in your yard announcing to any would-be troublemaker that your house is secured and monitored.

These security companies are marketing something intangible yet very real to people—protection. Some folk are willing to pay a lot of money because they don't want to feel insecure and unprotected in their homes. And since the September 11, 2001, terrorist attacks the issue of how to protect ourselves has become part of our national dialogue.

When it comes to protection, I have good news for you if you are a believer in Jesus Christ. God doesn't want you to feel insecure in His house as a member of His family either. In fact, security systems that afford protection are nothing new. God devised the first security system before the universe was created when He drew up the plan of salvation in eternity past. We have seen that each member of the Trinity was involved in delivering salvation to the human race, and we have spent a considerable amount of time discussing the roles that God the Father and God the Son play in the divine drama of salvation.

The Holy Spirit also plays a key role in salvation as the One who convicts us of sin and the truth of the gospel and implants the life of Christ in us through the miracle of regeneration (see chapter 6). I want to discuss two other ministries of the Holy Spirit relative to salvation because they are crucial to the security system God designed to protect and ensure our redemption. These are the Spirit's work in the baptism and sealing of every believer.

THE SPIRIT'S WORK OF BAPTISM

If you want to get a lively discussion going among a group of Christians, bring up the subject of the baptism of the Holy Spirit. Just mentioning the subject in today's Christian circles invites controversy, because if you get four people together you'll have five opinions about the nature and significance of the Holy Spirit's baptism. The fundamental statement of the Spirit's work in baptism is found in 1 Corinthians 12:13, where Paul wrote: "For by one Spirit we were all baptized into one body, whether Jews or Greeks, whether slaves or free, and we were all made to drink of one Spirit."

Every Christian Is Baptized

Now whatever the baptism of the Spirit consists of, it is something that every believer has experienced. That fact alone refutes the idea that Spirit baptism is a further work of grace that we seek after salvation, usually to be accompanied by special outward manifestations such as speaking in tongues.

My purpose here is not to debate the issue of baptism and tongues, so let me just make two observations before we move on. First, those who teach the necessity of tongues in Spirit baptism point to the several occasions in Acts when people who received the Holy Spirit spoke in tongues. Second, the problem with building our doctrine on events in the book of Acts is that Acts is a transitional book between the old and new covenants, recording many one-of-a-kind experiences. Once the Holy Spirit was given in fulfillment of Jesus' promise, the Spirit did not need to be given again and again.

Besides, we have Paul's clear statement that the Spirit's baptism is an accomplished fact for all Christians (both verbs in 1 Corinthians 12:13 are past tense). It is the Spirit's ministry by which He places a believer into the body of Christ at salvation. The Spirit's baptism is universal and equally applied to all believers. As a matter of fact, anyone who has not been baptized by the Holy Spirit is not saved.

Baptism Identifies Us with Christ

The key thought behind the doctrine of baptism in the New Testament is that of complete identification and unity with Christ. The Spirit's baptism of a new believer into the body of Christ identifies that believer with Christ and brings him or her into an organic union with Christ (Galatians 3:27–29). The church practices water baptism as an outward symbol of the inward spiritual reality that takes place when we are born again.

The Bible gives us a great picture of how this identification with

Christ in baptism takes place. In Romans 6:1–6, Paul rebuked the erroneous thinking that since God's grace continues to flow, we should sin more because it's all covered by grace.

After putting that bad idea to rest, the apostle wrote:

> Do you not know that all of us who have been baptized into Christ Jesus have been baptized into His death? Therefore we have been buried with Him through baptism into death, so that as Christ was raised from the dead through the glory of the Father, so we too might walk in newness of life. For if we have become united with Him in the likeness of His death, certainly we shall also be in the likeness of His resurrection. (Romans 6:3–5)

When we are immersed as believers in the waters of baptism, this symbolizes our identity with Christ in His death and burial. And when we come up out of the water, we are identifying with Christ in His resurrection. We are united with Him eternally and inseparably because everything that happened to Christ happened to us. In baptism we symbolically died with Christ and were raised with Him. Just in case there is any doubt, Paul continued: "Our old self was crucified with [Christ]" (Romans 6:6).

And not only are we buried and raised with Christ, but we also ascended into heaven with Him and are now seated with Him "in the heavenly places" (Ephesians 2:6). This is all possible because "the one who joins himself to the Lord is one spirit with Him" (1 Corinthians 6:17). As we said before, in the mind of God all true believers are already with Him in heaven (see Ephesians 2:6). That's about as secure and protected as our salvation can get. God is way beyond worrying about whether our salvation is assured, and we should be way beyond that too.

We Are United Forever with Christ

Our baptism into Christ by the Holy Spirit creates a new union so indivisible that God can already tell us what we are going to experience in the future with Christ. For example, the Bible says that we will be "revealed with Him in glory" (Colossians 3:4). According to 1 Corinthians 15:51, we will be changed when Christ returns. And in 2 Corinthians 4:14 we are told that God will raise us up with Jesus.

I like to illustrate this truth by using the analogy of a letter in the mail. If I have a letter I want to send, I first place or "baptize" the letter into an envelope. Now my letter is no longer an independent entity floating around by itself. It is joined to the envelope. And when I moisten the glue on the flap of the envelope and close it, I have sealed the letter inside the envelope. It is now secure and no one can open it except the person whose name is on the envelope. Then I address the envelope and put sufficient postage on it to ensure its arrival at its intended destination.

But there's more. My letter is backed by a postal system that has a tremendous network of technology and people to make sure that my letter is delivered to the proper address. This system even has security people whose job it is to make sure that no one messes with my letter on the way to its destination.

And on top of all this, I can register my letter to ensure even greater security in seeing that it reaches its destination. That's because a registered letter is monitored and tracked every step of the way, and you can be sure it's being protected and its contents are secured against tampering.

When you believed in Jesus Christ as your Savior, God placed you inside the envelope called Jesus Christ. You were baptized into Christ and sealed in Him with the "glue" of the Holy Spirit, and you don't have to worry about reaching your intended destination of heaven because Christ paid the price necessary to get you there. Your letter has all the postage it will ever need.

Since God owns the postal service that's designed to take you to heaven, and since everybody who works in His postal service has to obey God the Postmaster, He can guarantee you that the delivery will be made. And to ensure you even further, God registered you in the Lamb's Book of Life in heaven so He knows where you are at every moment on the way.

Because God is the only Person who is qualified to open the envelope with you in it because you are in Christ and sealed by the Holy Spirit, your safe delivery to heaven is as good as done already. Jesus paid the price to send you to heaven, so you can go to sleep tonight and let God's system take care of your arrival at God's intended destination for you.

THE SPIRIT'S WORK OF SEALING

One reason that genuine believers tend to doubt their salvation is that we don't receive all of it at once. Our full redemption is "reserved in heaven for [us]" (1 Peter 1:4). Until then, "We ourselves, having the first fruits of the Spirit, even we ourselves groan within ourselves, waiting eagerly for our adoption as sons, the redemption of our body" (Romans 8:23). The salvation we enjoy is just a small taste of the glory we will share with Christ in heaven.

But in the meantime, we have to live in this sin-ruined world in these sin-contaminated bodies. God has given us "His precious and magnificent promises" (2 Peter 1:4) concerning the certainty of our salvation and future glory, but being human we can forget these and begin to doubt ourselves and even God.

The Holy Spirit Is Our Down Payment

So what God has done is give us a down payment on His promises, a pledge or a reminder that our redemption is secure and will be consummated someday. This down payment is described in Ephesians as the sealing of the Holy Spirit: "In Him, you also, after listening to the message of truth, the gospel of your salvation— having also believed, you were sealed in Him with the Holy Spirit of promise, who is given as a pledge of our inheritance, with a view to the redemption of God's own possession, to the praise of His glory" (1:13–14).

When you were saved, the Holy Spirit not only baptized you into the body of Christ, but the Spirit Himself became your seal, protecting and guaranteeing your salvation forever. A seal in the ancient world referred to the wax with which a letter or other important document would be sealed. The king or official would press his signet ring into the hot wax, meaning that this document now bore his mark and his authority. Anyone who messed with that seal could lose his life.

The Holy Spirit's presence in our lives is our witness that God will fulfill all His promises. We know how a pledge or down payment works. It's a promise that the purchaser will pay the full price and take ownership of the property or whatever is being bought. God does not want His children to doubt either His capability or His willingness to redeem those whom He has purchased for Himself at the cost of His Son's life.

The Holy Spirit Is Our Protection

A seal also indicated protection because no one dared break it except the person whose insignia was in the wax or his duly authorized representative. This aspect of sealing is illustrated in Revelation 7:1–8, where God seals the 144,000 who are His special Jewish evangelists in the Tribulation period. God's seal is necessary for their protection because the Antichrist and his demonic forces are going to do everything they can to silence the witness of these evangelists. But God's seal protects them until their ministry is complete, and in Revelation 14:1 we find these same 144,000 in heaven with God. Not one of them was lost.

We Are Sealed for God

God's seal also represents ownership. When the Holy Spirit takes up His residence in our hearts at salvation, one of His ministries is to testify to us that we belong to God. "The Spirit Himself testifies with our spirit that we are children of God" (Romans 8:16). And because we are His children, God takes responsibility for our future. "Now He who establishes us with you in Christ and anointed us is

God, who also sealed us and gave us the Spirit in our hearts as a pledge" (2 Corinthians 1:21–22). If God promises to establish you and redeem your body someday, who can "un-establish" you?

If you belong to Jesus Christ, you are identified, marked, protected, and purchased by God for all eternity, and you have the Holy Spirit as a guarantee that every promise God made you will come to pass. Let me give you one more reason to rejoice, because a seal also signifies approval.

We Have God's "Seal of Approval"

Jesus said that God the Father had "set His seal" on Jesus (see John 6:27), meaning that Jesus and His ministry had God's "Good Housekeeping Seal of Approval." God the Father approved of everything His Son said and did, and the Father has pledged to make good on every promise Jesus gave us.

If God's seal signifies His approval, what does that say about our having the Holy Spirit's seal on us? It says that God has approved of us too—not because of who we are, but because He approves of Christ and we are in Christ. So as far as your salvation is concerned, you can sit back and sing, "Blessed assurance, Jesus is mine! O what a foretaste of glory divine!"

And by the way, you don't have to worry about God breaking His seal and withdrawing His approval, because we have been sealed with the Spirit "for the day of redemption" (Ephesians 4:30). Your seal is permanent until Jesus comes to complete your salvation.

We Belong to God

While you're rejoicing, let me also remind you of a responsibility we have as sealed believers. If God's seal means ownership, who owns our lives? Not us, but the One who bought us. We forget sometimes that we belong to God body and soul, which can lead us not only into doubt but into sin.

The first half of Ephesians 4:30 says, "Do not grieve the Holy

Spirit of God." And Paul asks this pointed question: "Do you not know that your body is a temple of the Holy Spirit who is in you, whom you have from God, and that you are not your own? For you have been bought with a price: therefore glorify God in your body" (1 Corinthians 6:19–20).

Somebody may say, "But, Tony, it's so hard to see heaven and experience the joy of salvation when I'm having such a hard time down here on earth." Then you've forgotten who lives inside you. Through the Holy Spirit, heaven has now been deposited within you . . . and you haven't seen anything yet! Pick your most joyful day as a saint, and it fades into nothing compared to the joy of heaven. Get your eyes off yourself and your circumstances and focus them on Christ.

We Have God's Engagement Ring

There is so much wrapped up in the Bible's teaching that the Spirit is our seal guaranteeing full redemption. I want to come back to the idea of the Spirit as a pledge, promise, or down payment because there is more truth to be mined here.

Perhaps the most enduring illustration of this that we know on earth is the engagement ring a man gives a woman he intends to marry. This ring is both a promise and a down payment of the good things that are to come, as well as a pledge that the man is committing himself to this woman for life.

Now if the guy is working this thing right and if he can afford it, he takes his girl to a nice restaurant with violins playing in the background and glowing candles, and at the right moment he looks into her eyes and says, "I want to spend the rest of my life with you. I want to be with you and love you forever. Will you marry me?"

What would a woman normally expect to happen next, assuming that she says yes? She expects the man to open up a little box, take out the engagement ring he has impoverished himself to buy for her, and put it on her finger as a pledge of his intentions to marry her and love her for the rest of his life.

That engagement ring means a number of things. It means this couple's love relationship has really just gotten underway. It means that there is a lot more to come. Everything about an engagement ring speaks of a promise to be fulfilled at a later date, because the woman doesn't even receive the wedding ring until the engagement is consummated on her wedding day.

In other words, the engagement ring is just a foretaste of the good things to come. The prospective groom is holding the wedding ring in reserve until he fulfills his promise and redeems his bride at the wedding ceremony. Likewise, the Holy Spirit's presence within us is a promise and a foretaste of good things to come.

I love this idea of a foretaste. You see, when a man gives his true love an engagement ring, he ought to be saying, "Baby, even though we don't have all of each other yet, what I am going to do during our engagement period is shower you with so much love and so much caring and so much commitment that it will give you a foretaste of what it will be like when we're together for the rest of our lives. I want to show you all the good things that are in store for you because of my love and commitment to you."

Now let's back up a minute. If a man proposes to a woman, and she accepts, but then all he does is say "Great" with no intention of giving her a symbol of his promise to forsake all others and love her only, what would that woman think? She would have every right to doubt the sincerity of his proposal and his promise. The engagement ring serves a very important purpose in the period leading up to marriage.

Once a prospective groom has pledged his love and sealed it with a ring, he has a right to start talking with his bride-to-be about their future life together. He can tell her all about the home he is going to provide for her one day and his plans for business and a family. They can talk about all the things they are looking forward to when they're together for the rest of their lives.

Human beings can't always fulfill their promises perfectly, of course, and we don't always keep our commitments. But God doesn't have that problem. When He gave us the Holy Spirit as a pledge of our coming inheritance, we can be sure that He will provide all the good things He has promised us. God is saying to us, "When I saved you, I gave you a pledge of My commitment because I want you to be My bride. You belong to Me, and even though we are not together yet in heaven, I will come for you and fulfill all My promises to you."

And just as an engaged man does everything he can to confirm and display his love to his intended bride during the engagement period, so God gives us foretastes and glimpses of heaven. The Christian life is not just "pie in the sky, by and by." Every time the Holy Spirit reveals more of Christ to you, brings you joy in the middle of a severe trial, or gives you the peace of assurance that you are saved and secured in Christ, you are getting a taste of heaven. It should make you look forward to the marriage ceremony.

We Have God's Miracle Seal

I recently saw a television advertisement for some kind of "miracle seal" system that guarantees no spoilage for your vegetables or other foods when they are sealed in the bag.

When God saved you, He sealed you with the "Holy Ghost Miracle Seal." You have been given the Third Person of the Trinity to save and secure you forever. Nobody can cancel your engagement or break God's seal on your heart.

① 22

THE
POWER
OF
ETERNAL SECURITY

When I travel to fulfill a speaking or other engagement, my assistant, Sylvia, or the host organization usually makes hotel reservations well in advance. Someone makes a payment by credit card or the room charge is automatically billed to a certain account, and I receive a confirmation number that assures me that the desired transaction has been made and a hotel room will be ready for me when the appointed day comes and I arrive in town.

A number of things may happen between the time that the reservation is made and the day it is realized. I may have days when I either forget that a certain hotel reservation has been made for a certain date or even doubt that the reservation is still in force. But if that happens, all I have to do is pull out my confirmation and see that everything is still in order for the trip because the price was paid to guarantee my room.

So even if I'm having a bad day or not behaving myself, it does not affect my reservation because the payment was made. When you accepted Jesus Christ He made a reservation for you in heaven. And to pay for your reservation, God paid the price of the precious blood of Jesus Christ.

Now of course, no human system is perfect and things can still get messed up. The computer system at the hotel where I'm supposed to be staying six months from now may crash and lose all its reservation data, or the desk clerk may have keyed in the information inaccurately. But if you belong to Jesus Christ, God has a reservation waiting for you in heaven that nothing on earth can mess up or cancel. True believers in Christ are as sure of heaven today as if they had been there ten thousand years.

How do I know that? Because two thousand years ago Jesus told us about the reservation He has made for His people. He even gave us a confirmation that's as good as His character. "This is the will of Him who sent Me, that of all that He has given me I lose nothing, but raise it up on the last day" (John 6:39). As far as Jesus is concerned, our "last day" reservation in heaven is confirmed. And just to make sure we don't misunderstand, Jesus said the same thing three more times in the same discourse: "I will raise him up on the last day" (vv. 40, 44, 54).

THE CERTAINTY OF GOD'S SECURING POWER

A hotel reservation, like all plans that we make for the future, is really a promise that certain things will happen at a certain time. Political candidates may make election promises that they have every intention of keeping. The problem is that they don't always have the clout to bring their promises into being, or they are unable to control circumstances that make the fulfillment of their promises impossible. You may remember former president George Bush's famous pledge: "Read my lips: no new taxes." But later he had to agree to a tax increase and try to control the resulting political damage.

The difference between our plans and promises and God's plans and promises is that He has the power to pull off every promise He makes. People have good intentions, but God has all-encompassing power. This is why I don't try to convince people to believe they are secure in Christ based on the persuasiveness of my argument. God has the power and ability to witness to their hearts that they are His children.

I have more good news for you. God is not running for election. He has already won. He is King of kings and Lord of lords, and He cannot be unseated or defeated, so He can control any person or any circumstance necessary to ensure that His promises come to pass. He's not dependent on advisory cabinets or on majorities in the House or Senate. He doesn't make decisions after reading the latest opinion polls.

God answers to no one but Himself, so you need to know that when God makes a promise to deliver every one of His children through this life and into heaven, you can rest your eternal destiny on His promise. If even one part of one of God's promises fell to the ground, He would not be the sovereign God we worship and in whom we trust for eternal life.

But the Bible affirms, "You know in all your hearts and in all your souls that not one word of all the good words which the Lord your God spoke concerning you has failed; all have been fulfilled for you, not one of them has failed" (Joshua 23:14). It would indeed be tragic if God had to attend a Promise Keepers convention to be reminded to keep His promises.

THE PURPOSE OF GOD'S SECURING POWER

God is going to deliver you safely to heaven because He has invested too much in you to let you fall away and be lost. God has a lot more at stake in this salvation business than we do. It cost Him everything to save us, and His character and integrity are on the line in His promise to glorify every believer whom He has predestined, called, and justified (see Romans 8:30).

God's purpose in securing His people is clearly stated in the opening verses of 1 Peter. The apostle addressed his letter to those "who are chosen according to the foreknowledge of God the Father, by the sanctifying work of the Spirit, to obey Jesus Christ and be sprinkled with His blood" (1:1–2). To these elect saints Peter said:

> Blessed be the God and Father of our Lord Jesus Christ, who according to His great mercy has caused us to be born again to a living hope through the resurrection of Jesus Christ from the dead, to obtain an inheritance which is imperishable and undefiled and will not fade away, reserved in heaven for you. (vv. 3–4)

Our Inheritance Is Incredible

These verses contain some wonderful descriptions of our inheritance, which is another way of talking about our salvation. It's a living hope because Jesus Christ rose from the dead never to die or perish again, which makes our inheritance imperishable. *Imperishable* applies to something that is not subject to decay and cannot be spoiled. There is nothing else in life you can say that about.

I got an expensive reminder of that truth not too long ago when I had some repair work done to our house. We have a lot of foundation problems in Texas because the soil is unstable and shifts back and forth. It's not unusual for cracks to appear in walls and over doors. My problem was that the patio had developed a crack.

The repairman assured me that after he redid the patio by putting in the new concrete and reinforcements I would no longer have any problem whatsoever with the patio. I believed him so much that I paid him to do the job.

Everything was fine for a while. But then I went outside one day and saw a black line running across the patio. It looked like someone had taken a marker and drawn a line across the surface. Unfortunately, it wasn't a marker but a crack. I cut my finger on it when I bent down and rubbed the line to see what it was. The "imperishable" concrete on my patio proved to be all too perishable, so I picked up my phone and called the repairman to tell him the bad news. Thankfully, his telephone number had not perished in the meantime.

Having a hope in heaven that cannot perish suggests security to me. So does Peter's description of our inheritance as "undefiled." This means it cannot be affected by contamination or stain or pollution. This is the other side of the coin because defilement has to do with what enters from outside, while perishable refers to decay that arises from within. Nothing from the inside or the outside can destroy our salvation—and since those are the only two sides that matter, that pretty well settles the matter.

This salvation and inheritance in heaven we have received from God also "will not fade away" (1 Peter 1:4). This means it won't lose its luster over time. What else on earth can make that claim? We are certainly fading away in our outer person, as anyone can verify by looking in the mirror day after day. That black hair is fading to gray, or maybe fading away altogether! That smooth, youthful complexion is developing some lines and cracks like my patio because we're all fading away. And that spring in the step has turned into a creak for some of us, because nothing on earth is designed to be permanent except our salvation.

But our salvation is as fresh and new today as the day we received it, and it will stay fresh for all eternity. I'm reminded that Jesus said the treasures we lay up in heaven will not be affected by moths or rust or thieves (see Matthew 6:20). It would seem odd for Him to urge us to lay up these treasures if there was a chance we might not make it to heaven to claim them.

Our Salvation Is Reserved for Us

Peter also referred to the fullness of salvation we will experience when we see Christ because our inheritance is "reserved in heaven for [us]" (1 Peter 1:4). The salvation that Christ purchased and secured for His own is being stored up in heaven for us. Paul said it so well: "I know whom I have believed and I am convinced that He is able to guard what I have entrusted to Him until that day" (2 Timothy 1:12). Notice that the One who is guarding our inheritance is the One we have believed in, who is Jesus Christ.

One thing that will help you grasp the security you have in Christ is the simple reminder that, as the old chorus says, "This world is not my home, I'm just a passin' through." We have sung that song in our churches for years without stopping to think that it is a great affirmation of eternal security. We discussed this point in the previous chapter, so we'll leave it there.

We Are Reserved for Our Salvation

The Bible also affirms that we are being reserved for our salvation. Peter continued talking about the greatness and the security of our salvation by saying that we are "protected by the power of God through faith for a salvation ready to be revealed in the last time" (1 Peter 1:5). The word *protected* is a military concept that pictures a garrison on guard to protect a city against the enemy.

Verses 4–5 form a strong one-two punch for the truth of eternal security. Verse 4 refers to that which is being reserved, while verse 5 has to do with the people who are being reserved. Verse 4 is all about the inheritance, while verse 5 speaks of the heirs. Verse 4 assures us that a reservation has been made in heaven. Verse 5 assures us that the reservation is in our name. God is saying to us in every way possible that He is not going to let anything happen to us or to our inheritance until He brings the two together in heaven.

THE POWER OF BEING IN GOD'S HANDS

There is power in the blood of Jesus Christ to save and keep His own. Jesus Himself had some very important words to say about the security of those who belong to Him. One of the most notable passages is in John 10, a tremendous chapter in which Jesus assured His followers that as the Good Shepherd, He knows His own sheep.

The particular text I want to focus on is John 10:19–30, but earlier in the chapter Jesus gave us a great word picture of His power to save and guard His sheep. "I am the door of the sheep. . . . If

anyone enters through Me, he will be saved, and will go in and out
and find pasture. The thief comes only to steal and kill and destroy;
I came that they may have life, and have it abundantly" (vv. 7, 9–10).
Note the contrast between any intruder who would try to harm one
of Christ's sheep and His assurance that they will find salvation and
life in Him.

Jesus' teaching on this occasion sparked disagreement among
His hearers, and John records that the Jews came to Jesus and asked,
"How long will You keep us in suspense? If You are the Christ, tell
us plainly" (John 10:24). Jesus' answer to those who rejected Him
led to the great statements on security for which John 10 is noted:

> I told you, and you do not believe; the works that I do in My Father's
> name, these testify of Me. But you do not believe because you are not
> of My sheep. My sheep hear My voice, and I know them, and they
> follow Me; and I give eternal life to them, and they will never perish;
> and no one will snatch them out of My hand. My Father, who has given
> them to Me, is greater than all; and no one is able to snatch them out
> of the Father's hand. (vv. 25–29)

We Are Doubly Secure

If we were having church right now, somebody ought to be praising God. In fact, it's OK to stop and praise God right now, wherever you are! Look at all that comes with the "sheep package" when
you belong to Jesus Christ. You are given eternal life as a gift of His
grace, and then you are promised that you will never perish. Peter
must have been taking notes in the background, because he used
the same root word for *perish* in the verses we just studied from
1 Peter.

If Jesus had stopped with the promise that no one can snatch His
sheep out of His hand, it would have been enough. But He doubled
the security by adding that He and His Father are both holding on
to their sheep. What a tremendous picture of the Trinity's work on
your behalf to make sure that you never perish. Jesus underscored

His Father's full agreement that not one believer will be lost when He added, "I and the Father are one" (John 10:30). This is truth you can rest your life and your eternity on.

After the September 11, 2001, terrorist attacks, security in a number of places all over the country was doubled and even more. Suddenly, we began to see uniformed officers and troops everywhere, including places like the sidewalks in front of buildings, in airports, and other locations where they had never been seen before in such force.

That's a small sample of the kind of security Jesus was talking about here. Can you imagine anyone, including Satan, who is the "thief" of John 10:10, slipping something past Jesus and the Father and coming in to steal, kill, or destroy you? It will never happen.

This double security that the Father and Son provide reminds me of a safety deposit box at the bank. That fireproof box is securely locked, but just to make sure no one tampers with the valuables inside, the box is placed inside a vault behind a very heavy steel door.

Now when you rent a safety deposit box, by definition you are trusting the safety of those valuables to the bank. You are putting something of great worth to you into the hands of your bank and saying, "Keep all of this safe for me until it's time to use it or take it somewhere else."

You can see where I'm going with this. When you received Christ, you placed your eternity into the hands of God the Father and God the Son for safekeeping until Jesus returns for you. Jesus chose the imagery of hands for good reason, because whenever you read about the hand or hands of God in the Bible, you're reading about His power (see Deuteronomy 26:8 and Jeremiah 21:5 for just two of many examples).

I know that we sing about the importance of holding on to God's hand, but that's not a reference to our salvation. We hold on to His hand in the sense of drawing strength and courage and comfort from Him. But when it comes to who is holding whom in terms of eternal security, the issue is not whether we're holding on to God so we won't fall. He is doing all the holding here.

We Have No Danger of Falling

I was walking with my granddaughter Cariss one winter day. It was icy and we had to be careful how we walked along. Cariss and I were holding hands, but she felt the slipperiness of the ice and said to me "Poppy, hold my hand."

I said, "Cariss, I am holding your hand."

"No, Poppy," she said, "I'm holding *your* hand. I don't want to hold your hand. I want you to hold *my* hand."

What she was saying, of course, was that she wanted to make sure I was doing my part in this hand-holding deal because I am a lot bigger and stronger than she. Cariss was worried that if avoiding a fall was up to her, she might slip. But if I held her hand, she wouldn't have to worry about falling. I can assure you that I was holding my granddaughter's hand firmly and was already watching to make sure she didn't fall.

We smile at the things kids say and the way they interpret the world through their childish eyes. But don't we do the same thing sometimes in our relationship with God? The Bible never exhorts you to hold on to God as tightly as you can lest you slip. Jesus said, "I am holding your hand, and no one can make you fall."

It makes a great deal of difference in whose hands you place your trust. Put a basketball in my hands, and you get a fair game. But put a basketball in Michael Jordan's hands and you get three championships in a row—on two different occasions! A golf club in my hands is a dangerous weapon, but let Tiger Woods wrap his hands around a golf club, and you rewrite the history of the game.

If keeping ourselves saved was in our hands, we'd mess it up for sure. But if we put our security in God's hands, it's a completely different story. Now we can talk about heaven as our home as though we were already there.

I love the phrases "no one will snatch" and "no one is able to snatch" of John 10:28–29. No one includes every "someone" in the universe. That means neither the devil nor any of his legions of fallen angels can take you out of your Father's hands. You can't even take yourself out of God's hands, because you are also a someone who is part of the "no one" of John 10. We've said it before, but it needs to be emphasized again. Instead of living in fear that you might mess up and slip from God's grasp, get on with loving and serving Him with all of your being, and He will minister assurance to your heart.

Let's face it. If we could forfeit our salvation, most of us would already be in deep trouble because of things we have said and done. You may feel as if you're holding God's hand but He isn't holding yours, but that's not the case. Both the Father and the Son are committed to your security.

The best antidote for worry and insecurity is commitment to Christ. I believe that the folk who have the most trouble serving God and who constantly worry about their security are those who don't really understand all that Christ has done for them. If He has promised never to let us go, who are we to tell Him we don't really believe Him? If we understand how much we are loved, returning that love will not be a chore or duty, but the delight and the consuming passion of our lives.

23

THE PERSEVERANCE OF ETERNAL SECURITY

A lot of great music is being written today for the church, but we still have a lot to learn from the classic hymns of the faith and the lives of the people who wrote them. A nineteenth-century British hymn writer named Frances Havergal is a good example.

Havergal was born in 1836 and only lived forty-two years, but she wrote a number of hymns. Perhaps the best remembered today is the classic, "Take My Life and Let It Be." For Frances Havergal, the words of this hymn were more than a collection of lines that rhymed.

Two of the lines that Havergal wrote had particular meaning to this dedicated Christian woman. "Take my voice, and let me sing always, only, for my King" was her response to the musical gifts God had given her. Havergal was trained as a concert soloist, and it was said that her talent could have brought her worldly fame. But her commitment was to sing only for her Savior and His glory.

Another line in this great hymn says, "Take my silver and my gold; not a mite would I withhold." At one point in her life, Havergal gave nearly fifty pieces of her jewelry to her church's missionary society to be sold and the money used to help reach the lost. Havergal later said she never had so much joy in packing a box. She didn't have to make such an extravagant gift, but it came from the heart of a person who could not get over the fact that God had given her such a great salvation.

We've said a lot about this great salvation and what it means to be totally saved. The Bible is clear that what God wants from His children is a life of faithfulness in gratitude for what He has given us. And the Bible is equally clear that God desires to reward His children when they are faithful to Him.

These are the two points or topics with which I want to conclude our study of eternal security in this chapter and the next. They're also a good place to end the book, because I want to leave you with a charge and an encouragement to give all of yourself without reservation to Jesus Christ for as long as you live. To put it in theological terms, perseverance is the appropriate response to grace. We should desire to live a life that is pleasing to the One who has granted us such a great gift.

THE IMPORTANCE OF PERSEVERANCE

In 2 Timothy 2:12, the apostle Paul made a very important statement about the great value of our endurance or perseverance in the faith: "If we endure, we will also reign with Him [Jesus Christ]." We've dealt with this verse and the crucial passage of which it is a part, so let me remind you that it deals with reward or the loss thereof in heaven, not the loss of salvation. The principle being taught is that the degree of our eternal reward depends on our faithfulness to Christ.

What It Means to Be an Heir

That's why the Bible has so much to say about remaining true to Christ, particularly in times of trial. Peter wrote to believers who were enduring a "fiery ordeal," and told them, "To the degree that you share the sufferings of Christ, keep on rejoicing, so that also at the revelation of His glory you may rejoice with exultation" (1 Peter 4:12–13).

Here's Paul on the same subject: "The Spirit Himself testifies with our spirit that we are children of God, and if children, heirs also, heirs of God and fellow heirs with Christ, if indeed we suffer with Him so that we may also be glorified with Him" (Romans 8:16–17).

Did you notice the conditional clauses in both of these passages? According to Peter, the degree to which we will exult in heaven, another way of saying the degree to which we will be honored and rewarded, is tied to the measure of our sharing in Christ's sufferings. Paul said that all children of God are heirs in terms of salvation, but the only ones who are "fellow heirs" are those who suffer with Christ.

There is a major difference between being a son or daughter and being an heir. This is true in many families. In our family, my oldest son, Anthony, is designated as the primary heir according to the biblical pattern, because in God's economy the oldest son was responsible to care for his parents in their old age and to carry on the family's legacy. The oldest son had more responsibility, so he was allotted more of the family inheritance.

But we also have a provision in our will that applies not only to Anthony, but to the other three children too. If any of them ceases to live a consistent Christian life and brings reproach on Christ, the will changes and that child forfeits his or her inheritance. Anthony and my other children are my children by birth, but they are my heirs by faithfulness. Their inheritance is a reward they must prove themselves worthy of receiving, because I don't want to turn our family legacy over to someone who is going to waste and destroy it.

The conditional statements made to believers in Scripture function in much the same way as the conditional clause in my will. That is, they have to do with our reward or inheritance. For instance, "Whatever you do, do your work heartily, as for the Lord rather than for men, knowing that from the Lord you will receive the reward of the inheritance. It is the Lord Christ whom you serve" (Colossians 3:23–24). In contrast, when the Bible speaks about the condition for salvation the language is very different. Jesus said, "He who has believed and has been baptized shall be saved; but he who has disbelieved shall be condemned" (Mark 16:16).

The Greatness of Our Reward

Jesus also had a lot to say about our service for Him and the reward it brings. One of the most concise summaries of His teaching on this subject is found in the Sermon on the Mount (Matthew 6:1–21). In verses 1–18, the Lord taught us how to do our giving, our praying, and our fasting in a way that honors Him and brings His reward. Two choices and a principle are given in each case.

The choices relate to our motivation for service. In each of the three cases He cited, Jesus made the contrast between the way "the hypocrites" serve and the way His people should serve. The former give with a big show "so that they may be honored by men" (v. 2); they pray in public "so that they may be seen by men" (v. 5); and they make their fasting obvious "so that they will be noticed by men" (v. 16). Notice that their reward in each case is commensurate with their goal. They receive human acclaim, but that's all the reward they get.

What a contrast to the kind of service that brings God's approval and His reward. Doing our service "in secret" (vv. 4, 6, 18) doesn't mean that we can't put our offering in the plate at church for fear that someone will see it, or that we should never engage in public prayer. Jesus was referring to our motive for what we do. If we are serving to please our Father in heaven, we won't worry about whether people notice us or praise us for it because our focus is on God.

It's not that the hypocrites Jesus was talking about go unrewarded. It's just that their reward, human praise and recognition, is so temporary and totally restricted to earth. It makes no impact whatsoever in heaven. That's why Jesus summarized this section of the Sermon on the Mount by saying:

> Do not store up for yourselves treasures on earth, where moth and rust destroy, and where thieves break in and steal. But store up for yourselves treasures in heaven, where neither moth nor rust destroys, and where thieves do not break in or steal; for where your treasure is, there your heart will be also. (Matthew 6:19–21)

I don't know anybody else in town who is offering the kind of eternal security on your deposits that Jesus offers. God is not a slave-driving Master looking to squeeze every ounce of service out of us while returning as little as possible. His rewards are so lavish that we can't even imagine what's stored up for us (see 1 Corinthians 2:9). Trading these for anything less is like Esau trading his birthright for a bowl of food (see Genesis 25:29–34).

The writer of Hebrews used Esau as an illustration of someone who made a very bad spiritual trade (see 12:16–17). Part of the reason that Esau is described as a "godless" and "immoral" person is that he showed his contempt for spiritual things by allowing himself to be ruled by his physical appetites. We are exhorted not to make the same mistake that Esau made in terms of sacrificing the spiritual for the material and the eternal for the temporal (see 1 Corinthians 6:9–10).

THE TEST OF PERSEVERANCE

There is no denying the fact that physical appetites have a strong attraction to our fleshly human nature, just as serving to collect praise and honor has a strong attraction to our human nature. They also offer an immediate payoff for comparatively little effort, in that like the hypocrites of Matthew 6 we get the pat on the back, the award, or our name in the paper, or like Esau we get our hunger satisfied. But afterward the emptiness returns and we start craving more praise or more physical gratification.

The Problem of "Lottery Christians"

It doesn't take much perseverance to reap a temporary earthly reward if that's what you're willing to settle for. But storing up treasures in heaven demands a mind-set of faithfulness that believes God when He says He will reward us for the service we do in His name and His power, and for His glory. The deposits we lay up in heaven are long-term investments, like the deposits people make in their retirement accounts.

The problem with a lot of Christians is that they are looking for the quick return or the big payoff that will bring them the eternal wealth they want without having to put in the time and the faithfulness it takes to build up their heavenly bank accounts.

I call these "lottery Christians." They don't want to work and save over time to get somewhere. They want to buy a one-dollar lottery ticket in the morning and watch television that night in the hope that they will hit the jackpot. They want the winner's van from the publisher's sweepstakes to show up in front of their house.

The opposite of the spiritual "get-rich-quick" mentality is the heart attitude that we are going to serve Christ with faithfulness out of love for Him because of what He has done for us. You may be saying, "Tony, that sounds good, but it's easy to get discouraged when you're trying to serve the Lord faithfully and you aren't seeing much happen or things get tough. How can I develop the kind of perseverance that gets the job done for the long haul?"

You have to take the long view and see the unseen, like the apostle Paul. Here's a passage you ought to memorize:

> Therefore we do not lose heart, but though our outer man is decaying, yet our inner man is being renewed day by day. For momentary, light affliction is producing for us an eternal weight of glory far beyond all comparison, while we look not at the things which are seen, but at the things which are not seen; for the things which are seen are temporal, but the things which are not seen are eternal. (2 Corinthians 4:16–18)

Now don't misunderstand. I'm not saying that if we just get the right spiritual attitude then a life of fruitful, consistent service will flow easily from our lives with no struggles. The interesting thing is that of all of Paul's letters, 2 Corinthians is the most poignant and revealing in terms of Paul's human weakness and struggles. He had "conflicts without, fears within" (2 Corinthians 7:5). But he was able to serve God consistently in spite of his weakness because he had learned how to access God's grace and the power of the Holy Spirit.

The World's False Advertising

You see, the problem is that we have been sold a bill of goods by the world, which tells us that anything worth having can be had now, for three easy installment payments or a few quick lessons.

That's false advertising. As a pastor, one area where I see a lot of the damage that this mentality does is in marriage, which serves as a good illustration of Christian service because the requirements for success in each case are very similar.

Anytime you hear anybody talking about the bliss of marriage with no arguments or differences of opinion or anything like that, you can be sure that one of three things is true: That person is either single, newlywed, or lying. Of course, marriage can be blissful. But anybody who has been married for very long understands that when you bring two people with different personalities, different genders, and different backgrounds together under the same roof, somebody has to do some work to make that marriage successful.

As great as marriage is, it is still a full-time job. The problem today is that everybody wants the smooth relationship without the work it takes to make the relationship successful. Putting it in the terms of salvation and reward, getting married is akin to salvation because it establishes the relationship. But a growing and dynamic marriage is a potential reward of that union, and that has to be earned by dedicated, diligent effort over a period of time.

The Problem of "Big-Play" Christians

I mentioned above the concept of "lottery Christians" who are looking for a quick, easy, and rich payoff. People like this are victims of the world's false advertising. So are "big-play" Christians, to change the analogy for a minute. These are the people who "come off the bench" every so often when there's something special going on in the church and make a splash, then disappear until it's time for their next big play.

I'm borrowing this "big play" terminology from the sports world. In sports there are actually two kinds of "big-play" athletes. Some perform consistently and dependably day in and day out, and when their team needs them to do something extra, they rise to the occasion and deliver the big play.

But the kind of big-play athletes I'm talking about are those who do the job for a quarter or a half, or put up some good numbers in one big game, but they fade away and can't do the job over the long haul of a season or a career. Big-play Christians can bring people to their feet for a moment, but after the applause dies down they disappear.

Too often churches look for big-play people who can make a splash, but the church is built and God's work is advanced by faithful believers who have the long view. I love what Paul said in 1 Corinthians 1:26–27:

> For consider your calling, brethren, that there were not many wise according to the flesh, not many mighty, not many noble; but God has chosen the foolish things of the world to shame the wise, and God has chosen the weak things of the world to shame the things which are strong.

I'm not saying that people who can do a lot in a short time cannot be used of the Lord. No category of people is that airtight. My point is that this is not God's normal way of getting things done. He can do a lot with a little if that little is given to Him in a commitment to daily faithfulness.

That ought to be an encouragement to us, because, let's face it, most of us fit in the category of the foolish and the weak as far as greatness in this world is concerned. You may not be able to bring the crowd to its feet, but you can be faithful and persevere in the place where God has put you.

I'm convinced that the people who will enjoy the greatest reward in heaven are those who didn't give up when the storms came. We'll see in the next chapter that in one of Jesus' most familiar parables about heavenly rewards, the only servant who wasn't commended and rewarded by his master was the one who quit and simply hid what the master had given him (Matthew 25:14–30). We are called to fight the good fight, finish the course, and keep the faith (see 2 Timothy 4:7), not necessarily to win every fight or finish the race ahead of everyone else. God's standard is faithfulness, not greatness (see 1 Corinthians 4:2).

WHEN QUESTIONS COME

What about those times when we are tempted to question our salvation as doubt takes hold of us? The best example I can give you in this case is what John the Baptist did as he languished in prison and began to wonder if Jesus really was the Messiah. John sent two of his disciples to Jesus with the question: "Are You the Expected One, or do we look for someone else?" (Luke 7:19). Jesus demonstrated His power to John's disciples, then sent them back with the unmistakable testimony of His deity (vv. 21–22).

God is not afraid of your questions, so if you're struggling He knows it and you might as well talk to Him about it. Don't hide when you have questions and doubts, because God can deal with them if you'll be honest with Him. Now let me point out that Jesus' answer to John didn't get John out of jail. His circumstances didn't change, but it makes a big difference in trials whether you know that Jesus is the One and you belong to Him, or whether you're not sure. That can make the difference between persevering and giving up.

Now let me turn this issue of questions around and talk about what happens when God has questions to ask of us. God would ask some of us, "I have given you a great salvation and secured your future in heaven. What are you doing with what I've given you?" We've promised God that if He would meet this need or get us out of that tight spot, we would serve Him faithfully. Have you ever done that?

This question of what we are doing with our salvation is one that all of us need to ask ourselves. We're secure in Christ, but what are we doing for Him in gratitude and love for what He has given us? If you are a spiritual dropout, then get back in the race. Pick up the pace to make up lost ground. Every day you delay is another day of lost opportunity. "Let us not lose heart in doing good, for in due time we will reap if we do not grow weary" (Galatians 6:9).

24

THE
PRIVILEGE
OF
ETERNAL SECURITY

In the summer of 2000 a highly touted race in Sacramento, California, during the Olympic trials ended in a very unusual way. Because of this, the race serves as an apt illustration of one of the most important principles of the Christian life and a fitting way to conclude our study of what it means to be totally saved.

The 200-meter race pitted Michael Johnson and Maurice Greene, the two greatest sprinters in the world, against each other in head-to-head competition. There had been some trash talking and boasting beforehand, and this was supposed to be the battle of the titans. But a funny thing happened on the way to the finish line. Both Johnson and Greene pulled up lame in the middle of the race and neither sprinter even made it to the finish line, much less won the race. The rest of the sprinters, who had been obscured and overshadowed by the superstars, finished the race, and a lesser athlete in terms of ability wound up winning.

The surprising and unexpected outcome of that race reminds us that, as Solomon put it, "The race is not to the swift and the battle is not to the warriors" (Ecclesiastes 9:11). Another way of saying it is that faithfulness is what counts the most with God, not just ability (see 1 Corinthians 4:2). The truth of eternal security gives us the unshakable confidence we need to run our Christian race with perseverance and concentrate on crossing the finish line instead of worrying about whether we're still in the race. All of us can receive the winner's crown from Christ because all of us can be faithful. It matters more that we run our own race with faithfulness than that we get to the finish line ahead of someone else.

The grace necessary to finish well is one of the privileges we have the opportunity to enjoy because we have been saved, sealed, and secured forever by the precious blood of Christ. I want to talk about some of these privileges that can be ours in Christ, in the hope that you will come to appreciate and value your salvation in new ways and determine that nothing will keep you from serving Him faithfully and running your race to His glory.

I refer to these privileges as opportunities because they are not automatic. That is, these things we're going to discuss are tied to our faithfulness in living for Christ. They don't determine how much salvation we get, because we get all of it. But they do help to determine how much we will enjoy our salvation.

WE HAVE THE PRIVILEGE OF
BECOMING PARTAKERS WITH CHRIST

One of the privileges available to us as believers is the opportunity to become "partakers" of Jesus Christ. The writer of Hebrews addressed his readers as "partakers of a heavenly calling" (3:1), and then he told them, "For we have become partakers of Christ, if we hold fast the beginning of our assurance firm until the end" (v. 14).

Let me deal with the last part of verse 14 first, because on first reading, it sounds as if the writer is making salvation conditional. We've covered enough biblical ground in this book to demonstrate

that these conditional phrases refer to the potential loss of privilege and reward, not salvation. So let's lay that issue to rest right here.

The Greek word translated "partakers" in this text is a special
word that has a tremendous meaning. In biblical days it referred to
a ruler's cabinet or inner circle of friends and advisers. Interestingly, this same word is translated as "companions" in Hebrews 1:9
in reference to Christ's pre-eminence. These companions are believers, the same ones who are later called "brethren" (Hebrews 2:11).
That makes Jesus Christ the most special Person among those who
are His partakers or companions.

A Special Group of People

Partakers are a special group of people in God's kingdom. This
term refers to those who are close to the king, much like the mighty
men who were elite members of King David's army (see 2 Samuel
23:8–12). Another example from the Old Testament could be the
advisers that Rehoboam consulted after the death of his father, King
Solomon (see 1 Kings 12:9–16). Every person in Israel was a member of the kingdom, but not everyone was a member of the king's
inner council or closest associates.

We have pointed out before that when it comes to our service and
usefulness for Christ here on earth, all believers do not have the same
depth of relationship with Christ. Nor does He commit Himself
equally to all believers (John 2:24). He is the Savior of all who believe,
so that's not the issue. But the privilege of being a partaker with Him
is for those who prove themselves worthy, who "hold fast the beginning of [their] assurance firm until the end" (Hebrews 3:14).

You've probably heard it said that the reason God doesn't take
His children home the moment we are saved is that He has work
for us to do. From the day of our salvation until the day of our death,
we have the incredible privilege and opportunity of participating
with God in bringing His kingdom agenda to pass. Unlike earthly
rulers, God does not pick out certain people for places of honor in
His kingdom while bypassing others because they aren't as talented

or wealthy or don't have as much training or clout as other people. The privilege of being a partaker with Christ is available to any believer. The only criterion is faithfulness.

Staying True to Our Calling

The problem is that being human, we can get sidetracked from the work God has called us to do. Although in one sense that's understandable, and although it happens to all of us at one time or another, it's not an excuse for a failure to be faithful.

Jesus made some strong statements about what it takes to have a place close to Him in terms of our earthly service. "Whoever does the will of My Father who is in heaven, he is My brother and sister and mother" (Matthew 12:50). "You are My friends if you do what I command you" (John 15:14). Again, these are not conditions for salvation, but conditions for being what the book of Hebrews calls a partaker of Christ.

Sometimes we distract ourselves from following close after Christ, and sometimes others put distractions in front of us. During the 2000 George W. Bush/ Al Gore presidential campaign, one of the television networks called my office and asked for an interview. When the crew came to our church, I was asked for my view of the presidential race from a faith standpoint because, as you may remember, religion was a major issue in the campaign.

Then the interviewer asked me, "If one of the candidates were to call you and ask you to be one of his advisers, would you accept?"

My answer was, "Well, that would depend on whether the candidate was interested in counsel from a biblical frame of reference, because that's the only one I know." I didn't expect to get such a call, and it never came. And even if it had come, it would have been basically irrelevant, because my calling is as a pastor. There's nothing wrong with being a political adviser, but for me that would be a distraction from my commission in the kingdom of God.

One of the things Jesus Christ is doing today in preparation for His millennial reign on earth is assembling His "cabinet," His close advisers or special administrators or whatever term you want to use. He's looking for people who are faithful until the finish line so He can award them special responsibility in His thousand-year kingdom —which, by the way, includes more than just His church. The Lord is going to need a lot of sub-rulers to oversee a kingdom that will encompass all the earth and all the nations.

Partakers are those who don't quit. They are fiercely and fearlessly loyal to the King. If you think it would be an honor and a privilege to be asked by the president or the governor to accept a position of special responsibility, imagine what it will be like to be a partaker of Christ.

WE HAVE THE PRIVILEGE OF ENTERING GOD'S REST

If you've studied the book of Hebrews, you know that one of its key themes is what is called God's rest. Hebrews 4:1 contains a conditional statement regarding God's rest: "Let us fear if, while a promise remains of entering His rest, any one of you may seem to have come short of it."

A Special Kind of Rest

Now someone may be saying, "Hey Tony, that rest thing sounds good to me. I'm tired all the time, and I could use a good rest." Well, that's not exactly what God's rest consists of, although it does involve the cessation of work. Hebrews 4 goes on to explain what God's rest is and the privilege we have of entering into or sharing in His rest. We need to know what this is, because it's obvious from the verse above that it's possible to fall short of achieving God's rest.

According to Hebrews 4:4, "For He has said somewhere concerning the seventh day: 'And God rested on the seventh day from all His works.'" This takes us all the way back to Genesis 2:2, where we read, "By the seventh day God completed His work which He had done, and He rested on the seventh day from all His work which He had done." God did not rest because He was tired and needed some sleep. The idea here is that God sat back, if you will, beheld His creation, and felt complete satisfaction in what He had done. In other words, God thoroughly enjoyed what He had created.

Enjoying Our Work

God's rest is crucial for us as human beings because He consecrated the seventh day and built the principle of rest into human life. Sabbath rest is one of the Ten Commandments, as a matter of fact. The portion of this teaching I want to pick up on for our purposes is this concept of rest as the capacity to enjoy your work. Now I'm not talking about your vocation as such, but the whole of your Christian service.

God offers you and me the privilege of feeling the same way about our work as He felt about His work. Not because our work is perfect, by any means, but because when we are fully participating in His plan for us and are serving Him to the limits of our ability and faithfulness, we can enjoy a tremendous sense of satisfaction and spiritual fulfillment. The opposite is that sense of guilt and frustration so many Christians testify to because they are knocking themselves out trying to please God.

Now in case this idea of rest sounds a little dangerous because it could lead to a sense of pride and spiritual smugness, let me say very clearly that entering God's rest does not mean becoming prideful about what you are doing. Nor does it mean putting your feet up and going to heaven on a spiritual recliner. Knowing that we are saved and secure forever should motivate us to serve God with everything we have—a message I hope you take away from this book if you miss everything else. The offer is there, because the Bible says, "There remains a Sabbath rest for the people of God" (Hebrews 4:9).

How to Miss God's Rest

That might seem like a strange way to lead off a section, but that's exactly what Hebrews 4:3 deals with as the writer pointed to Israel as a negative example. I want to pick up the verse in mid-sentence: "Just as [God] has said, 'As I swore in My wrath, they shall not enter My rest,' although His works were finished from the foundation of the world."

This is a reference to the nation of Israel as they traveled through the wilderness on their way from Egypt to Canaan. God set His people free with the goal of entering Canaan, inhabiting the land, and enjoying His rest as He drove out their enemies and presented them with a fertile land flowing with milk and honey.

But it didn't work out that way. In Numbers 13–14 you find the story of the twelve spies who went into Canaan and came back with reports of giants that made the people melt with fear and turn on Moses in anger. The Israelites stopped believing God and started believing the enemy, and that angered God. So with the exception of Joshua and Caleb, that whole generation was judged and refused entry into the Promised Land. They missed out on God's rest not because they weren't His people, but because they were unfaithful and unbelieving when it came to taking God at His word and obeying Him. So the warning comes to us not to come short of God's rest through faithlessness.

WE HAVE THE PRIVILEGE OF EARNING GREAT REWARD

I've referred to Jesus' parable in Matthew 25:14–30 that teaches the principle of reward for faithful service. We don't have the space here to quote the entire passage, which you can read for yourself. I want to summarize the story and highlight the principle.

The parable involves a man who goes on a long trip and leaves various amounts of his money to three of his servants to manage and invest for him. You may recall the story, in which the first two servants double their money while the third hides his allotment in the ground and does nothing with it.

When the master returns and calls for an accounting, he commends the two diligent servants and gives them a reward that is described as being put "in charge of many things" (vv. 21, 23) and the extra blessing of entering into his joy. Whatever this involved, it was very good. But the third servant is judged and stripped of his money because he was faithless with what the master had given him. He had nothing to present to the master in return for the privilege of having charge of some of the master's money.

It's true that the servants were given different amounts of money to work with. But the reward for those who were faithful is identical. And the third servant had the same opportunity to hear the master say, "Well done, good and faithful servant" (vv. 21, 23 KJV). The only difference was that this servant didn't persevere in faithful service.

God is watching carefully what we do with the salvation we have been given. When you know you are being evaluated, it affects what you do.

WE HAVE THE PRIVILEGE OF FINISHING WELL

It has often been said that it doesn't take a whole lot to start well. Whenever I think of this I picture the thousands of runners massed at the starting line of a major marathon like those in Boston or New York. The cameras are always there as the gun sounds, and the runners burst from the starting line with smiles on some faces and fierce determination on others. But making it to the finish line is another story for many of those runners.

Aren't you glad that God gives us the privilege of finishing well? That's important because as so many have said, the Christian life is a marathon and not a short sprint. This takes us back to Hebrews 3:14 and the exhortation to "hold fast the beginning of our assurance firm until the end."

In one sense, the truth of eternal security assures us that we will finish well, because every person whom God saves makes it to heaven. But there's something even better than making heaven. It's finishing well and entering heaven with a lifetime of rewards from

Christ instead of merely making it through the fire of Christ's judgment seat (see 1 Corinthians 3:15).

As I write this book, my youngest son, Jonathan, is at Baylor University in Waco, Texas, on a football scholarship. Jonathan's situation at Baylor provides an example of the difference between being saved and finishing well.

Remember I said at the beginning of the chapter that the privileges of security are not automatic, even though our salvation is assured. Jonathan's education is being provided for by his scholarship, which assures him a place on the Baylor football team. But his performance on the team is not at all assured by his scholarship. He has to win a starting position and then "hold on" to his spot and do the job faithfully over the course of several seasons to "finish well" as a member of the Baylor Bears and maximize the opportunity he has been given.

Of course, no human illustration perfectly pictures spiritual realities. But the difference between Jonathan's scholarship, which gave him admission to Baylor and a place on the football team, and his performance on the field is the difference between grace and good works. Grace is what God gives us; good works are what we are responsible to do. Grace gains you heaven. Works gain you reward in heaven. But we must hold our confession to the end (see Hebrews 3:14).

WE HAVE AN UNSHAKABLE KINGDOM

This concept has new meaning because of the events of September 11, 2001, that shook our world like nothing else this nation has ever experienced. As the old song says, "There's a whole lotta skakin' goin' on" in this fallen world we live in. But I want to encourage you with the truth of your security in Christ and urge you to persevere, with a final word from Scripture: "Therefore, since we receive a kingdom which cannot be shaken, let us show gratitude, by which we may offer to God an acceptable service with reverence and awe; for our God is a consuming fire" (Hebrews 12:28–29).

This world may be shaking, and things may get a lot worse before God decides it is enough and Jesus returns for His own. But as believers in Christ, we are in the most secure position we could possibly be in. We are part of a kingdom that cannot be shaken by the instability around us, because our kingdom is not of this world.

What can we do to express our appreciation for this secure position? The answer is in the text. We need to show gratitude to God by serving Him "with reverence and awe." In other words, God is like loving parents who take care of their children and meet all of their needs, but who have to say sometimes, "How about a little gratitude here? How about a little help with the chores and the responsibilities around the house?"

We are saved and secure, and God wants us to be grateful for our privileges by serving Him in a way that is acceptable to Him. God will not make us be grateful, but neither can we make Him reward us for our lack of gratitude. There's a whole lot of shaking going on out there in the world, and if anything ought to make us grateful, it is our security in Christ.

HOW GRATEFUL ARE YOU?

For a number of years our church has hosted the commencement services for my alma mater, Dallas Theological Seminary. Being a graduate theological institution, the expectation has been that there will be a certain amount of decorum during the presentation of degrees. Those in charge of the ceremony ask family and friends not to shout out or scream or make a scene when their graduate's name is called.

Now you know a lot of folk don't pay any attention to that request. At the seminary's 2000 ceremonies, one of the graduates was our associate pastor, Martin Hawkins, who was being awarded a Doctor of Ministry degree.

Pastor Hawkins worked very long and hard for that degree, and being Pastor Hawkins, he wasn't about to walk nonchalantly across the stage to receive his degree. He was so grateful to be there and so thankful to have all those years of work behind him that when his name was announced, he went dancing across the stage. Then some people in the audience started clapping and standing up, and soon this huge commotion erupted because one of our own was being honored.

I was kidding Pastor Hawkins about it afterward. "They told you to chill, and you go dancing across the stage!"

But he said, "No, they don't understand. They don't understand how hard I worked and how long it took to finish this degree. They don't understand how many nights I stayed up trying to finish my dissertation. There was no way I was going to graduate quietly, because I was so excited to be on that stage."

God has saved and secured you and brought you into His unshakable kingdom. He has promised to keep you from falling. He loves you that much. His question is, How grateful are you for His presence in time and His promise for eternity?

Are you excited enough about your salvation to let the whole world know, and grateful enough to serve God with everything you have for as long as He leaves you on earth? If so, you are getting hold of the fullness of what it means to be totally saved.

In one of my favorite old *Superman* episodes, the "man of steel" rescued a man from a burning building and flew through the air with him before bringing him down to safety. The man was a little shaky on the flight as he dangled in midair in Superman's strong arms, but he was secure.

If God rescued you from the flames of hell, He's not going to drop you on the flight to heaven, no matter how shaky you feel at times. The knowledge of our security in Christ should cause us to show God our gratitude by our love and service, so that one day we can hear Him say, "Well done, good and faithful servant."

CONCLUSION

The largest bulldozer in the world is the Kosmatsu D575A. It is sixteen feet tall, twenty-two feet wide, forty-one feet long, and weighs 291,000 pounds. It holds 440 gallons of diesel fuel. In a ten-hour shift it can push or pull 250,000 tons. It was recently used in Collin County, Texas, to dig a hole that was so massive all of the county's trash was buried in it.

When Jesus died on the cross, God dug a hole big enough, as it were, to bury all of the "sin trash" of all people for all time. God applies the benefits of the Cross to all who embrace Christ as their sin-bearer, and they are gloriously and eternally saved. A Christian is someone who has brought his or her sin to Christ and will never face it again, because it is buried in the deepest hole in creation.

To be totally saved means that God has completely, eternally, and irrevocably forgiven us as believers of all our sins—past, present, and future—and has adopted us into His family. We are assured a place in heaven as well as God's ongoing presence during our lives on earth.

The only appropriate response to such a great salvation is to fall down before God in love, commitment, and worship. When you know you've been delivered and no one can bring a charge against you, it ought to make you want to shout. May the realization that you are totally saved produce gratitude in your heart that results in exuberant, uninhibited, and unabashed praise and worship of our great God. And I'll be right there praising Him with you!

WHAT ABOUT THOSE WHO CAN'T BELIEVE?

I'm asked a lot of questions as a pastor, many of which are not easy to answer. More than once, a mother who has just lost a baby through miscarriage or stillbirth, or who has suffered the death of a child, has asked me, "Is my baby in heaven?"

Other parents with a mentally handicapped child have asked me, "Will God hold our child spiritually accountable?"

And numerous times I have been asked about people around the world who have never heard the name of Jesus Christ and so have had no opportunity to be saved. What happens to people who die without ever hearing the name of Jesus and having the opportunity to be saved?

These are controversial questions, and most difficult to answer to everybody's satisfaction. They all boil down to this basic issue: What about those who can't believe?

What happens to those who lack either the maturity, the mental capacity, or the knowledge of Christ necessary to respond to the gospel? Do these people have any hope of heaven? Are they covered by the redemption Christ provided on the cross?

We need to face these questions and find out if God's plan for the ages includes people who can't believe. I want to address this in what I hope is a clear and unambiguous way by dealing with four key aspects of this issue.

THE PROBLEM OF THOSE WHO CAN'T BELIEVE

The problem is that at any given time there are countless millions of people on earth who cannot obey the Bible's command to repent of their sins and believe in Jesus.

The Problem of Sin

This is a theological and biblical problem because the Bible declares that all people are born in sin. Paul writes, "There is none righteous, not even one" (Romans 3:10). Later he declares, "Through one man [Adam] sin entered into the world" (Romans 5:12). David said, "I was brought forth in iniquity, and in sin my mother conceived me" (Psalm 51:5).

Every human being born since Adam has inherited Adam's sin nature. The Bible says that we are "by nature children of wrath" (Ephesians 2:3). The reason you don't have to teach children to lie is that the bent toward lying is already present in their hearts. They just need the maturity and the opportunity to express their sinful nature.

The problem of our human sin nature leads to the problem of eternity, because the Bible teaches that those who die without Christ will spend eternity separated from God.

Some people deal with the problem by arguing that a God of love simply would not send such people to hell. But that's not an adequate solution in itself, because many people go to hell despite the fact that God loves them.

Every unrepentant sinner who chooses hell does so in spite of God's love. So the love of God does not automatically guarantee everybody heaven. If it did, everybody would go to heaven, because God loves everybody.

Others try to solve this problem, at least for little ones, by baptizing infants and teaching that they are now full-fledged members of the church in good spiritual standing. But the Bible is very clear that water does not wash away sins (see 1 Corinthians 1:17), and the only baptism the Bible knows anything about is believer's baptism. Also, what about infants who die without being baptized? So infant baptism does not address the issue satisfactorily.

The Problem of Faith

Another side of the problem is that the Bible states unequivocally that people go to heaven based on their faith in Jesus Christ. The most famous verse in the Bible says that "whoever believes" in Jesus is the one who will not perish, but have eternal life (John 3:16).

In other words, faith is given as the condition by which salvation is obtained. Since that's true, and the Bible affirms it in many other places, what happens to people who cannot believe and express their faith in Christ?

This is also a crucial question in light of another truth the Bible teaches over and over again—that Jesus is the only way of salvation (Acts 4:12). Jesus Himself said in John 14:6, "I am the way, and the truth, and the life; no one comes to the Father but through Me." There are no side roads to heaven.

Therefore, to biblically address the problem of those who can't believe, we need to see their condition against the backdrop of the Bible's clear teachings on sin and the necessity of faith in Christ alone for salvation. God does not skip or ignore the issue of sin to get some people into heaven. Sin is far too costly for that.

THE PREMISE TO ADDRESS THE PROBLEM

Now that we have laid out the basic problem of people who can't respond to the gospel, I want to offer a premise in an attempt to deal with the problem biblically.

The premise is this: God's invitation to all people to respond in faith assumes that those who have been invited have the capacity to respond. To put it another way, God's command to believe is only applicable to those who can heed it. Jesus said in John 3:18, "He who believes in Him is not judged; he who does not believe has been judged already, because he has not believed in the name of the only begotten Son of God."

An Assumption of Ability

This is a very important verse because it sets belief in opposition to the refusal to believe in Christ, which results in condemnation. God does not ask us to do something we are incapable of doing. To ask me to believe when I am not capable of believing, and then to condemn me for not believing as if I had willfully rejected Christ, is doubletalk.

What I'm saying is that those who can't believe also can't reject. This is a very important point to understand. Those who can't say yes to Christ also can't say no.

Both John 3:16 and 3:18 demand an act of the intellect and the will. Jesus went on to say, "He who does not obey the Son [that is, by believing in Him] will not see life, but the wrath of God abides on him" (v. 36). Again, He tied eternal condemnation to a deliberate failure to obey the gospel by believing in Him.

In John 5:40, Jesus told the religious leaders of His day, "You are unwilling to come to Me so that you may have life." The key word there is "unwilling." Belief or lack of belief involves a choice. God may not send people to hell, but He will allow them to choose hell for themselves by refusing to trust Jesus Christ. People are lost because they reject the revelation of God.

God's Infinite Justice

The fact that "faith comes from hearing, and hearing by the word of Christ" (Romans 10:17) does not hinder God from accomplishing salvation in those who can't hear and believe the Word. Faith is not a work we perform to earn our salvation. It is simply the condition for receiving Christ.

God would not be just if He held people accountable for that which they cannot do, and for knowledge they do not possess. It is a sin not to do right only if a person can choose between right and wrong (see James 4:17).

In a class I once taught at Dallas Seminary, I inadvertently asked an exam question on material I had not covered in class. One of the students brought that discrepancy to my attention. To be fair, I had to rescore all of the test papers because I could not hold the students liable for information they had never been given.

God is infinitely just. No one can question His fairness. Abraham asked, "Shall not the Judge of all the earth deal justly?" (Genesis 18:25).

So the premise is that God will not hold people accountable for a decision they cannot make, based on information they have not received.

But this still does not completely solve the problem of those who cannot believe, because God's purity and holiness will not allow any sin to enter heaven. Even people who can't believe still carry the stain of their sin nature. And people in faraway lands who have never heard the gospel still have their own sins to answer for. This means we need to talk about the provision God has made for those who cannot believe.

THE PROVISION THAT
VALIDATES THE PREMISE

As we build the case for people who don't have the capacity or the information necessary to believe, we need to see that God has revealed Himself to mankind in two ways. We call these general and special revelation.

Special revelation refers to any direct revelation from God, especially the Scriptures, the full and final revelation of God's will. People who have the Bible available to them are especially blessed, because they can know exactly what God expects of them.

But even those who don't have the Word, and don't know who Jesus is, can know enough about God through general revelation to seek Him. The gospel is not contained in general revelation, but it demonstrates enough of God's reality and nature to lead people to seek further light. This fact is crucial in the case of those who have never heard about Jesus Christ.

God's Witness in Nature

General revelation is God's disclosure of Himself in nature. One of the clearest statements of this doctrine, and of mankind's responsibility in light of this truth, is found in Romans 1. Paul writes:

> The wrath of God is revealed from heaven against all ungodliness and unrighteousness of men who suppress the truth in unrighteousness, because that which is known about God is evident within them; for God made it evident to them. For since the creation of the world His invisible attributes, His eternal power and divine nature, have been clearly seen, being understood through what has been made, so that they are without excuse. (vv. 18–20)

God has revealed enough of Himself in creation that He can hold people responsible for the truth and the light they have. He can do this because all of creation points to the Creator.

If you go to a museum and see a great work of art, you don't have to know or see the artist to know that an artist had to be behind the creation of this masterpiece. Creation is God's masterpiece. People say, "I wish I could just see God, or hear Him speak. If I could do that, I'd believe in Him."

The psalmist said God is shouting out His presence: "The heavens are telling of the glory of God; and their expanse is declaring the work of His hands. Day to day pours forth speech, and night to night reveals knowledge" (Psalm 19:1–2). Verses 3–4 go on to explain that while creation doesn't speak with words, it still shouts out its witness to the presence of God.

Suppressing the Truth

The problem with general revelation is its limitations. In addition, according to Romans 1:18, wicked people suppress the truth they have. It's like trying to hold a beach ball under water. If you've ever tried that, you know how hard you have to work to hold the ball down. It keeps wanting to pop up.

When a person sins, no matter if that person is living in the most primitive society on earth, an internal witness says, "That was wrong." If the person who doesn't know about Jesus Christ follows that internal sense, and if he looks up in the sky and says, "Someone great has to have made all of this," he is responding to the light he has. And God is faithful and just to respond to anyone who seeks Him.

God never leaves Himself without a witness (see Acts 14:16–17). Therefore, any person who can see the witness of God's reality in creation has started on the path to knowing God. Someone who has never heard the name of Christ may not know God personally and intimately, but he can grasp the reality of God's existence and power.

The Savior of All

With this information as background, I want to consider 1 Timothy 4:10, which is a very important verse in dealing with God's provision for those who can't believe.

Let's focus on the last half of the verse: "We have fixed our hope on the living God, who is the Savior of all men, especially of believers." This verse says God saves all people generically, but He saves some people particularly. Now this statement needs careful explanation, because I am not saying that there are two ways to get to heaven, or that everybody will be saved.

Paul mentions two groups of people here, "all men" and "believers." Let's take the second group first.

God saves believers "especially," or in particular, because they are the ones who both have the capacity to believe in Christ *and have made their decision to believe in Christ.* So far there's no problem, because this is what the New Testament teaches from beginning to end. The death of Christ is sufficient to save all who will believe in Him.

But here's something else we need to understand. The death of Jesus Christ also removes the guilt of original sin for all people. It's in this sense that God saves all people generically, for lack of a better term.

Remember that for infants, their only sin is the stain of original sin they inherited from Adam. It's still sin, and every baby born into the world is guilty of Adam's sin, for "in Adam all die" (1 Corinthians 15:22). God can't skip any sin, and He doesn't have to, because He put Jesus to death on the cross to pay for sin.

In other words, because of the death of Christ people no longer go to hell because of what Adam did. They go to hell for what *they* do. Adam infected the human race with sin, but God took care of Adam's sin on the cross. He paid for original sin. That is why Paul can say God has reconciled the world to Himself (see 2 Corinthians 5:19). That is why the Bible says Jesus has "taste[d] death for everyone" (Hebrews 2:9).

Another important Scripture in this regard is Romans 5:18, in which Paul says, "So then as through one transgression there resulted condemnation to all men, even so through one act of righteousness there resulted justification of life to all men."

Paul can say this because all life is justified with regard to original sin, but not with regard to personal sin. This is the way in which Jesus "enlightens every man" (John 1:9).

This provision of God for the guilt of original sin is the reason infants and children go to heaven if they die before reaching the age of accountability. The same is true of those who become mentally incompetent before reaching accountability. The sin that would take them to hell has been paid for by Christ on the cross.

The situation is different when people reach the age at which they can understand the revelation of God and are accountable for their actions. The Bible doesn't give a definitive age at which each person is accountable, since it varies for each person.

The only indication we have in Scripture of a specific age being connected with accountability to God is in the case of Israel in the wilderness. When the people came to the edge of the Promised Land but turned back in unbelief, God said no one age twenty and over would enter Canaan as a judgment on the people's unbelief (Numbers 32:11).

That's an advanced age for accountability, but this case is not the norm for every person. Anybody who can understand that he or she is a sinner and in need of salvation is capable of responding to God's grace, and is responsible to believe the gospel for himself or herself.

Those Who Have Never Heard

How does God's general provision of salvation apply to those who haven't had an opportunity to hear, understand, and respond to the gospel of Jesus Christ?

We touched on this issue earlier, so let's carry it through to its conclusion. Consider a person who doesn't know anything about Christ, but who responds to the spiritual light God gives him through natural revelation rather than suppressing and denying it. He welcomes the knowledge of God he has.

The Bible declares that whenever anybody, anywhere responds to the light he has, God will give him more light. Hebrews 11:6 says God "is a rewarder of those who seek Him." God says in Jeremiah 29:13, "You will seek Me and find Me when you search for Me with all your heart."

Here's the spiritual principle at work: When people respond to what they do know of God, He takes personal responsibility for giving them more information about Himself.

The most obvious way is by sending someone with the Word of God who can say, "Let me tell you about the true God and how He became a man and died on the cross to save you."

It's also possible that apart from someone bringing the Word, God can supernaturally reveal Himself to a seeking heart. There have been missionaries who have gone to remote tribes and told the people about Jesus, to which they have responded, "We have been worshiping Him. We just didn't know His name."

Applying Another Dispensation

Now there's a third way God can deal in grace with those who can't believe because they have never heard the gospel. He can apply another dispensation and its criteria to them. A dispensation is simply an economy or an administration of God, a way in which He deals with people based on the information He has given them.

For instance, people in the Old Testament were saved without hearing the name of Jesus, because Jesus hadn't come to earth yet. But they were saved because they believed the revelation of God.

The Bible says Abraham believed God and was accounted as righteous, or saved, for believing in God's promise of a son and a seed (Genesis 15:6). This was long before the Mosaic sacrificial system was even begun.

Abraham believed without hearing about Jesus, but I am *not* saying that people can be saved apart from Jesus. Never. Nobody can get saved without Jesus, because He is the Savior of all men, as we read in 1 Timothy 4:10. Everybody is saved through Christ, even those who lived before Jesus came, because in the mind and heart of God, Jesus was already sacrificed to pay for sin before the world was ever created (see Revelation 13:8). So a person can be saved without knowing Jesus' name, but not without Jesus' provision for sin.

In the case of a person who never hears the gospel and never knows the name of Jesus, but who responds to the light he has, God treats that person like an Old Testament saint, if you will. That is, if the person trusts in what God has revealed, God deals with that person based on the knowledge he has, not the information he never received. I call this transdispensationalism.

By this I mean if a person is sincerely seeking God and desiring to know Him, and is responding to the truth he knows, if there is no missionary or direct manifestation of God, then God judges that person based on his faith in the light he has received. And as in the case of Abraham, God will retroactively count this person as righteous by applying the death of Christ from the dispensation of grace.

In Revelation 7:9, John said he saw people from "every nation and all tribes and peoples and tongues" in heaven. How is this possible when we know that not every single tribe or language on earth today has been reached by missionaries, or has the Scriptures in its own tongue? In fact, this has never been the case in history. The reason every tribe and language is represented is that God will never let anyone who sincerely seeks Him fall by the wayside.

God is not some monster in heaven tossing people gleefully into hell. "[He is] not wishing for any to perish but for all to come to repentance" (2 Peter 3:9). The only thing God will not tolerate is people who willingly suppress His truth and reject His salvation. Jesus did not just die to make people "savable." He died to save people.

An Objection to the Premise

Now you may have been reading this with an objection rolling around in your mind. "Tony, if you say people can be saved by general revelation, why preach the gospel? Why bother sending missionaries around the world and translating the Bible?"

There are two answers to this. First, we go because Christ has commanded us to go and tell the world the good news of His salvation. And second, we go because the process I just described for those who haven't heard of Christ is far from automatic. Whatever we may try to deduce from Scripture about those who have never heard about Christ, we know without a doubt that those who hear and believe the gospel will be saved.

Remember, those who haven't heard the gospel are still sinners by nature and by their actions. They are under the condemnation of their sin, and their natural tendency is still to suppress the truth and reject the light God gives them. They need to hear the gospel so the Spirit of God can bring conviction of sin and salvation.

It's the gospel that opens people's eyes to their need of Christ. Satan is so powerful and sin is so pleasurable, even in the deepest jungle, that he will blind hearts to the truth if he can. We need to preach the gospel to help pry people loose from their suppression of the truth.

PROOF OF THE PREMISE

God's Word gives us at least one very intimate glimpse into the death of a baby, which helps us understand what happens to those who can't believe.

The story is in 2 Samuel 12, in the aftermath of King David's adultery with Bathsheba. A baby boy was born from that sinful encounter, and God judged David by declaring the baby would die (v. 14).

David fasted and prayed and sought the Lord for seven days, but the baby died (vv. 15–19). David stopped his fast, got cleaned up, and worshiped God. Then he ate and resumed the normal routines of life (v. 20).

When David's servants expressed surprise at his calmness, he made the statement I want us to notice: "While the child was still alive, I fasted and wept; for I said, 'Who knows, the Lord may be gracious to me, that the child may live.' But now he has died; why should I fast? Can I bring him back again? I will go to him, but he will not return to me" (2 Samuel 12:22–23).

This is a great statement of hope and faith on David's part. He knew his baby was with the Lord, and he was looking forward to the day he would be reunited with his son in heaven.

How do we know David was referring to seeing his son in heaven, rather than simply joining him later in death? One indication is the fact that the first thing David did after the baby died was worship God. Why worship if you have no hope? David reaffirmed his hope that he would not only go to heaven himself, but be with his son again.

Another argument in favor of heaven as the focus here is that the phrase "go to him" (2 Samuel 12:23) is a term of reunion and relationship. It's a term of fellowship. Parents don't get close to their children in death. You may be buried next to your loved one at the cemetery, but that's as close as two people come in death. David was looking beyond the grave to being in God's presence with his baby.

For those who have lost babies and children, the bad news is that the children can't come back to their parents. But the good news is that their parents can go to them if the parents are trusting Jesus Christ for their salvation.

What about unborn children who were lost through miscarriage or abortion before they were fully formed? I believe Christian parents will not only see these children in heaven, but see them as they were meant to be, without the limitations of their earthly form.

Jesus and the Children

The strongest affirmation of the spiritual welfare of children came from Jesus Christ Himself, a fact for which every believing parent should be very grateful.

In Matthew 18 we have this wonderful scene in which Jesus brought a little child before the disciples to settle their argument about who was the greatest in the kingdom (v. 1). Then He said, "Truly I say to you, unless you are converted and become like children, you will not enter the kingdom of heaven" (v. 3).

What is it about conversion that makes it childlike? The usual answer is that we have to shed our pretenses and be open and trusting in heart like a little child to come to Christ. Jesus later referred to the openness of children in coming to Him (Matthew 19:14).

That's certainly true. But I also think Jesus is referring to the removal of the guilt of sin. In other words, little children—those who can't believe—have had the guilt of Adam's sin removed through the sacrificial death of Christ. The removal of sin's guilt is what happens at conversion.

When Mark tells the story of Jesus bringing a child into their midst, he notes that Jesus took the child in His arms (Mark 9:36). That's what it means to believe—placing yourself in Jesus' arms. A child who cannot believe is in Jesus' arms.

We pick our children up and hold them when they are small. But as they get older, they want to wriggle out of our arms and go their own way. That happens spiritually too, at the age of accountability. That's when children must believe for themselves. But until that point, they are covered by the blood of Christ.

Let me show you one more proof that little children are safe in God's arms. Jesus was still teaching about children when He said, "See that you do not despise one of these little ones, for I say to you that their angels in heaven continually see the face of My Father who is in heaven" (Matthew 18:10).

Jesus said children have "their angels." Now according to Hebrews 1:14, the only people angels minister to are believers. So Jesus' statement is wonderful affirmation that children who are not old enough to understand and believe the gospel are assured of heaven if they die.

Seeking the True God

Before we close this discussion, let me show you a biblical example of our premise that if people who don't know about Christ truly seek God, He will give them further light.

The story is in Acts 8:26–40, the encounter between Philip and the Ethiopian eunuch. This man was reading the prophecy in Isaiah 53 about Jesus' death, and wishing someone could explain it to him, when Philip supernaturally appeared, explained the gospel to him, and led the man to faith in Christ.

It's true that this is an exception to the normal pattern of evangelism. But God can make exceptions to His rules to accomplish His purposes without compromising His integrity. For example, the rule is that it is appointed to human beings to die once (see Hebrews

9:27). But every person whom Jesus raised from the dead is an exception to the rule because each of these people died twice.

When it comes to salvation, God always makes a way for those who seek Him. He will never leave Himself without a witness. Because He is God, He is free to deal in grace with those who can't believe, either by sending them the gospel through a missionary, by giving them a direct supernatural revelation of Himself, or by applying to them the criteria of another dispensation. God will not hide Himself from someone who is truly seeking Him.

INDEX
OF
SCRIPTURE

INDEX
OF
SUBJECTS

Further Insights by Moody Press

Understanding God Series - by Dr. Tony Evans

Our God Is Awesome
Encountering the Greatness of Our God

"*Dr. Tony Evans has done a masterful job of unfolding the rich truth about God and who He is. Dr. Evans writes with uncommon clarity, accuracy and warmth. This book will be a treasured resource for all who desire to know God better.*"
– John MacArthur, Pastor / Teacher, Grace Community Church of the Valley.

ISBN: 0-8024-4850-X, Paperback

Returning To Your First Love
Putting God Back In First Place

"*Dr. Evans has done to us all a service in focusing the biblical spotlight on the absolute necessity of keeping our love of Christ as the central passion of our hearts. Any earnest Christian knows how easy it is to become so absorbed in doing things for Christ that we forget to cultivate our love relationship with Him.*"
– Charles Stanley

ISBN: 0-8024-4851-8, Paperback

The Promise
Experiencing God's Greatest Gift—The Holy Spirit

"*Here is a book that points us to the Spirit's way to purity and power. Every chapter is appropriately titled "Experiencing the Spirit's . . ." May this work help all who read it to do so.*"
– Dr. Charles Ryrie

ISBN: 0-8024-4852-6, Paperback

Further Insights by Moody Press
Understanding God Series - by Dr. Tony Evans

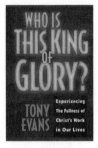

Who Is This King of Glory ?
Experiencing the Fullness of Christ's Work in Our Lives

In this practical, biblically-based volume, Tony Evans examines Jesus, "the greatest of all subjects," from three different perspectives:
1. His uniqueness
2. His authority
3. Our appropriate response to Him

ISBN: 0-8024-4854-2, Paperback

The Battle is The Lord's
Waging Victorious Spiritual Warfare

We're in a war, but Christ has given us the victory. In *The Battle Is the Lord's,* Dr. Tony Evans reveals Satan's strategies, teaches how you can fight back against the forces of darkness, and shows you how to find deliverance from the devil's snares.

ISBN: 0-8024-4855-0, Paperback

The Best is Yet To Come
Bible Prophecies Through the Ages

Tony Evans propels you past the hype and confusion of prophecy, straight to the Source. He skillfully unlocks the secrets of the prophetic program, simultaneously unveiling the future for all to read and understand.

ISBN: 0-8024-4856-9, Paperback

What Matters Most
Four Absolute Necessities in Following Christ

God's goal for believers is that they become more like Christ. But what does that mean? In *What Matters Most,* Dr. Tony Evans explores the four essential elements of discipleship:

1. Worship
2. Fellowship
3. Education
4. Outreach

ISBN: 0-8024-4853-4, Paperback

MOODY
The Name You Can Trust
1-800-678-8812 **www.MoodyPress.org**